CLOAKED IN DEATH, WRAPPED IN LOVE

A MEMOIR

JILL BARNES

First published in Great Britain in 2018 by Aldersey-Harrap Publishing

Copyright © 2018 Jill Barnes

www.cloakedinwrappedin.com

This is a work of non-fiction based on the life, experiences and recollections of the author. Some names and identifying features have, on occasion, been changed to protect the privacy of others.

ISBN: 978-1-9164628-1-6
ISBN (eBook): 978-1-9164628-0-9

Cover Design and Photography by Alexander Barnes

Edited by Cally Worden
www.enigmaeditorial.com

In memory of Heather, Felix and Oscar Bickley

In June 2010 Heather Bickley, forty-six years of age, and her two sons, Felix, ten, and Oscar, six, died at home in a house fire. A fire-service investigation established the seat of the fire as an electrical fault in an old fridge-freezer situated in the kitchen pantry. The subsequent inquest concluded that, had a smoke alarm been installed at the property, their deaths may have been prevented. Their husband and father, John, survived.

For John
and my son, Alexander.

ACKNOWLEDGEMENTS

This memoir could not have been written without the will and desire of John Bickley, both to keep the memory of his wife and sons alive, and in the hope that something positive could be salvaged from the tragedy of their deaths - the hope that those readers who do not have smoke alarms installed in their homes, ensure that they do so after finishing this book.

As much as it is my hand that has written the following words, John has stood alongside me every step of the way. When I wavered at the thought of placing so much of our private lives into the public domain, his unswerving encouragement, support and belief that we should share our story, spurred me on. However many tears I shed as I wrote about the deaths of Heather, Felix and Oscar, and John's life after, they are incomparable to the number he shed in repeatedly revisiting the most painful of spaces in order for us to recall the events and conversations that bring our story to life, and this book to its conclusion. He has been, and remains, my inspiration.

To the courageous firefighters who attended John's home on the night of the fire. In their efforts to save Heather, Felix and Oscar, they chose to enter the unsafe property and in doing so placed themselves at immense risk. Public servants who undeniably went above and beyond their call of duty.

It is without doubt that the big-hearted community of Benllech, Anglesey, gently wrapped themselves around John in the immediate aftermath of his loss. So many kind and generous people made him feel he was not alone: personal friends, childminders, the school, and Heather's work colleagues, to name a few. And, although he was unable to comprehend at the time the true magnitude of such love and support, their powerful presence, humility and capacity to embrace him, closely or from afar, truly made a difference as he faced each day. He will never forget them.

To Cally, my editor, in whom I found the gentle hands needed to ensure that, in writing this memoir, the memories of Heather, Felix and Oscar were handled with the utmost care. As she took hold of the editing reins, her natural ability to empathise repeatedly led me to a space in which we could discuss openly and honestly how the words being written could do justice to the story being told. I couldn't have arrived at a finer door.

To the late Linden Stafford, editor for drafts one and two, who gently and with humour pointed me in the right direction.

And last, but by no means least, my son, Alexander, a teenager at the time John came into our lives but whose young shoulders embraced him and his loss with a maturity way beyond his years. He, too, has walked closely alongside John and, during the last eight years, has borne witness to John's efforts to find a way forward. His enduring love, support and tremendous humour have been a welcome breath of fresh air. But most treasured of all, are his wonderful big hugs. As he wraps his arms around me through the window of John's life, I breathe in slowly and deeply, savouring his presence in my world, and truly know how lucky I am.

INTRODUCTION

When I attended the funerals of Heather, Felix and Oscar Bickley I could not have predicted just how their lives would become so embroiled in my own. I had not known them, our only link being the husband and father they had left behind: John, a man I had met at school at eleven years of age, who gave me my first kiss at thirteen and another, years later, at twenty, brief encounters that he had, confusingly, both sought and immediately rejected in equal measure before our lives took very different and distant paths. It was unrequited love on my part; he hadn't wanted me then but, almost three decades later, he certainly needed me now.

Around the time of the funerals, life had brought me to a natural junction of my own. I was forty-six, had been a single mother of a fifteen-year-old son for thirteen years and had a relationship history that, despite my fun along the way, was hardly the advert for success and longevity that John's marriage to Heather had been.

Compared to him I'd had a bumpy ride, and one that had eventually led me, some years earlier, to a counsellor's door. It was a door that, once I had entered and over time, had painfully illuminated my own dark shadows: the death of my father when I was seven years of age, the impact his loss had had on my subsequent adult relationships, and my desire to be a 'responsible' person, an unconscious process that had often drawn me – as my counsellor unflatteringly put it – to 'any lame dog in the room'.

I'd now been single for about five years and was safely ensconced with my son in our impenetrable home, the brick wall around us growing higher with every passing year. Men were better kept at bay.

I had a choice: to hug John goodbye after the wake and return to my own life over two hundred miles away, a distant bystander to his tragedy, or to stand firm and offer a hand of friendship in his darkest hour. This, in the full knowledge I was not only placing myself in proximity to a grief-stricken and vulnerable man, but also to *the* man who had rejected me years earlier and *a* man who I had always found very attractive. He was now, sadly, that 'lame dog in the room'. This was a path well trodden, and one I should not have been venturing down again.

I chose to offer a hand of friendship.

This memoir, although born of a tragedy, is not the story of Heather, Felix and Oscar.

It is the story of how their lost lives brought the paths of two people careering back together unexpectedly, of how one renewed friendship managed to find and hold tight to the most fragile of tethers in the wilderness of raw grief – volatile, unseen and without boundary.

This friendship managed slowly to steer a course through darkness, strengthening with every tear and, eventually, every smile. It allowed love to blossom in a space where love had died. But this new love posed more questions than answers. Just how altruistic and healthy were my own motivations as I became lost in the intoxicating allure of a man in need, of a previously unrequited love, and of love itself? In my quest for answers, it was not only John who was stripped bare in his grief; my own human frailties lined up before me, as I faced not only John, but also myself.

These were not normal times. We were in a room where the space was defined by multiple and young deaths. It was a room where Heather, Felix and Oscar sat, where their senseless and preventable deaths reverberated off the cold hard walls, where their lost futures, hopes and dreams lay in shattered pieces on the ground. The brutal reality of their demise repeatedly stabbed at our feet as John and I walked side by side. It was a room of extremes, where John pushed himself to emotional and physical limits, challenging life itself and his desire to remain in it. It was an ugly room where suicide danced menacingly alongside regret, anger, searing pain and a million sweet yesterdays. It was a room where death lay side by side with life.

I can't pretend that what follows in these pages is just a story of friendship and love. Nor can I pretend you won't be taken to the darkest of spaces as you bear witness to one man's struggle to survive following the loss of his wife and sons. Neither of these stories would exist without the other. What I *can* say is that along the way you will also bear witness to the life-affirming human capacity, when pushed to emotional extremes, to find a strength not previously found, to find hope when hope was lost, and to emerge from the edge of darkness and find a reason to live.

The question was whether we would emerge together.

CHAPTER 1

I just knew I was standing in the wrong place, but I had feet of clay which, with every uncomfortable second that passed, sank deeper into the ground. Like most of those present I was dressed head to toe in black, which no doubt rendered me invisible in the large crowd, but blinded by my growing anxiety I felt ridiculously self-conscious. As I continued to watch others arrive, the air heavy and sombre, I silently repeated the instructions John had given me the previous evening when we'd shared a few hours together. He was now a distant, unreachable figure as he faced the cremation of his family – I was most definitely on my own.

'Make sure you go to the front of the queue and then wait in the vestibule with the others that have been given a seat inside. You won't be able to go into the crematorium as there's another funeral beforehand, but you can wait with everyone else until they let you in.'

Well, this wasn't the front. It was midway, and the queue in question ran long and snake-like up a small slope to the left of the crematorium's mahogany front door. Nor was it clear to me whether it was the queue for the funeral I was attending or for the one beforehand, but having made my choice I wasn't about to march past those in front of me. Heaven forbid I should gatecrash a service that hadn't yet finished, and the formal atmosphere had frozen any personal desire I may have had to start asking strangers if they could clarify whose funeral they were attending and who should be where. It was an impersonal conveyor belt of grief – one in, one out, one in, one out – not helped by the bleak and harsh appearance of the isolated crematorium building. Set back from the road, in grounds surrounded by black railings, it was approached by a sweeping tarmac drive that weaved downwards through perfectly manicured grass. The austere, deep-pitched, grey slate roof, gave it a dramatic and stark outline, the front facade split, with sandstone on the right and rendered cream on the left. Over the front entrance, a flat roof metal canopy, extended outwards by some four metres, supported at the corners by two metal poles, accentuating every chilly contour. I shivered. I still couldn't quite believe I was here. Mid-July it may have been, but the sun was nowhere to be seen, the overcast sky placing another layer of despair over the growing, muted and waiting crowd.

As I chastised myself for my confusion, a man I did not immediately recognise suddenly approached me. He had dark brown, slightly wavy hair, gelled and combed back, brown eyes, and he was about five feet seven inches tall, of medium build and wearing a dark suit. Gently taking my hand, and in a hushed but strong and assured northern tone, he said, 'Jill, you're in the wrong place.' Not so invisible after all. Instant relief filled me; someone who knew where I should be. Despite not being able to place him, I found his calm and concerned manner instantly reassuring. As he pulled me from the queue and towards the front door of the crematorium he must have sensed my uncertainty. He turned towards me and said, 'Jill, it's John Lyon.' The years instantly melted away and I could now see the face from high school thirty years earlier, albeit a little heavier. Small in height he may have been, but he was imbued with a quiet authority and dignified air. I could have hugged him right there for discreetly saving me from my lost self.

Continuing to hold his hand I followed him down past the long queue and into the packed and dimly lit crematorium vestibule. It can't have been more than nine metres square. Turning left as we entered, I was immediately hit by an intense and intangible sense of desolation. I took a deep breath to steady myself as we slowly pushed our way through the crowded space. Within moments my eyes fell upon more faces from the past in an instant school reunion, childhood friends all huddled together: Amanda Williamson, still with her blonde, wavy shoulder-length hair and not looking much older than when I'd last seen her at school. I made a memo to myself: recalibrate, Jill, you're about to walk into a funeral for three. How old Amanda looks right now is insignificant and shallow. I had no idea how many more similar mental memos I'd be sending to myself in the ensuing months. To Amanda's side stood dark-haired John Columbine or, as he preferred to be known, 'Colly'. Then tall, slender and blonde Michael Hutson, 'Hutty', with his wife, Katie. And finally, there was

Ian Gamble, 'Gammie', John's closest friend, small in height and slim, with blue eyes and a youthful abundance of thick, blonde, straw-like straight hair; he had travelled all the way from Australia to support John. As my eyes passed from one face to another and quiet 'hellos' were spoken while we waited to file in, the loud and distressing wails of a blonde female who was sitting in a corner on the perimeter wall bench filled the small space. A dark-haired male tried to comfort her, to no avail, and her relentless, seemingly uncontrollable weeping filled the air with a combustible pressure, transporting me back to my father's sudden death when I was seven and my mother's ceaseless crying that had filled our home. Tears without end forever etched into my soul.

A frenzy of emotions filled me: a bizarre joy at the meeting of old school friends mixed with overwhelming, crushing sadness and utter disbelief at the enormity of what had happened, and that it had happened to someone I knew. These things didn't happen to people you knew. And although I was physically present, I felt strangely disconnected from the people and events surrounding me, as though I were having an out-of-body experience, not quite able to grasp what I was standing in the midst of. It was surreal: a tragedy, a funeral for three and a school reunion, all wrapped up in the unbearable sobbing of the female I was later to learn was Mel. She and her husband, Kev, the man sitting by her side in the vestibule, were close friends of John and had cut short their overseas holiday with their two young daughters to come to the funeral.

As I wondered how much longer I could wait in that suffocating space, my own painful memories, the enforced proximity to others and the dark atmosphere weighing heavily upon me, the doors into the crematorium suddenly opened. Had I imagined our collective sigh as we all surged forward, as though being released from a locked pen? There was a polite, mini-stampede of desperation as toes hit heels and shoulders jostled for space. Death's formality added under-the-breath, barely-audible apologies that stopped short of their destinations.

The palpable relief was to be short-lived. The room into which we emerged may have been a larger and brighter space, but once the sole central seating area was filled it immediately became a continuum of the room from which we'd just escaped. It was packed, with every possible seat and standing place taken, the rapidly enmeshed emotions of hundreds hanging in the air. More loud crying from within the congregation filled the atmosphere, travelling with ease across the higher ceilinged room, creating an intimate encounter with people I couldn't even see.

I found myself sitting approximately halfway back with Hutty on my left and Colly on my right. I was thankful we were at the end of the pew, so if it all became too much and I felt the need to flee the room I had only Colly to squeeze past. It was a fantasy, of course. I knew I would stay for the dura-tion; in comparison to John's, my experience was a breeze, but my mental escape plan gave me some much-needed breathing space.

Once the seating area was full, colleagues of John's wife, Heather, a serving detective constable at the time of her death, filed in on both sides, standing shoulder to shoulder and facing towards those sitting. Wearing formal 'No. 1' police tunics, they looked so smart and upright and were a commanding presence, creating a cocoon of support around us. Their own grief was clear as they shed silent and mesmerising tears, which rolled down their cheeks untouched as they stood to attention, placing duty first.

As John approached the centrally placed lectern at the foot of the altar, the cries of those present seemed to stop abruptly, and silence fell. I felt a lump in my throat, and my heart was thumping as he looked up to face the congregation, outwardly calm in his demeanour but so ashen-faced and ghost-like with the shock of his loss. His dark suit served only to add to the translucency of his skin. He opened his mouth to speak and his failed attempt, with voice broken, passed through the microphone and filled the room, his distress and pain clear, a life force of its own that screamed silently at us. A second failed attempt to start followed. It was truly distressing to listen to him trying to form his first word. Time stood still. I and, I have no doubt, every single person present willed him to find the strength to speak. *Go on, John, you can do it,* I repeated to myself. *You can do this. Please speak and break this silence, this unbearable silence.*

I fought against my instinct to stand up, push past Colly and run down to him. Perhaps if someone was standing by his side he would be able to speak. How long would, or should, we all sit and bear witness to his broken, crumbling form before one of us stepped forward to rescue him – and the rest of us – from the immense discomfort of the situation? Each second floated by in some sort of extended time frame; it felt interminable.

My head was bowed, and tears streamed down my face as

I was transported back to Parrenthorn High School, with John as Head Boy and me as Head Girl, to another lectern where John had stood, facing a different crowd. I remembered his nervous voice as he had spoken to attentive parents in the large sports hall with me standing behind him, pea-green with envy: he always got to do the speeches.

Two lecterns representing such differing times and emotions. Lectern one, 1980, and John as Head Boy doing what John always did best: taking control, facing the situation head on and leading the way. Catapult forward thirty years to lectern two, 2010, and John as bereaved husband and father doing what John always did best: taking control, facing the situation head on and leading the way. But what brutal differences. Gone, the eager parents. Gone, the lightness and joy of youth. And gone, gone, gone my envy. As I digested these two cruelly different images, and felt a searing relief fill my body at the knowledge that my own fifteen-year-old son was alive, John finally found his voice.

'Well, firstly thank you all for coming. I can't quite believe that so many people are here and if Heather could see you all now she would be amazed. My wife was truly the rock and driving force behind our family, doing absolutely everything for us. She adored the family life we shared, and I have a million memories to fall back on because she made them happen.'

He had steadied himself and, despite the fragility in his voice, his words slowly became a little more fluid.

'Felix loved football, and fish and chips. Oscar just loved jumping on the trampoline in our garden every day after school. He was always so happy and forever saying he loved you.'

As I sat listening I struggled to remain composed, trying to stifle my distress and the need to blow my nose as his emotionally charged voice filled the small space, describing the many happy family holidays they had all shared: skiing, repeated visits to Disney World in America, and to Center Parcs in the UK.

'I'm not sure when I tell these stories that I am portraying the amount of fun and warmth we shared and incredible bond we had, but I can stand here today and say that in his short ten years Felix had an absolute blast. I just wish it could have been longer. As for Oscar, it was a six-year gift to see the world through his eyes. There is absolutely nothing I can say to express how much I will miss him.'

How he managed to stand in front of us all and speak of his wife and sons with such heartbreaking pride and love I will never know. He delivered such beautiful words, at such a devastating time, in such an eloquent way. Where many of us would have lain down, curled up in a ball and given up, John stood tall, leaving the rest of us to crumble in our seats. In all his raw, exposed glory he did what John had always done: he took control, faced the situation head on and led the way. In his weakest hour, he stood the tallest amongst us.

As the service ended, Colly grabbed hold of my right knee and gave it an affectionate squeeze. 'Are you okay?' he said, his gentle and warm northern tones conveying genuine concern. I passed him a tissue, his own distress visible; his eyes were deep pools of glossy brown as they struggled to hold on to the tears that were seeking release, and his intermittent sniffling becoming louder.

It was reassuring to be sitting next to such a lovely man. I hadn't seen him in years but that didn't seem to matter. I could have broken down and bawled loudly with him right there and then in the full knowledge that he'd have stayed beside me and probably cried more himself, too. He was one of life's good guys. It was all I could do to nod in the affirmative to him as I tried to compose myself.

The vicar then asked everyone to file out from the front to the back, not through the door by which we had entered, but through a door situated to the back left of the altar. Just as I thought it couldn't get any worse, people in the rows in front of me started to file out of their pews. Silently and with small steps they moved gracefully to the left like cascading slow-motion dominoes and, as they gently rippled away, my view of the floor to the front of the altar, that had been blocked until that time, cleared. There, sitting parallel to each other on separate trestles, were three coffins, one large, two so very small: Heather's, oak and central; Felix's, a *Doctor Who* coffin emblazoned with a large dalek, to the right; Oscar's, a red, white and blue Lego coffin, to the left. Felix loved *Doctor Who* and Oscar loved playing Lego. Sitting on top of the coffins were their respective pictures. Dark, wavy-haired, hazel-eyed, handsome Felix, and sweet, cherub-faced, blue-eyed and blonde-haired Oscar, either side of their mum, blonde, blue-eyed and with such a kind and gentle face. I felt winded. As the queue continued to move forward I was transfixed, unable to divert my gaze from such a distressing sight, as if by looking longer I might convince myself that what I was seeing was not real.

The chilling reality of the situation smacked me in the face again.

The queue continued to move out onto a covered patio area facing a small, immaculate garden enclosed by a fence at the rear of the crematorium. As I came through the door I could see John ahead, standing at the front. No wonder it was taking so long to move forward – John, at the helm again, was greeting and hugging each person as we filed out. His sister, Sue, looking drawn and tired, was supporting him by moving down the queue, hugging and thanking guests too. As they did this, the summer sun, which had been absent earlier when we had entered the crematorium, suddenly emerged, flooding the terrace and shining brightly down. It was a wonderful, welcome blanket of warmth in such a desperately sad and emotionally draining day. For a brief moment, its beauty fooled me into thinking life was okay again, but the grim reality of death – and such young death – wore a heavier coat that continued to hang over the assembling crowd.

'How are your daughters doing?' I asked Colly, trying to make some light conversation as we moved slowly along in the queue.

'They're doing really well, Jill. Both at university. One's studying fine art and the other pharmacy, so very different subjects.'

'John says you have a great relationship with them both.'

'Yes, I do. I'm very proud of them. What about your son? Remind me, what's his name?'

'Alexander to me, but all his friends call him Alex. He's fifteen now and studying for his GCSEs. We're very close.' I broke momentarily, before continuing. 'Thank God we've still got them, Colly. The thought of being where John is right now makes me feel ill.'

'Yeah, I know,' he said. He paused before slowly leaning in towards me and whispering, 'But they can be little fuckers can't they? ... Right little fuckers,' he muttered again, shaking his head knowingly as he pulled back and winked at me.

Little fuckers! Did he just say that? His blunt but funny words sliced through the thick air, hanging provocatively in front of me. I managed to suppress my immediate desire to laugh out loud, both at the truth of his statement and my shock at its timing, mumbling quickly in agreement to try and move the conversation on. This was the gentlemanly Colly all over, delivering a verbal atom bomb like he was talking about the price of fruit and continuing without any outward expression or emotion, leaving others at the wayside, reeling. No offence was meant or taken – he was very bright, with a razor-sharp, wry humour. And perhaps that day his observation, however out of place, was an understandable effort to keep his own emotions in check.

I pondered his words, knowing that in their tragically young deaths Felix and Oscar would now be immortalised as perfect, just as my father had been. They had never been little fuckers, and sadly would never have the chance to be.

As I reached John, he wrapped his arms around me and hugged me tight. 'Thanks again for coming, Jill, making such an effort to be here and travel all the way from London. It really does mean a lot.'

I whispered in his ear. 'Please stop thanking me. London really isn't that far away and I wanted to come. I'm right here for you and don't worry, I'm going nowhere.'

Going nowhere – what was I thinking? Of course I would be going – straight back to London, back to my own full life and my son. My living, breathing, lovely son. Thank you, thank you, thank you – my son is alive. I've lost track of just how many times I repeated that to myself, the fragility of life dancing around me, invisible but so very present.

As I walked away from John and headed towards the car park I breathed a sigh of relief, selfishly envisaging my welcome return home; this was his nightmare, not mine. I just needed to face my car south and keep driving, his life a disappearing vision in my rear-view mirror. He hadn't played any significant physical part in my life over the years. But there my thoughts paused, and I smiled inwardly as I acknowledged the emotional presence he most certainly had.

CHAPTER 2

It had all begun in 1978: thirteen years of age, a school skiing trip in Italy, a basement disco and a kiss. My first kiss, as it happens, and apparently only John's second. I was smitten. I still have a picture of us standing outside our accommodation after a day of skiing, a beautiful blue sky and two tall fir trees in the background. Strangely, there is no snow on the ground – as I recall, it had started to thaw. His right arm is wrapped protectively around me; he has short, straight, chestnut-coloured hair with a fringe, and is wearing dark, flared trousers, a pale, collared shirt and a light-grey fitted woollen jumper – very 1980s. His left hand is casually placed halfway into his trouser pocket and he looks confidently at the camera – quite the cool dude. I, on the other hand, look quite overcome in his presence, shy and unsure. I have one arm around him but the other hanging loosely at my side as he pulls me in towards him. My hair is a similar colour to his, but shoulder length and in a rather unattractive basin cut, and I'm still wearing my dark blue salopettes and boots, a light blue jacket with red piping down the front and have my white-framed goggles hanging around my neck. My dull, mismatched outfit hangs shapelessly on my young shoulders, screaming out for something a little more stylish. Thankfully, I recall thinking otherwise at the time.

It was young, sweet, innocent love but sadly it was to be short-lived. Just that one week, in fact, followed by the briefest of contact in two separate lives over thirty-three years, as mismatched became something of a theme between us, extending way beyond one forlorn ski outfit.

John says today that when he returned from the skiing trip he just couldn't find the courage to step forward again. Well, of course he would say that, wouldn't he?

'Honestly, Jill, I did fancy you back then, I just didn't have the confidence to make a move.'

'Oh, please! You don't expect me to believe that explanation, do you? You had the courage on our skiing holiday. It can't have just disappeared.'

'I know. It doesn't make sense, does it. But it's true. When we returned from Italy I just bottled it, and the longer it went on the harder it became.'

In fairness to him, in the weeks that followed the skiing trip I do remember spending many lunch breaks sitting on the steps outside the school block, facing the expansive playing fields that surrounded the school as he circled from behind with a seemingly troubled and tortured expression. I willed him to make a move but, regardless of his apparent desire, his own forces willed him to stay put. It just wasn't to be; or it just wasn't *meant* to be.

Two years later, in 1980, and at fifteen years of age, we were elected Head Boy and Head Girl. John's forces continued to keep him firmly in his trenches, while mine still carried the torch I had lit for him two years earlier. I was unable to shake off my youthful infatuation with a brief and unrequited first love and, worse, I was now forced into his direct path with the joint responsibility we shared. That which I could not have was paraded daily in front of me: it was a permanent close-range reflection of rejection. It might have been easier if he'd retreated with overt disdain after our ski-trip encounter, indifferent to my presence. But instead, he oozed warmth and charm around me, ensuring I knew he enjoyed being in my company.

'Wow, well done, Jill. It's fantastic, isn't it?' he said, as we left the Headmaster's office having just been told we'd been selected for the Head Girl and Boy roles.

'I'm a bit shocked actually. I didn't expect it.'

'No way,' he said, incredulously. 'Don't be ridiculous. It was always going to be you, and I couldn't think of anyone I'd rather be sharing the role with.'

And with that one sentence and a bucketload of flattery he kept me hooked and hoping that one day he might return. I looked on admiringly, buoyed by his compliment.

I consoled myself with the knowledge that we were friends, a friendship that was formed despite, or maybe because of, our secret and mutual admiration. I loved our time working together as Head Boy and Head Girl, managing prefects and their rotas, being central to school parent events and being involved in overall student activities. It was a platform on which our friendship could grow.

'It was a complete disaster,' John said one day after a prize-giving speech to hundreds of parents had rendered him almost voiceless. 'I feel so embarrassed.'

'Honestly, John, it was fine,' I lied. Green-eyed envy or not, I couldn't possibly have taken joy in his overt discomfort at underperforming. If I had hardly heard him, standing no more than a metre away, no one else had stood a chance.

'Are you sure?'

'Absolutely. I could hear you clearly, so stop worrying. Your mouth's too big and loud not to be heard,' I joked.

'Very funny.'

It was enough to make him feel better, enough to feel like we were a team, enough to generate a lovely feeling of closeness. It was enough.

Regardless of his apparent lack of romantic interest in me, I loved being around him.

He exuded confidence with his constantly positive and upbeat nature, generously giving out energy to others around him, lightening the mood of wherever he found himself. He was a breath of fresh air.

'Congratulations, Jill,' he said, as he walked towards me on the school playing field at the end-of-year local schools' athletic championships. I'd just won the final of the four-by-one-hundred-metre baton run with three other girls. He loved and excelled at sport, and my achievement was now the welcome focus of his attention. 'Absolutely fantastic.'

My heart swelled as he showered me with praise. Coupled with the hot and sunny day, his words made life feel good and full of possibilities.

'Thanks. We trained hard and so it felt great to win. But it doesn't touch your own success. I hear you've been awarded Sportsman of the Year. Now that's something to shout about. Well done!'

'It was a foregone conclusion,' he joked. 'I mean, who else was going to get it?'

Despite his never-ending bravado, and outward geniality and warmth, I always thought he kept others emotionally at bay, an instinctive sense that an invisible moat floated around him, a boundary wall behind which he hid. He was an apparent contradiction, or just very well defended. I couldn't imagine having an open conversation with him about personal aspects of our lives; he didn't engage in that way. Well, not with me anyway. Not then.

And then it was upon us – the end of school, a parting of the ways, though the only crisis I vividly remember from this time was spectacularly failing most of my exams, rather than any sweet longing for John as we waved goodbye. I'd passed my English O level the previous year, but sadly this early promise was soon forgotten in the face of such humiliation. I was Head Girl and I had let myself and the school down. John was the last thing on my mind.

This academic failure, born from a sheer lack of study and focus – which I believe stemmed from the continuing trauma of my father's sudden death – was, and remains, the biggest single regret of my life. As a rule, I don't like to view any of my life experiences in this way. I prefer to say I've made choices, some better than others but all ultimately bringing either great highs, great lows or something in between. But on this occasion, and on one other in my life some years later, it was exactly what I felt. (The second regret comes from my time in the armed forces, when I foolishly turned down the offer to be put forward to Sandhurst Officer training to see if I could pass their selection procedures. I left, and joined the police instead.)

I have digressed somewhat from the object of my affections. As another year spent retaking exams loomed in front of me, there was little room left in my world for any wistful romantic thoughts and musings.

Our paths would not cross daily again, but our friendship continued as we regularly met up with Colly, Gammie, Amanda and others; rollerblading, parties, walks and other social activities brought us into repeated contact. On one occasion, John joined me and my family at a golf club party. But nothing changed; I continued to hope and he maintained his emotional distance.

Venturing to pastures new at the age of seventeen, I left the UK to spend one year in Belgium as an au pair; letter writing kept the strings of our friendship tied. I remember sitting next to the floor-to-ceiling window in my small bedroom, looking out over the beautiful large garden to the front of the house and penning letters to him full of my experiences of living with an American family with three young children, and of my gallivanting as I forged new friendships:

Hi John,

Hope all is good with you. I'm settling in well and have met some other au pairs to go out with socially. We've found this nightclub out in the sticks called the Black Beauty, and we go there most weekends. Last week was a disaster though; I was coming home in the early hours and as I stepped onto the train one of my shoes fell off onto the track – a nightmare! I was so embarrassed as I crawled home looking like some dirty stop-out and quietly opened the front door at 5 a.m. so that I didn't wake any of the family. Thank goodness they didn't see me – would have given the wrong impression.

Looking forward to receiving all your news

Jill x

Hi Jill,

Only you could lose a shoe as you board a train. Oh, how I wish I could have been a fly on the wall. As for dirty stop-out – that's exactly what you were! I'm great. My pattern-making apprenticeship is going well, even though it's an eleven-mile cycle ride both ways and I've got to leave home at 4 a.m. each day. I've never been bothered about learning to drive before, but think I may have to save the money for some lessons. It's a long day otherwise.

Have you met any Belgian hunks yet?

John x

Hi John,

Believe it or not I'm more interested in dancing the night away to Michael Jackson. The Black Beauty plays 'Thriller' and lots of his other tracks obsessively. It's great! The only Belgian hunk circling is a waiter at the club called Xavier, who I am currently keeping at bay.

What about your own love life? Girls galore?

Jill x

Hi Jill,

Xavier sounds very exotic to a northern boy like me and why, just why, are you keeping him at bay? He must be ugly or have ears as big as mine? Life here busy, lots of gigs, football and no girlfriend right now. Surprising I know, being the handsome catch I am. Relieved to hear that your taste in music is the great Michael Jackson. I'm prepared to let you dance to him.

John x

Hi John

You are correct. Xavier is a tall, dishy blonde whose alluring mystery is only heightened as he speaks not a word of English and, as my Flemish is non-existent and my French weak, we communicate non-verbally. It's much easier. He's moving in slowly with his blue eyes and sexy foreign accent. I may be out here for longer than my intended year.

Jill x

PS Please stop asserting your musical yardstick on my life.

Another letter posted, another ping-pong ball sent back. We got on so well, and our shared humour and relaxed ribbing of each other ensured my affection for him continued. In view of his responses I could only believe he felt the same way. But the threat of the lovely Xavier failed to catapult him forwards.

My three-year psychiatric nursing course on my return to the UK at eighteen and John's continued apprenticeship, both in our home town of Manchester, returned us to proximity, as did both of us working in a wine bar in the evenings in the city centre, in the same pedestrianised shopping square, to supplement our incomes. The same square maybe, but in keeping with the forces of nature that still weaved their web around us, different bars. John worked at Horts and I worked at The Conservatory. Positioned opposite each other, no more than two hundred metres apart, they were so tantalisingly close but with what felt like an ocean between them.

Our friendship continued and John took me to my first concert when we were about nineteen. He loves his music and took me to see Animal Nightlife. I wasn't aware of it at the time but this was apparently a 'sort of' date – a covert dummy run that John was quietly entertaining. I obviously didn't pass muster, as there was no subsequent outing or clear declaration of desire from him.

As he danced the evening away, submerging himself in the experience, I momentarily stepped back a few metres and quietly watched him, rather than partaking and letting myself go. I could see John clearly – full of life, free and completely unaware of my observation – and soaked up the joy of being in his company even though, despite his physical proximity, he was an emotionally distant figure, beyond my reach.

'So, I didn't pass the John-Bickley-potential-girlfriend test then?' I said, recently.

'That sounds awful. It wasn't quite like that. I was overawed in your company and I still couldn't find the courage to make a move.'

'You were nineteen,' I laughed, 'not thirteen, and we were good friends. You knew I was attracted to you and wanted more.'

'I know, but maybe I didn't want to risk our friendship. If I'd said something and it hadn't worked out, we'd have probably lost that.'

By around twenty years of age John was in an established relationship and I, as a late starter, was not. He became, if it were possible, even more unobtainable. We were maturing, and with that maturity I began to accept that we were destined for different romantic paths. I surrendered, letting go of my long-held desire for more from him; he clearly wasn't interested and I had to stop wallowing in some romantic notion that he ever would be.

Surrendering in life can often lead to that which we think we want or need actually presenting itself to us and, as if by magic, shortly after my resolve to let go, events transpired that allowed us to take a closer look at each other. John's relationship faltered and, newly single, he placed himself momentarily within reach of me once more. Being brave or reckless, he decided to cross the platonic boundary during a night out together. We must have been about twenty-one.

We returned to my nursing-home room in his car and parked outside. He leant in, stealing a kiss, the eight years that had elapsed since our last one fuelling our shared passion and eager consumption of each other. A couple of his open shirt buttons revealed his very hairy chest, something which, years later, he delighted in reminding me I couldn't keep my hands off.

'Your hands were all over me,' he teased. 'You wanted me, I know you did. I could have had you!' he confidently asserted, the male fantasy of female submission in the face of his assumed charms colouring his judgement.

'I don't remember that – well, not in the way you describe,' I responded, indignantly. 'You were hardly an unwilling participant. And let me tell you, I was never going to succumb to your charms. I was still a virgin and not about to relinquish *that* to you.'

But boy, he'd been sexy. There was something so very masculine about him beyond his physicality: his heady, powerful aura and essence, that intangible hypnotic something that our unconscious animal instincts can become alerted to in another. At the time I was quite overcome by it. My virginal and youthful inexperience only served to exacerbate the impact. This was new territory, his body a land not yet traversed but somewhere I wanted to travel to, explore and become lost in and on.

We fell onto my single bed fully clothed, arms and legs entwined, kissing passionately. And then without notice and brutal in its immediacy he suddenly jumped up, his whole demeanour changing. I just didn't see it coming. We can only have been in the room for a matter of minutes.

'I'm sorry, I'm really sorry. I have to go,' he spluttered, and fled without further explanation, like a wild horse bolting in fear. I was left reeling again. Had I been about to sleep with him? No, but the possibility of a future intimacy had been placed tantalisingly close, and I had momentarily become beguiled as he had offered, and I had readily taken, a few more sips of the elixir of John.

This was his second hurtful brush-off and despite the eight years that had passed since the last, this time the sting truly stung, placing an invisible but defined and painful line under us. His silence in the following weeks only added to my hurt and confusion. We were two people who could not find the courage to speak to each other, either by way of an explanation from him to me, or my own enquiry regarding his behaviour.

What stopped him from moving in close and developing a relationship with me? He was the only one with the answer, and was clearly not about to provide any explanation at that point. Maybe he didn't even understand himself. I berated myself repeatedly: you foolish, naive woman. Don't. Let. Him. Do. That. To. You. Again.

His rejection was something I reflected on throughout the years, and the fact that I continued to reflect in this way was a source of intrigue to me: why should I care about something that had happened such a long time ago with someone I had barely seen over the years? Was it the mistaken hero-worship of my first love, with all its rose-tinted glasses, coupled with the fact that on two separate occasions he'd shown an interest and then inexplicably withdrawn? I couldn't quite define it, but I knew that the affection I felt for him at school had never left me, and I instinctively felt he was still drawn to me too. Perhaps because of this I would always look back and wonder why he had been unable to progress a romance with me. What had he feared so much?

A year or so after this second rejection, in 1987, I was twenty-three years of age and seeking adventure. I joined the

Royal Military Police, and with that one move I put a sea between us. During two years in Germany my love of letter writing continued:

Hi John,

I'm just back from a field exercise when it rained non-stop for a week. I was filthy! The dirt engrained on my body will take months to clean away. I slept in a soggy sleeping bag in a dug-out trench. Absolutely no room for mascara or beauty regimes my friend – being smeared in camouflage paint was as close to a moisturiser as I came! But all great fun; the physical and mental challenge, the sense of camaraderie and adventure.

I'm off now to my clean bed sheets. Bliss.

Hope all is well in your world.

Jill x

Hi Jill,

Life's great. I went to three gigs last week, all at the Manchester Apollo: The Style Council, The Communards and Joan Armatrading. A fantastic week of music and a whole lot more enjoyable than sleeping in a soggy sleeping bag in a trench! Crikey, it sounds awful. You're turning into a real-life *Private Benjamin* and I've got to say it takes some guts to put yourself through that – I'm impressed, I really am.

Outside of music, I met a lovely girl called Heather a few months ago at a nightclub. I'm officially off the market – it's a huge disappointment for thousands of other women, I know, but what can I say? We get on great and it's all going very well. She's a nurse – a general nurse though, not psychiatric like you were.

Looking forward to your next instalment.

John x

I reread his words slowly. He was my friend, and one who, above all the friends I'd had at school, I had actively kept in contact with. My attraction to him, his apparent attraction to me, our wonderful ease together, shared humour and the intangible and unexplainable bond that seemed to exist between us, had kept us glued together. It was a friendship sustained, despite our confused earlier emotions and our youthful inability to understand or articulate our feelings; a friendship valued, despite the distance and the very differing paths of our lives.

I was now twenty-three and had accepted he was never going to be anything other than a platonic part of my life, but to read of the warmth he clearly felt for his new girlfriend was difficult. He was moving on, and in the opposite direction to me. It hurt. Thank goodness I was in a different country:

Hi John,

Your life sounds very exciting for very different reasons to mine. My idea of fun is now making sure that I can strip and reassemble a nine-millimetre handgun quicker than the instructor or face doing repeated press-ups for every mistake I make. The other day I barely made it off the floor! But I'm getting there slowly and by the time I come in under his timings I'll clearly have a six-pack!

I'm so pleased that you've met someone. You sound so taken with her. Boy, she must be something to stop you in your tracks.

I'm still single but always on the hunt for my next prisoner!

Jill x

Hi Jill,

Just a very quick letter to say that Heather and I have decided to go and live in Jersey together. Gammie and Kev moved out there a few months ago and are loving it, so we thought we'd join them. I'll forward my new address when we've settled.

Hope all is good with you.

John x

His new address didn't materialise and twelve years rolled by when, with one short email, he dropped back into my life effortlessly, sounding as upbeat and positive as always. He'd found my contact details on the new Friends Reunited website:

Hi Jill,

It's me! How are you? It's been so long since we last spoke. I lost your address when I moved to Jersey and so couldn't write to tell you mine. We're back in the UK now, living in

Wales, married and we've just had our son, Felix. So much has happened since we last spoke!

Life's just dandy here. It would be great to hear all your news.

John x

I now had one three-year marriage behind me, had separated from my subsequent partner of a further five years and was raising our son alone. Twelve years, two failed relationships and one child. I was clearly a little more bruised from life's romantic path and challenges than John appeared to be. I had also left the armed forces after three years, was serving in the Metropolitan Police and living in London. We'd certainly had different experiences:

Well hello my friend!

Wow – what a surprise after all these years. Lost my address? Likely story.

Huge congratulations on becoming a daddy!

I'm now a parent too, and like you, to a son. He's five and called Alexander. Sadly, I separated from his dad when Alexander was around eighteen months and so it's just the two of us. But we're very happy.

I left the army after three years to join the Met Police, so life on the work-front has changed – admittedly just from one uniform to another.

It's lovely to hear from you, John. We must try and keep in touch this time.

Jill x

Three more years passed, the strings of our distant friendship remaining loosely tied with annual emails.

Suddenly, another opportunity to meet: John was coming down to London for a few days to work and was free to meet up. He'd taken me by surprise, unexpectedly calling to see if I was too. His voice had been instantly familiar and reduced years of little contact to insignificance.

'It'd be great to see you again. We're doing a job in central London for a couple of days and I can leave the guys on one of the evenings so we can have a drink together. I want to know all about the men in your life.'

I laughed loudly. 'Really, there's not a lot to tell you on that score. It's just me and my son, which is much simpler, trust me.'

'I can't believe you haven't got lots of admirers,' he jokingly offered.

Well, that's an inadvertent irony, I thought. *I was such a catch you'd walked a country mile to avoid me in our youth.* I let it pass without comment. The observation would have been far too direct and it was a subject we had never permitted ourselves to talk about – well, one he'd never wanted to entertain, and so it would have been out of place in our first conversation for years.

'Yes, of course I can make it. It'll be lovely to have a proper catch up after so long. Crikey, how long has it been?'

We mulled it over and decided it was about sixteen years since we had last seen each other. It was early 2003, and our last encounter had been the 1986 momentary bed scene, though I resisted making that observation. We'd moved on, hadn't we?

It was an out-of-the-blue call and completely unexpected, but a wonderful surprise.

A few weeks later I found myself outside the Hippodrome night club in Leicester Square, standing discreetly against a wall to the side of the front door as I waited for him to arrive. *Relax*, I told myself, as I tried to calm the knots in my stomach. *He's just an old friend passing through.* It was a dark early-winter evening, the pavements heaving with people and the surrounding roads busy with the traffic and noise of central London. The atmosphere was buzzing. I melted into the background as I collected my thoughts. I was no longer the young, adoring woman he'd last seen, but thirty-eight years old and a devoted mother to my eight-year-old son. Despite this I still felt both nervous and excited at the thought of seeing him after such a long time. My expectation of romance had now gone but what remained, and was carried deep, was huge affection and a childhood love for him. This feeling was beyond even my own understanding and comprehension, an innate part of me, possessing a timeless and pure quality.

I was intrigued; just how would he look and, more importantly, in his physical presence how would he make me feel? Would he still affect me as he had always done? We had joked about holding a red rose to make sure we would recognise each other. I recalled that when I was about thirteen he had insensitively nicknamed me 'Big Jill', for the simple fact that I had left school at the end of one year flat-chested and returned to school in the September with a substantially bigger chest. My oestrogen had clearly arrived, and the soft curves of womanhood had rapidly flourished over the six-week summer break. As a self-conscious teenager I was mortified at John's adolescent attempts at humour and the subsequent repeated use of this nickname by him and Gammie for many more months to come. John had meant no offence – he just didn't think sometimes.

Well, I was now a modest 34B, so hardly 'Big Jill' material. In my efforts to hide some emerging grey, my hair was blonder than before but I thought it was a similar style to when we had last seen each other – slightly wavy and falling a couple of inches below my shoulders. I hoped I looked good. I was determined to look as fantastic as I could, my wounded pride at his rejections, despite the years gone by, vainly marching on. I was a young thirty-eight, I told myself.

As I stood contemplating my feelings, attempting to appear outwardly calm and nonchalant, I suddenly saw him walking towards me through the crowd, his stride and poise as confident and determined as it had always been. As he reached me I could see his blue-green eyes looking down, absorbing my face as he smiled broadly, immediately wrapping his arms around me in a big bear hug.

'Great to see you Jill. It's really great to see you,' he said, enthusiastically.

'And you too, John. It's been far too long.'

He had less hair now but it was still his own dark colour.

He was ever so slightly heavier, but still athletic in physique and as attractive to me as he had always been.

We made our way to a nearby busy pub and found a booth behind the bar; the gentle noise of people chatting filled the air. He hadn't changed, still teetotal and drinking Diet Coke with ice. I hadn't changed either, choosing a large glass of red wine. It was an evening of chat and laughter where, as I sat opposite him, I can recall so vividly still thinking that I'd just not been his type. Why did this man still pull at my heart-strings? Sitting there in his thick, cream woollen jumper, there was something so reassuringly solid and earthy about him, and he had a wonderful glow as he spoke with such warmth about his life in Wales with his wife and son. We studied each other intently as we spoke, and I sensed what I had always sensed: his own attraction to me. Our mutual attraction weighed heavily on the wooden table between us, an intan-gible presence. The simple, unexplainable chemistry of two people who, despite opportunity, had somehow managed to teeter around the perimeter of a controlled and safe friendship without ever jumping feet-first into the unknown, risky and deep abyss of romance.

'So come on then, tell me all about your life in Wales. I think you said you moved there from Jersey when Heather joined the North Wales Police?'

'Yes, that's right, about eight years ago. She'd always wanted to leave nursing and go into policing. She applied to North Wales because her family used to live in the area and she liked it, and because it was close to Manchester where some of her family live.'

'So, did you have a job sorted before you moved, then?'

'No, once we arrived I managed to find one at a place called Knights Shopfitters, and I eventually became one of the partners. It's doing very well too, which is great. We absolutely love living in Anglesey. It's such a beautiful part of the world and being near the sea is just fantastic, particularly with Felix.'

He shone with pride as he continued to tell me about becoming a dad three years earlier.

'I just love it. We waited until we were a little bit older before having him but I can't tell you how much I love it. I've even given up playing football on my Saturdays off, which says everything. Anyway, enough about me. What's been happening to you? I've got to tell you, you look great.'

'I know, I know,' I joked, brushing him off in my embarrassment at his sudden observation.

'Well, look at me – I've not fared so well,' he laughed, pointing at his thinning hair.

'Life's good. Just like you, I love being a parent and I just adore my son. We're a very close unit.'

'It must be hard, though, raising him alone and working full-time in a job like policing?'

'Yes, when I have to do long hours it's particularly hard, but I'd rather be a single parent and happy than in a relationship that's not good. I do envy the fact you've been with Heather for years and are happy. I just haven't managed to find that long-term success with anyone. I get a five-year itch!' I said, making light of the situation to inject some humour into the conversation. This was an evening to be light and celebratory at seeing each other again. I didn't want to get into heavy waters about my past relationships.

And so the evening continued, taking turns to share snippets of our lives from all the previous years we hadn't seen each other and, as always when engrossed in another's company, the time sped by. Before I knew it, we were walking out into the cold night air and had arrived at the top of Leicester Square tube station steps. It was bedlam, with people pushing in opposite directions as they tried to progress through the crowds. One final hug and, after I pulled back from him and we'd said our goodbyes, I descended quickly into the Underground, not wanting to extend the moment more than was necessary. I decided not to look back to send him another wave. In all his vibrant, technicoloured unavailability he looked gorgeous; I didn't need to cast my eyes further on his departing figure to see or feel his effect. He says now that he stood at the top of the steps waiting and wanting me to turn around, and felt huge disappointment when I didn't. Not for any desire on his part to flee his marriage and suddenly do what he had been unable to do before – he was so very happily married – but because of the unspoken bond we had had from childhood.

I found myself a window seat on the train home and closed my eyes to reflect. It was over two decades since we'd left school, during which time our contact had been mainly distant and sporadic. Yet, we could meet up sixteen years later and slot back in together seamlessly, as though we'd never been apart. Life may have changed over time for us both, but our natural connection had not. It remained as strong as ever.

Seven years passed. John was now the proud father of a second son, Oscar, born one year after our London meeting, and I remained single with the rare and generally short-lived foray into dating and romance, ensuring the emotional wall around me and my son had become higher and higher. Alexander was my joy and we had a safe and happy ship; romantic ventures rocked the boat – they were to be kept at bay. My mating radar was not to be trusted!

My mothering radar, on the other hand, despite the challenges posed as a single parent, was a finely-tuned and trusted tool. My easy motherly devotion and perpetual inability to attract the 'right' man rubbed together like sand on wet skin. But I was very content in my single state. A cherished son, a reliable job and good friends, and for all the inevitable sporadic loneliness that the inconsistency of my love life brought, I had a happy and full life in every other respect.

It was June 2010, and my last email contact with John had been about eighteen months earlier, so I decided I'd send him another to see how he was doing:

Hi John, just wondered how you are my friend?

Hope all well with you and your family? Would be good to catch up again.

Jill x

Good morning, Jill. Great to receive your email, life's just dandy. We've moved house, still in Anglesey but into the country with a big field for Felix and Oscar to play in. I'll assume you've just kicked your chap into touch and you're in need of comforting. Only kidding. I'm sure you've replaced the front door six times by now due to the constant beating down by would-be suitors. Would love to keep in touch. Have a groovy day.

John x

Hi John, no door beating going on – I'm happily single, with a very busy life that leaves no time for men! We've now moved to a lovely house overlooking a river in Weybridge and nearer to my son's school. And I'm studying for my Inspectors' exam, so I'm under a lot of pressure. But life's good.

Jill x

John now poked fun at my inability to maintain a long-term relationship, his life being the complete opposite of mine – settled when young, and happily married. It seemed our love of our respective children was now the only similarity we shared.

Some two weeks later I stood in my living room watching the scrolling Sky News bulletin at the bottom of the screen, blinking to make sure I'd read it correctly and waiting for it to scroll round again to reread it. Disbelief at first, then the slow and awful realisation that it could only be them. There it was in unmistakable black lettering:

Detective Constable Heather Bickley and her sons Felix, 10, and Oscar, 6, have died in a house fire in Anglesey.

Life wasn't dandy for John any more.

CHAPTER 3

It was just before the thirtieth anniversary of my father's death that I realised I had not actually grieved his loss. In 1973, counselling was either not easily accessible or just didn't have the wider and more receptive audience it has today. So, I was seven years of age and, along with my siblings of five, nine and eleven, supported only by our mother who was herself bereft and, for some time after his death, unable to see beyond her own overwhelming grief. The love of her life had been snatched away, leaving her widowed at thirty-two, with four young children to raise alone.

I say this in utter appreciation of, and sensitivity towards, her position. However much love she gave, we were like scared chicks clinging on for dear life and fighting for a piece of her as we dealt with the sudden death and disappearance of our father – a big, strong, fun man who was such an enormous presence in our lives, but who with a click of a finger was gone, taken from us forever, leaving a gaping hole in our lives.

He was not so strong, apparently, and had died from a huge heart attack, or what is medically referred to as a myocardial infarction.

Left in his space was our mutual young confusion, shock, distress and bewilderment, which crashed together like ships in a storm without a compass, struggling to stay afloat, struggling to keep our heads above water and breathe, but slowly drowning in our mother's relentless tears as they fell down her cheeks. They were coloured black with her mascara, the contrast stark against her pale skin. Some were smudged across her face and some escaped and trickled downwards to her neck. In their darkness they provided a haunting visual image, a screenshot of our collective distress; these weren't just her tears, they were ours too.

As she lay unmoving on the sky-blue woollen settee, sobbing loudly, we would huddle on the floor around her, just watching and absorbing the trauma within and around us, bereft of our father and, for some time, our mother too. Her vibrant and energetic presence had disappeared as quickly as had our father's, temporarily extinguishing her guiding light that should have lit the road ahead. We were in turbulent and frightening waters.

It took me ten months of counselling to unravel the lifelong and traumatic impact of losing my father at such a young age. I walked through the door for appointment one almost foetal-like and emotionally buried and out of the door after appointment forty feeling reborn. I will forever be indebted to my counsellor, who provided a safe and protective haven in which I could talk without fear of judgement, with whom I could cry my own pain-filled tears – enough for a sea – for the father I had lost and never really known, and who guided me gently in an environment of trust and acceptance. It was in this cocoon that at long last I felt able to take myself back to my seven-year-old self and slowly examine the personal impact of my father's death and, in laying myself bare, come to a far greater appreciation of myself and my life. I was finally able to grieve his death, set free years of unconscious hurt and distress, and so begin to heal my own deeply submerged, but exposed, raw wounds. Thirty years later it may have been, but when the flood gates opened and those same wounds were given free rein to have a voice – boy, did they speak!

What had I learnt from those ten months and how did this impact my relationship with John, who was now in a world of grief all of his own?

Two distinct threads had emerged. The first was how I was a *responsible* person, which is a theme apparently linked to childhood parental loss. Overnight my life had changed from being a seven-year-old child who played, to a seven-year-old child who had responsibilities, and the first one of those was to care for our mother. As she lay sobbing, my siblings and I had to put things right and make it all okay somehow. We were not children any more; we had more serious worries to consider.

The central role of a *responsible* person is to *save* others around them. This was not something I had been consciously aware of in myself; rather, it was an unconscious process. Having been inadvertently given the role as a child, this had manifested as I became older into an actual *need*. *Needs* are an unconscious driver and lurk below the surface wreaking havoc with what we believe are our conscious choices, our *wants*.

My saving sonar was literally on red alert, detecting any needy soul within a ten-mile radius. Not great when seeking out a potential partner.

The second thread to emerge, again operating unconsciously, was my perpetual search for my father incarnate. From the moment of his death my mother had immortalised him as some perfect God, encased him in a glass tower and placed him on a sky-high pedestal of perfection. He was what every man should be: a tall, dark and handsome gentleman, decent, loyal, dependable – the list of qualities was endless. Importantly, he was without fault or weakness. Perfect, just perfect! I *could* find him! I *would* find him!

The combined strength, but very different agendas, of these two aspects of the deeper recesses of my being charged forward, unseen and most definitely in control, determined to seek out the food of their survival: to find someone to save, and a template of my father to adore. The former generally bore no resemblance to the latter in terms of personality traits – on the face of it, yes, but time usually exposed something very different.

Once I had met the unsuspecting individual I would unconsciously, and with insane immediacy, project my father's apparent qualities onto him and convince myself I had found the man for me. He did not have to earn respect or love; it was instantly given by me on a plate. I had found him – my father, he did exist! Oh boy, the high of all highs, the sweet nectar of my needs and the rush through my veins as those needy bones of mine ran amok, tingling with the excitement and thrill of it all. Absolute mayhem then ensued as that wonderful initial high was then followed by the crashing inevitable low, with the slow and painful realisation that this man was not my father, that he was not strong but weak, weak and in need of my strength, in need of someone to take care of him, in need of a *responsible* person.

I was now *his* sweet nectar, the high of *his* highs, the rush through *his* veins! Oh, the tangled web we weave, the madness within the illusion. I had drawn-in the complete opposite of what I *wanted* but, true to form, exactly what I unconsciously *needed*, and the difference between the two was the hardest of realities. It was just devastating.

However, despite the pain of this realisation, after years of roaming in my unconscious wilderness the light bulb in my conscious mind had at last been switched on, and it was blindingly bright. That's not to say I could immediately change years of conditioned responses; counselling – and I speak from my own experience here, not from any particular body of research – does not cure, but having gone through the process I was finally alive to what had been operating within myself. I had a new set of eyes, a different vision and, in the words of my counsellor, a new 'set of tools' to use. I hoped that, over time, I would be able to identify and completely circumnavigate, negative and damaging relationships or, at the very least, extract myself from them if I had been unwittingly drawn back in. It was not a prescriptive 'this will not happen again' result. So, forewarned, forearmed.

I had also, throughout the process, painfully brought my father out from his glass tower in all his perfect glory, this untouchable presence and shadow who walked by my side, and dared to take a closer look. Slowly I had peeled back his seemingly perfect layers and realised that, just like us all, he was imperfect and flawed. He had become human. At long last my beloved father had become human.

I think it important, by way of balance, to state that despite not having met someone to share life with in a long-term and stable relationship I had had my fun along the way. I do not view any of my previous relationships with regret; to do so would devalue the whole sum of my life. They had naturally brought highs and lows, laughter and tears; I've loved or been enamoured by, and believe I've been loved or enamoured with, and I've thought I was loved but realised I wasn't or didn't. I've felt the unadulterated joy of being pursued, and the pain of being ruthlessly dispensed with. I've soaked up the flattery, and stood waiting for flattery to arrive which never materialised. I've been wined and dined, and I've wined and dined too. I've been treated like a lady or not, and thoroughly enjoyed being in the company of some lovely men, not all of whom needed saving.

I've had some wonderful sex, some average sex and some not so wonderful sex. I've been the recipient of a range of seduction techniques. I'll never forget returning home one evening with one date, whose impeccable manners and soft, cut-glass tones suggested a man of propriety. Coffee was my only offering. I think we'd had a few nights out by then and he clearly thought it was time to progress matters. As I returned from the toilet to the kitchen I found him leaning confidently against a countertop with his trousers and boxer shorts around his ankles and a very large grin crossing his face. He couldn't have looked prouder. I noticed his bottom was conveniently blocking the cutlery draw. I was shocked, and am certain it was the momentary loss of blood from my brain as it fled to my major organs – as his had clearly done – and the accompanying dizziness that propelled me forward into his arms in need of support and most definitely not coffee.

He was such a lovely man, and I know in the final hour I hurt him and for that I'm genuinely very sorry.

It's the rich tapestry of life, of my life, and I like to think I've learnt from it all and from them all. In each case we just weren't the right fit for a longer-term commitment or the timing wasn't right. However, underneath all these experiences lay my own less-than-healthy dynamic, waiting to find a suitable cause.

As John crossed the threshold back into my life, the ground on which I stood began to shift. His presence was a threat to my own well-being: my school sweetheart, a man I had carried a torch for throughout my life and who, with the heady and hypnotic allure of an unrequited love, had garnered untouchable and saintly qualities, just like my father. John, the gentleman – dependable, decent, loyal, just lovely and, from where I sat, without apparent fault or weakness – but now in the midst of an immense tragedy. He was vulnerable, cut adrift from life as he knew it and emotionally weakened.

And here was I, responsible and strong. I could feel my needy bones tingling already as they prepared to mount another operation. Up the M6 they sprinted in some out-of-body experience, the normally packed motorway empty for once. Not a car in sight, just me and the open road. I was in the outside lane, backpack on and full to the brim with my 'saving' tools. This was my biggest saving job yet – my last before retiring. I *could* save him! I *would* save him! Where was the bloody M6 traffic jam when I needed it? Bringing with it an enforced and prolonged conversation with myself. A chance to realise my own insanity at such a move and, at the next available turn-off, sneak down the slip road, duck my head and breathe a sigh of relief that I had not been ensnared again as I circled the roundabout and headed back south to safety. It was too late. I was already in Wales and the funeral was the next day. Life was never that simple.

CHAPTER 4

I don't recall how many times I read it – how many times it took before the reality of those simple black words sank in:

Detective Constable Heather Bickley and her sons Felix, 10, and Oscar, 6, have died in a house fire in Anglesey.

I stood staring at the television and within minutes the burnt shell of a house was beamed onto the screen where a reporter was standing in front, talking. The rafters hung from the collapsed roof, their dark and charred remains stark against the crisp, clear, pale-blue morning sky. A graphic, eerie picture, haunting in the still aftermath of the previous night's fire. A house destroyed, and with it the lives of three; a family wiped out in an instant – two young boys and John's wife, only forty-six herself.

What to do? How could I offer some form of support and help? His mobile was the only mode of communication I had with John, but I couldn't begin to be so intrusive as to call in the immediate aftermath. I was now a distant friend and, in any event, it would surely have been futile. I visualised him curled up in a ball somewhere, unresponsive and mute, struggling to breathe with the shock and distress. Calling was clearly not an option. I decided I would have to send a text. Regardless of its impersonal nature, the risk of easy misinterpretation and, I felt, such an arid, harsh manner in which to offer words of support at such a time, I didn't think there was any other way. I had to contact him somehow, so a text it had to be.

Struggling to compose an appropriate message, everything sounding so ridiculously trite, I eventually settled on a few words I hoped would say something of value. Value! There it was again, surely nothing would have any value to him now. It was an impossible task, so I was just going to have to go with my instinct. I phoned my sister to run through what I had managed to compose before I pressed *Send*. It was never going to be the right way to communicate in such tragic circumstances, but it was the only one open to me. It would have to suffice:

Dear John, this is Jill Barnes. I cannot begin to comprehend what you are going through.

The loss of your wife and sons is truly devastating. I just wanted to say you are very much in my thoughts. If there is anything at all I can do for you, please let me know. I hope you are able to find the strength to deal with such a tremendous loss. Take much care. Jill

One week later, he called. He said he was managing to breathe. He wanted to thank me for the text I had sent and said he was receiving lots of support from his family, friends, the community and the police. How lovely it was to hear him, to be able to ask him directly how he was and offer my support. But at the same time it was tremendously difficult to ask the right questions or make the right enquiries. Just where does one start in such circumstances? Perhaps not to ask too much at all. *Let him do the talking,* I said to myself, *just listen and be guided by him.* As we spoke, I became aware that my tone had become lower and sombre and my delivery slower, as if this would somehow wrap a gentle layer of concern and warmth around him.

'Thanks for calling, John. I really didn't expect you to. I just can't imagine where you are right now.'

'To be honest, I've just been focusing on the funeral arrangements which have kept me busy. I need to keep moving or I'll not survive.'

'I'm amazed you're standing. Have you got support close by?'

'Yes, the police have been fantastic. They've found me a flat to live in temporarily and some furniture too, and so many other people have been offering their help. It's quite overwhelming.'

He began to tell me some of the circumstances of the fire. He thought it had started at about 11 p.m. and John, who often worked late, had not been home. He had returned from work to find the house engulfed in flames.

'Do they know what caused the fire?'

'Yes, the fire brigade said it was an old refrigerator that had been left by the previous occupant. It was in the utility room next to the kitchen. We'd only moved in six months ago and we thought it was okay to use.'

I didn't push it any further. His voice sounded heavy, trembling with emotion, and now wasn't the time to ask probing questions.

As I sat on the stairway at home listening to him talk, I thought how unusual it felt. Watching the news, like all television viewing, enables you to absorb events in some surface way and then detach from the reality of those things reported upon, switch off the television and carry on with your life. As John spoke, the graphic image of his former home that had been beamed onto the television screen a week earlier rapidly flooded back into my mind in all its harrowing form. I struggled to let go of the image of the hanging black rafters. There'd be no switching off the television now as his voice, full of pain, passed down the telephone line, bringing the brutal reality of what had happened back to me. Death hung in the air; no skirting around it as it sat heavily between us. Life unexpectedly taken; no waking up in a sweat and breathing a sigh of relief that it had only been a nightmare; no more chances to speak to those suddenly taken; no more hugs and kisses. The only reality was the finality of his sudden and immense personal loss.

He wanted me to come to the funeral and, of course, I wanted to, but after years of distant contact and not having known his wife and children, I envisaged finding a hidden space outside the crematorium amongst the crowds where I could quietly pay my respects. His vision was somewhat different. He was having none of that and said he wanted me inside the crematorium with other school friends that were attending, where I was to be given one of the few seats available.

'Honestly, I don't need a seat inside,' I protested, 'I'm not close family and I didn't know your wife and sons. I'll be fine standing outside and in the circumstances would prefer it.'

'I'm not having that, absolutely not,' he said. 'You're travelling a long way and I'd really like you to be inside with the others that are coming from school.'

His pleading, emotionally charged voice silenced my own, placing me exactly where I hadn't wanted to be: in the middle of it all.

I had been catapulted to a ringside position: there'd be no discreet hiding outside now. Furthermore, he asked that, as I was travelling up the night before, could we spend the evening together? He wanted some space from family and friends closely affected and I was to be a welcome distraction.

Seven years since our last meeting and I had been thrown back into his path and the midst of an unimaginable tragedy. Driving to Wales, my mind had been full of all manner of thoughts and feelings: the cruelty of life events, striking without notice and leaving devastation in their wake; the blade-thin line between life and death; the warm feeling the long-held affection and regard I had always had for him gave me; and the prospect of meeting old school friends after thirty years. Thank goodness for the last of these. Despite the circumstances bringing us back together it would be so lovely to see them all.

As I pulled into the hotel car park in Bangor, John called: he could be with me in forty minutes. Crikey, only forty minutes! That was just enough time to check-in, find my room and do a virtual turn around. He said he would meet me in the hotel car park. Suddenly, I felt like a rabbit in the headlights. No time to compose myself either physically or emotionally, I was to be ejected rapidly from the safe confines of the hotel room and into his trauma-filled life.

As I walked out of the rear of the hotel I could feel my anxiety rising rapidly, my mouth becoming drier and my heart pounding against the wall of my chest. As I desperately tried to calm my breathing and to locate wise words of comfort that had now, despite my frantic efforts, inconveniently deserted me, I continued along the side of the building and around a corner, taking me immediately to the side area of the hotel. As I looked up the small slope leading towards the almost empty car park, my eyes instantly fell on him. There he stood, still as a statue, so terribly pale, bereft and stripped bare in his grief, a shadow of his former self. His pain was etched deeply across the gentle face I had known for so many years, and an aura of darkness and devastation surrounded him. I had known him from boy to man, but he now stood in front of me, broken and utterly alone, and bearing no resemblance to the John I had seen before.

Warning bells started to ring loudly. Had I learnt nothing from my life experiences? This was the exact moment I was supposed to start walking rapidly in the other direction. This was what months of counselling had been about: to understand my own dynamic and unconscious need to emotionally rescue vulnerable people.

As he stood facing me, now no more than a metre away, I was full to the brim with conflicting emotions. My own natural need to take full responsibility for him, to wrap him up and make sure he was okay, had saturated my motionless form, trying to seize control and lead the way while for the first time in my life a bright red *'Danger!'* alert bulb had begun flashing in my mind. A feeling of distinct unease descended upon me as I felt myself being pulled towards his magnetic aura. His emotions and need for support oozed out of his every pore like slow-running treacle spreading down onto the car park floor and wrapping around my feet, making it impossible to move and choose a direction. The combined force of our mutual presence was overwhelming.

This infuriating man who I was still so hugely drawn to, who had never needed me before but now stood before me weak in his loss, distraught and in the darkest of spaces. This man and his vulnerability, my nemesis, cruelly placed in my path, baiting me forward. As my mind exploded with the intensity of it all and I studied his broken form, instinct kicked in and propelled me slowly forward towards him. I had to find a way to be the friend he needed right now, and so I did what any friend would do: I wrapped my arms around him and we hugged while he cried, his heartbreaking sobs shattering the silence around us, his taller and bigger body slumping over me as he crumbled in my arms. There was no need for words. In those few brief minutes nothing else mattered; the rest was inconsequential. My bag of tools was laid to rest at the side of the road; they were not needed. I was simply being a good friend.

I don't know how long we stood holding onto each other. I don't know if anyone walked past. We were oblivious to our surroundings; the world had stopped moving, and time with it.

Eventually he pulled away, wiping the tears from his blank face. His eyes looked shut down and without depth – flat and dead.

'Thanks so much for coming. It's such a long way to have driven and I'm conscious of your son and your work commitments too.'

'There's no need to thank me. I'm just glad I can try and support you in some way. Are you sure you'd rather not be with your family this evening?'

'No, I need some space from them. It's too distressing when we're all together. Being with someone who isn't family is what I need right now – so long as you're okay with that?'

'Of course. What would you like to do?'

'Well, I've had an album of family pictures put together professionally for the wake and I need to collect that first. I can drive past the crematorium to help you get your bearings if you'd like, and maybe we can go out for some food later.'

I climbed into his black work pickup truck and secured my belt. It felt strange to be sitting next to him as we drove and spoke, to have been catapulted back into his life all these years after our last meeting in London.

'Is everything sorted for tomorrow?'

'Just about. I've found my conversations with the vicar difficult, but I think we've agreed the service now.'

'What was the difficulty?'

'Two things. Firstly, he wanted three hymns to be sung and I said I only wanted two. I'm an atheist and Heather wasn't much further from that position. And if I'd been a God-believer before the fire, let me tell you, I certainly wouldn't be now. I'm not about to have a religious service forced on me or my family. Then, when I was discussing my eulogy with him and who I was going to thank for all their support, he disagreed with me not wanting to include the National Health Service. This was despite me telling him that, following my check-up on the night of the fire to make sure I was physically okay, and with no home to return to, they insisted I leave the hospital. I'd asked if there was a room I could stay in and was told "No" very clearly.'

'Oh really? It doesn't sound like your mental welfare was considered at all.'

'No, it wasn't, so I'm not about to thank them for care they didn't provide, whether the vicar thinks I should or not.'

'You're right to stand your ground. It's your eulogy and your family, and you have to do it your way.'

'That's what I'm trying to do.'

Minutes later, we pulled into a large industrial park. He disappeared into one of the small business premises, returning after five minutes with a square black box about A3 in size and no more than three inches deep. He placed it on the seat beside me. I hid my immediate alarm and distress; we had just collected the visual remnants of his life with his family. His wife and sons were now sitting next to me, hidden from view, but filling the space with their deathly presence and the tragedy of their sudden demise. One innocuous box containing three lives. I wanted to tenderly place it in my lap and caress its hard exterior to soothe them as they lay inside, and to soothe my own unravelling emotions. I gulped quietly and looked towards him to see how he was. Still the same blank, distant expression.

'How about we go back to my flat for a coffee now? I'd like to look at the album, and I was going to ask you if you'd read my eulogy. I understand you might not want to, so please say if you'd rather not.'

I quickly thought over his request. Boy, I needed to steel myself for the next few hours alone with him where, it seemed, we would be sitting together in his dark world, he using me as a buffer in his rapidly changing existence.

'Coffee sounds wonderful, and of course I can read your eulogy,' I said. 'I'm touched that you've asked. Are you sure you want to share it before tomorrow? It's such a private and personal thing.'

'Yes, I'm sure. I've already shared it with my mum, who says it's beautiful – but she would say that, wouldn't she. If you could tell me what you think I'd appreciate your views.'

Ten minutes later, and we were walking through the door of his ground-floor flat into a narrow corridor with two small bedrooms and a bathroom off to the left and which led into an open-plan, cream, carpeted kitchen and living room that was about four metres by six metres in size. The kitchen area was situated in the right-hand corner, and to the left was a square table covered in various papers and 'In sympathy' cards, with two wooden chairs. French doors and a window to their right looked out onto a small patio that overlooked the sea. A black leather recliner was situated opposite the window. Devoid of the usual pictures, ornaments and lamps that all add a certain warmth to a home, it was a basic, but modern, clean space for him to retreat to, and in which to be safe from the world. No obvious home comforts, but right now, his home.

I sat down at the table and he immediately handed me his eulogy, handwritten on sheets of paper that had been folded together, their repeated opening and closing thinning the creases and bringing an aged and delicate feel. The hand-writing that I remembered from our school days jumped from the page and momentarily took me back, but as I slowly read his words, the past evaporated as his family surrounded me: their favourite things, their shared holidays, their shared laughter and years of a shared life.

Heather's favourite songs were from The Sound of Music, *and that's why we chose to play them today as you entered the crematorium. She'd taken Felix to see the show in Llandudno only a month ago.*

Felix was so competitive. He loved playing games but couldn't bear losing – even cheating at draughts to beat Oscar.

Oscar was as bright as a button, always coming home with stickers for good work or for helping the teacher.

He placed a large mug of coffee on the table. 'Thanks,' I said, as I took a deep breath and wished the mug held something a little stronger. But I would be driving everywhere in the next few days, so coffee was as strong as it was going to get. No warming glass of red to soften the edges of misery.

When we first met, Heather was very sociable and loved parties, and we were lucky to live in Jersey from where we flew to Paris, to see Prince and Michael Jackson. But then when Felix was born she changed and became more private, and the good thing was that I changed with her. We didn't want that lifestyle any more, we wanted to give all our time and effort to our boys.

I took a sip of coffee and continued. I was being given a preview into not just his yesterday but his tomorrows. Tears rolled down my face.

'I'm sorry, I didn't mean to upset you.' John was now sitting at the table too, leafing through his newly composed album.

'Oh, John, it would be impossible not to become upset. How you describe your life together and who they were. Your mum's right – it *is* beautiful.'

'Would you like to see the album?' he asked, as he passed it over to me without waiting for an answer.

I opened the first page and confronting me was a glossy professional picture of Felix and Oscar taken a few years before their deaths. They were lying close together on the floor, with beaming smiles and arms crossed as they looked at the camera, peachy-skinned and innocent. I turned the page to find another. This time both were kneeling close together in the snow, wrapped up in woollen hats and coats, Felix with his arm wrapped around his younger brother's shoulder, pulling him towards him affectionately. There were pictures of them at the seaside, at Disney World and at Christmas; pictures of Heather and John on their wedding day and, over the years, with their sons; and a menu Heather had written for a meal she prepared for John one evening, titled 'Bickley's Bistro', her surrounding words full of love and affection and providing a window into their life together and into Heather herself. It was a normal family album, portraying normal family life that within hours would be passed around mourners in anything but normal circumstances. Its glossy finish and neatly contained pictures challenged the reality of their deaths.

'Come on,' he said, 'let's go for a drive to the crematorium – so you've got half a chance of finding it – and then we can go and get a bite to eat.'

'I don't know about you but I need a hug right now,' I answered. I was here to support *him*, but was feeling bruised already by eulogies, albums and joyous pictures, all waiting to attend an imminent funeral.

He walked towards me, arms outstretched, and we held each other tightly.

It was a relief to leave his flat and breathe the outside air. A quick drive to, and past, the crematorium and twenty minutes later we found ourselves in a large, busy open-plan pub with different levels of secluded seating areas. 'My treat,' I offered, as we ordered our food and found a table with our drinks.

'What are you going to do, John, have you any idea?'

'No, not really, but I don't think I can stay here. For now, I'm going to take the next month or so off work to give myself some time to think it all through.'

'You're okay for money, though?'

'Yes, the police very generously gave me some to help tide me over, and I'll be earning once I return to work. So, I'm fine. Tell me about your son. We need to focus on something other than my family if we can.'

'Of course – I'm just sensitive to how you'd feel about that.'

'It's okay. My boys were much younger, so I'm okay listening to you talk about Alexander. Honestly, I'd like to know more about him.'

I reached for my purse and produced the picture I carried with me always: my son's face, shining back with his thick, dark eyebrows, dark brown eyes and mop of dark brown wavy hair in his sky-blue school blazer. 'Oh, Mum, that's not the best picture of me. Can't you choose another?' I could hear him say. But to me he looked exactly as he was: a young man on the verge of adulthood, testosterone rapidly changing his appearance.

'He's a handsome buck,' John generously offered.

'Well, of course I'd agree with that,' I laughed.

My mind was on overdrive, rapidly trying to filter my words for anything that could possibly cause him upset once they had left my mouth:

'He's lovely, but boy, getting him out of bed is the most frustrating thing. I swear he could sleep on a washing line.' No, you can't say that – if only he could stand by his son's beds trying to unearth them.

And another:

'He's lovely, but boy, getting him to focus on his homework and study for his exams is the most frustrating thing.' No, you can't say that – if only he could be supporting and encouraging his sons to study.

I wondered if my face was a contorted vision as I considered and dispensed with a range of options, finally arriving at something I thought was safe, my anxiety levels running high.

'But he's lovely with it too. He's so laid back, and as frustrating as that is sometimes I adore this bit about him. We move at different speeds!' I joked.

John might have been comfortable with this but I wasn't. His sons might have been younger, but with every word I spoke I was excruciatingly aware that Alexander had reached an age that Felix and Oscar never would. I quickly changed our conversation to neutral territory.

'Enough about my son. Did I mention that I'm studying for my Inspectors' exams this September?'

'No, I don't think you did. That's fantastic.'

I exhaled slowly as the undoubtedly boring subject of my study programme, normally capable of inducing instant narcolepsy, suddenly seemed very attractive.

'Well, it's hard work actually – six months of study around work and my son.'

'Heather wasn't interested in promotion at all. Did I tell you she'd been accepted by the Adelaide Police last year?'

'No, you didn't.'

'We were all ready to emigrate. Our visas had been processed, our house sale was going through, and then her posting arrived last September and changed it all. It was about four hours from the city and far too remote for us. So we changed our minds and bought the house we were living in. If only we'd gone. They'd all still be alive.'

'I'm sorry, John. That's awful for you – but you can't punish yourself for staying. We all make choices every day of our lives that take us down different roads. You must have felt it was the right decision at the time.'

'Yes – but right now that gives me no solace.'

He dropped me back to the hotel and we shared one final hug in the car park.

'If you need anything just let me know.'

'Thanks, Jill, for this afternoon and tonight. I appreciate it can't have been easy to be in my company.'

'Take it easy tomorrow, John. We're all here for you, so remember, you're not alone.'

He got back into his truck, and as he drove off I breathed a sigh of relief. Relief that that was his life not mine, that I could return to my hotel room and, for the next few hours, step back from the distressing space I had entered; relief that I could speak with my son and hear his lovely deep voice telling me how he'd get around to his homework later, reminding me we were due at the early 5.30 a.m. ice hockey training slot on Sunday and sharing with me what he'd been doing at school – a voice full of life.

'Hi, it's me. How's your day been?'

'Hi, Mum. Good so far. Nan's treated me to a delivery pizza which is about to arrive so I haven't got too long to talk.'

A welcome shot of soothing reality: his stomach taking priority over chats with his mum.

I laughed. 'Pizza – what happened to healthy living and a plate full of vegetables?'

'One pizza won't harm me. We're going to watch a movie together and Nan's going to have a glass of wine.'

I closed my eyes and listened to his familiar voice, happy and full of warmth, describing a picture of domestic bliss. I wanted to step through the phone and join him. My boy: the centre of my life.

'I've got to go, Mum. The door bell's ringing.'

'Okay. What are you having?'

'You know me – the usual large Hawaiian and some chicken wings too. Oh, and some barbecue sauce.'

'So a small meal, then?'

He laughed, taking pride in his substantial appetite; his twice-a-week hockey training and matches thrown in at the weekend consumed endless calories and maintained his slim physique.

'Before I go, how's John?'

He was fifteen, with his adored nan and had a pizza at the door. Talk of John could wait. I didn't want to bring darkness to his evening, however mature and capable he was of managing it.

'I'll tell you when I call back later. Go, before the pizza ends up next door. I love you loads.'

'I love you loads too.'

I stood under the shower, the hot reassuring water and lather gently cascading over my hair and body, cleansing me of the sadness of John's world. I crawled into the crisp, white cotton bed sheets and fell asleep instantly, exhausted by my day.

I woke early the next morning and decided to send John a text:

John, take a deep breath ... one step at a time. When you read your eulogy just remember to shut everybody else out and speak from your heart. You can do this, and Heather, Felix and Oscar will be proud. I know we can't hug and be together like yesterday but I will be with you every step of the way. Jill x

One final look in the mirror: black fitted short-sleeved, knee-length dress, black court shoes and a black bag; hair pulled back loosely with a conservative brown hair slide.

I was most definitely attending a funeral.

Taking a deep breath, I opened the door and walked to my car.

CHAPTER 5

After the emotional intensity of the funeral it was a relief to drive from the crematorium to the wake, a journey which John, who had given me directions the previous evening, assured me would be about fifteen minutes. It was a welcome respite from the intense atmosphere and sadness, and a chance to catch up with my school friend Amanda who was coming with me. Marvellous: bubbly Amanda; just the tonic.

Once in the car, we took our place in the queue of vehicles driving slowly up the long slope from the crematorium to the main road, at which point I was to turn left. If only it were that simple. So many had attended the funeral that the police were managing the traffic out of the crematorium. As I reached the junction, a larger-than-life uniformed police officer was waving vigorously and directing me to turn right. I looked tentatively to the left, wondering if I dared to feign confusion and break free in the direction I should have been going, but there stood another policeman in the road, stopping the traffic coming and indicating that I was not to turn towards him. For those with an in-built, natural sense of direction this would have posed no problem. However, I had not been blessed in this way and my first wrong turn, as is often the case, led to another wrong turn and to another and another. Oh, the gods weren't looking down on me! There we were, lost in Wales, with a wake to get to that would soon be over. Add to that my absolute hatred of being late and my stress levels were riding high.

Poor Amanda. Her regret at opting to take a lift with me was well hidden. She'd had no idea she was about to be given an inadvertent scenic tour of the Welsh countryside.

'Oh, Jill!' she eventually exclaimed. 'You haven't changed a bit. You're still ditzy.' Ditzy! I had clearly failed in my mission as Head Girl. Of all the lasting impressions I had wanted to leave, this particular personality facet had not been one of them, yet my inability to identify the correct route was doing everything to confirm this view and nothing to negate it.

I can't remember how long it was before I pulled into a lay-by and admitted defeat. But to sit there laughing and lost at the side of the road was truly a welcome relief. Simple laughter at the absurdity of it all. We were supposed to be at the wake by that point, but instead we were parked at the side of a dual carriageway with not one navigational bone between us.

'Oh, Amanda, I'm so sorry, I haven't a clue where we are. Do you have any idea at all?'

'Me neither, I'm afraid. My sense of direction isn't much better than yours,' she answered.

'Well, we can't miss it. How awful would that be. I'll never forgive myself if we don't get there in time.'

And then, as I looked in my rear-view mirror, I saw a lone, middle-aged male pedestrian approaching. I could have jumped out of the car and kissed him. *Please let him know how to get us back on the right track, please, please, please,* I muttered to myself. My prayers were answered. He was a local; he confidently asserted we were facing in the wrong direction, and provided us with a detailed route of how to get to our destination.

Forty-five minutes after leaving the crematorium we arrived at the wake, which was being held at a detached, traditional-looking pub called the Breeze Hill, and walked into a packed and loud large square room. Immediately to the left a long bar was positioned, where many people were standing and chatting in groups. Beyond that, dark wooden tables of varying sizes were dotted about, crowded with people, and along the end wall was an oblong buffet table laden with sandwiches and the usual cold-food spread.

Wakes, what strange affairs: full of sadness, full of people from years gone by, full of people you don't always know and, at times, full of unexpected laughter, be this in celebration of those who have died or a human coping mechanism through which to channel the intensity of emotion. I will never forget the wake of my stepbrother, who took his own life suddenly and without warning at the age of twenty-one: I was eighteen at the time. Family members had stood in the hallway of his grandparents' home as we left at the end of the night, and I can still hear the unexpected laughter we shared as we hugged goodbye. Perhaps, when walking so close to and in the midst of death, with its floor of shifting sand and the feelings of utter loss of control this can create, laughter keeps us sane; it is something easy and safe to hold on to.

We made our way through the crowd and sat with the rest of our high school friends at a table along the rear wall. It was good to catch up with them after all these years.

John Lyon, the cheeky Del Boy of the north, was still bemoaning the fact he had not been selected as a prefect: 'I mean, I still can't understand why I wasn't chosen. What was wrong with me?'

'John, you're on the way to fifty. It's time you let it go!' I answered. He was a lively and welcome presence at the table. He'd neither married nor had children, but had a girlfriend.

There was Colly, the charismatic sweet-talker, easy on the eye and divorced some years earlier from the mother of his daughters. And Hutty who, like Amanda, was married with two young children – serious and banker-like in manner, quietly spoken, and gentle in demeanour. He and John had often got together with their respective sons who had been a similar age.

While we chatted John moved around the room talking to other guests, returning to us occasionally and, as the wake drew to a close, joining us for a picture taken outside by his sister, Sue, to capture us all together again after thirty years. It was a moment of relief from the heavy atmosphere inside, and a time to share some uneasy laughter while we stood tightly together, arms around shoulders attempting to squash into one picture, clinging onto this shred of normality that allowed us to relax and breathe a little more easily.

I returned inside and decided to grab myself some sandwiches from the buffet. As I placed a few items on my plate, a slim, short-haired blonde lady in her early forties approached me. I thought it was the distressed female from the vestibule earlier but couldn't be sure.

'You must be Jill,' she said.

I smiled and answered, 'Yes,' not knowing how she had identified me.

'I'm Mel. My husband Kev and I have known John for years. I just had to come and say thanks so much for spending the evening with him yesterday. We were worried sick that he'd be alone. We said we'd travel up earlier, but he insisted he'd be fine as you were travelling from London and he'd be with you. I said to Kev, "Who's this Jill?" and he said you'd been at school with John. Thanks for looking after him for us.'

'There's really no need to thank me. He said he needed to be with someone outside of his close family, and I fitted the bill I suppose.'

'But he obviously feels close to you, otherwise he wouldn't have wanted to be with you on the eve of the funeral. It was a relief to know he was with a friend on such a difficult night.'

'It's very kind of you to come and say that, and it's lovely to meet you. John's very touched that you cut short your holiday in Spain to return for today.'

'We're devastated. We have two daughters of a similar age to Felix and Oscar. We used to meet up and they'd all play together. I almost didn't walk through the doors into the crematorium I was so distressed in the vestibule.'

'But you did,' I said and hugged her briefly before she left with talk of meeting up again in the future. It was the sort of passing conversation that fills uneasy gaps with vague plans you know are unlikely to come to fruition; the social niceties that weather the storm.

Slowly people started to leave, until eventually only a small circle of about fifteen men sitting on chairs were left, with a few others sitting close by; men who lived locally and knew John through work. I sat amongst them and John came and joined us, sitting next to me. This was the first time we had had a real chance to talk since the funeral.

'I just want to say how lovely your eulogy was. The way you spoke about your wife and sons – it was beautiful and I'm sure they'd be very proud.' I turned my body towards him slightly and spoke quietly, attempting to ensure our exchange was private. He was listening intently.

'Thanks, it's very kind of you to say, but I don't want them proud – I want them alive.'

A large smack to my face had just been delivered. I winced a little inside, but dared to continue.

'I'm excruciatingly aware that nothing I say in this respect will have any value to you at all right now, but I don't know how you managed to stand before everyone in that way. To have done them all such justice when you're in such a painful space must have taken an iron will.'

'I had to. I had to find the strength to talk about who they were, to tell everyone what they meant to me. But words on paper can't convey our lives together, how special they all were, how happy we all were together.'

'I know, but it was very moving. I wanted to acknowledge that.'

The chatter between others in the group had now increased and become louder, with laughter, and even jokes, being shared. It was a moment to behold: stoic Welshmen, some sitting quietly and appearing reflective, others boisterous and loud, sitting in the final moments of the wake and wrapping themselves around John, not in a physical sense, but by the sheer strength of their collective presence, while simultaneously possessing a gentle and protective aura.

Micky, his closest friend, sat nearby and was particularly vocal. In his mid-forties, with short, fine, mousy hair, he was tall and lean, his long legs, crossed at the ankles, stretched out in front of him, shouting over to others sitting opposite, clearly making a huge effort to make sure everyone gelled and the mood was kept more positive. His bellowing voice filled the air. John had worked with him for twenty years, the last ten in partnership, and such was the strength of their friendship that it was to Micky that John had turned on the night of the fire. They were chalk and cheese: John, teetotal and measured; Micky, a man who liked a few pints and could successfully work any room with his gregarious nature and charm. But they had a solid friendship that endured years, and when John had sat waiting at a neighbour's house to see if the fire brigade had managed to save his family, it was Micky who sat waiting with him. It was also Micky who had got out of bed hours later when John had called him to say that he'd been discharged and sent away from hospital with nowhere to stay. Micky had immediately gone to fetch him and had taken him home.

Sitting to the side of the circle was Elwyn, John's work colleague of about fifteen years, a gentleman, and a 'gentle' man, of few words. He was built like a rugby player: strong and stocky, and about five feet eight inches tall. 'He's so generous with his time,' John would later say. 'If he's ever asked for favours outside of his working week he'll drop everything and make your needs a priority. It doesn't matter what he's doing. He's such a genuinely lovely man.' Elwyn sat facing the centre of the circle in silence and was very still, looking down towards the floor. He obviously didn't want to talk and that was fine, but he was clearly going nowhere. He didn't need to speak a word; his quiet, powerful presence was enough to convey to John that he was there for him if needed.

Directly across from us there was one other friend called Fitzy, who John had known for fifteen years through work. He was a warm Irishman who sat observing all. I could see him looking at me from across the circle; eventually he approached and introduced himself.

'So tell me, how do you know John then?' he enquired.

Crikey, how long had he got to hear my tale of romantic woe and unrequited love? As we hugged goodbye later, he whispered to me, 'He's listening to you, Jill.'

More goodbyes, and then John and I sat in my car in the pub car park waiting for Gammie to come out. He was staying with John for a couple of weeks and I was driving them back to his flat so we could all spend a little more time together.

As we stared silently through the windscreen towards the rear pub door, I mulled over whether it was right to broach the subject that many must have thought was a distinct possibility with John: suicide. When was it right to enquire whether this was something he was considering? Immediately? In one week? One month? There would never be a right time, and I was not someone who was afraid of raising the simple fact that, after his loss, this may have been something that had already crossed his mind. For one thing, I had experienced suicide close-hand in my own family, and my four years as a psychiatric nurse had involved caring for many who had been suffering from severe depression. From both these experiences I knew only too well that if someone wished to take their own life then, with a persistent intention, they would do just that. This was not to underestimate the value of medical intervention, to which I had often borne witness in my years in nursing, or the support of family and friends, but rather to acknowledge the will of an individual. Unless someone is sectioned and hospitalised then it is generally not possible to be with them twenty-four hours a day and, consequently, the opportunity will always exist.

I quickly considered whether our distant friendship and history placed me on strong enough ground to risk his wrath if, by enquiring, I was taking a step too far. Did my invitation to spend the evening before the funeral with him permit me to make such a sensitive enquiry? I thought of my stepfather, a man I love dearly, but whom I had been unable to protect when his son had taken his own life. I had been unable to bring his son back, unable to remove his pain. If I could have relived that time, I'd have risked the wrath of the world if I thought I could have prevented my stepbrother from ending his life.

I knew my enquiry might not make one bit of difference, but I knew it might make the world of difference, and I knew I was going to risk John's wrath. Friend or stranger – and it mattered not to me – I was not going to be cowed by suicide's unpalatable door, turning away before I'd attempted even a feeble knock.

I took a deep breath. 'You're not going to do anything silly, are you?'

'What, take my own life?' he replied. He sounded unsurprised at my enquiry.

'Yes,' I said.

'No, it's not an option. It's just not me. No matter how bad things are it's not something I would ever consider.'

There it was, right there in the car with us: suicide, in all its ugly and unwanted, brooding presence. My enquiry had been so simply delivered, straight to the point and without fuss, and so simply answered too, but so powerful in its implication. Maybe I hoped that by saying it out loud we'd be giving it a punch in the face, rendering it useless, removing its power and possibility. I sincerely hoped these were not just empty words rolling easily off his tongue, belying some other darker intention. One thing I knew for sure was that the walk ahead for him could push that position to its limits.

A moment later saw Gammie emerge and join us, sitting in the seat behind John. He had always been energetic, vocal, fun-loving and hard-partying, though he had now settled with his own young family. His non-stop talk filled the car all the way back to John's temporary home, and then filled the air for the next few hours, too, in the flat the police had miraculously found for John within twenty-four hours of the fire and managed to fill overnight with furniture – begged and borrowed. This had been the police at their absolute best, looking after the bereft partner of a colleague and friend, just as they had done for my mum when my dad had died. He'd been a serving police sergeant in the Manchester Police at the time of his sudden death, and they had been wonderfully supportive. I can recall, for many years after, the annual visit to the house of a male police officer bearing a Christmas plant and being taken with my three siblings to the police Christmas party.

However, as I returned to John's new home – without eulogies to read and albums to look at – and as I sat and slowly absorbed my surroundings, it was depressingly clear that, despite the huge efforts of the police, there was no getting away from the fact that this was plain, bland and soulless. The contrast for John couldn't have been starker. He'd gone from a lovely detached family home in a Welsh inlet, full of the sounds of children and family life, to a home without personality where he would spend many hours alone in deafening silence. Yes, it was a roof over his head, and one for which he was extremely grateful but, from where I was sitting, I could see how it would also serve as a constant reminder of what he had just lost.

But for now, three old friends filled the space. Gammie, having had quite a few drinks at the wake it would seem, was lying on his back on the living room floor, extremely angry and upset. Looking physically younger than his years, he resembled a Peter Pan-type figure, but his natural effervescent spirit, passion and zest for life now lay in pieces around him. Like the rest of us, he was broken and desperate as he walked through the devastation of John's life.

As I sat next to the dining room table less than a metre away, he began shouting, verbalising what we all felt with repeated expletives.

'It's fucking shit … life … it's just fucking shit … I can't believe what's happened. John man, just what are you going to do? ... Come to Australia. Yes, come to Australia. Get away from here. I'll always be there for you, John, you know you can come and I'll look after you. You can rely on me.'

As he filled the flat with his inebriated ranting, anger and uncontrollable distress, I listened without interruption, sensing he didn't want one. This was an unstoppable juggernaut and I wasn't going to stand in front of it. Vomiting his emotions into the air and wiping tears from his face as they tumbled down his cheeks, he was simply distraught and beyond consolation.

John stood silently on the patio outside. With the French doors wide open I could see he was facing the sea, motionless like a statue, the dark, clear sky and the street's overhead lighting outlining the contours of his body, the calm summer evening creating a sense of peace around him. The contrast between the two friends couldn't have been greater. The increasing volume of Gammie only served to emphasise John's silence and stillness, the doors a natural open threshold between the two scenes. My eyes darted from one to the other as I struggled to absorb the two very different visions, both conveying equally painful images of strong but broken men.

It was simple: fuck the world, this cruel, unjust world, just fuck it. Right here, right now. That's exactly how it felt. Just no rhyme or reason to life's random events. What had happened to John, a man born to be a dad and who lived for his sons, was utterly incomprehensible. It was not possible to make sense of such a tragedy.

A few hours later I decided to leave. I was exhausted and I thought it was right to give them some space. Gammie objected loudly.

'You can't go yet, Jill. Come on, please stay. You've not been here very long. You can stay overnight and have a proper drink with us. Can't she, John?'

I didn't want to see John put in an uncomfortable position and realised instantly that in the circumstances he might not want me as an overnight guest. So I immediately shut the idea down. Nor did I want to stay.

'No, really, it's great to see you but I'm going to go. It's been a long day and I'm very tired. I just need my bed.'

'Oh, come on, you can't leave us. *Please* stay a bit longer.' I resisted again.

John intervened. 'What time do you have to leave to drive back home tomorrow? If you could spare a few hours in the morning you could come over for breakfast, and then we could all go for a coffee and a walk.'

'Are you sure? I thought you two would want to spend some time alone?'

'Absolutely. It would give us all some extra time together.'

'Okay, that sounds lovely. I'll need to be leaving around lunchtime, though.'

'Great, that's sorted. By the way, as my cooking skills are useless Gammie's going to make us sausage and bacon rolls. We've already got the food in.'

'I'm impressed at your culinary know-how, Gammie,' I joked.

'You will be tomorrow,' he boasted light-heartedly. 'No doubt about it – they're the best. You're in for a real treat.'

'Anyone cooking for me is a treat. So I'm going to enjoy being waited on for a change.'

Good old Gammie, full of heart. Of course he would be

making sausage and bacon rolls; what else would he be doing? He was just not the sort of guy to sit with a bowl of muesli for breakfast.

Eat, drink and be merry should have been his motto and, despite his momentary breakdown in John's flat, there'd be no sitting around moping while he was in town. Understandably, the sheer weight of emotion had finally overcome him, just as it had for the rest of us, but his emotional outburst had somehow cleansed him. He'd vented his anger, refocused, and was back doing what he was great at – being a sheer energy force in the room. He had the capacity to raise the roof, and although it was not a time for celebration he was just what John needed: a lifelong, very close friend who would keep pushing his head above the waterline to stop him from drowning.

I left, having made an arrangement to return about ten the following morning, and drove back to the hotel in silence. I felt drained, and the peace of the hotel room was a welcome haven after such an emotionally charged day. As I lay on the bed, I decided to send John a text. After his earlier irritated response to my words of kindness at the wake, I wasn't quite sure whether the words I chose and sentiments I tried to offer would be welcome or not. What I did know was that if he spat back in anger it wouldn't deter me from offering support; it wouldn't deter me from trying to provide a platform on which he could talk. From the aftermath of my father's death I knew that grief was a remote, uninhabited island in a full room, surrounded by noise but deafeningly silent, surrounded by people just out of reach, surrounded by life – just out of reach.

Grief needed friends who placed themselves close enough

to be heard and to hear, close enough to be touched and to touch, and close enough to be called on.

John, just wanted to say again that your eulogy was truly remarkable, what you said and just how you said it. Thank you for allowing me to share it with you. Jill x

CHAPTER 6

I checked out of the hotel the morning after the wake and drove straight over to John's. The flat was full of the heavenly smell of bacon and sausages cooking, momentarily kidding me that this was a normal home and life was good, the comfort food an inviting blanket of warmth. Amazing how something so simple can create such a feeling of well-being. Gammie was standing at the cooker smiling, busying himself at the grill and adding to the cosy, welcoming feel.

'Morning, Jill. Now what's it going to be – one roll or two?' He sounded chirpy and light.

'Just the one. I'll have sausage, thanks, and a strong coffee with just a little milk would be lovely too.'

'Coming up, coming up. Take a seat, I've got it all under control.' I soaked up his buoyant mood.

Half an hour later and with only a few hours to spare before I left to return home, we climbed into my car to drive to the village of Moelfre, Anglesey, for a walk along the coastline.

Gammie took the back seat and John sat next to me in the front. The fresh air beckoned, as did, later, the obligatory coffee and cake. Even more comfort food and, quite frankly, the way I felt I could have stuffed my face with all manner of fattening and forbidden goodies. John subsequently divulged that in some of his truly dark moments, his own consumption of chocolate and cake had increased significantly, bringing layers of sweet and much-needed comfort into his world.

As I drove from the flat, John unexpectedly suggested we visit his old family home, the most private and painful of spaces for him.

'I'd like to take you there, so long as that's okay with you both. We can go straight there before our walk.'

'Are you sure?' I asked gently, trying to concentrate on my driving as I flinched at his suggestion. I was being propelled at speed towards a place of immense sorrow, a place where life had ended. I looked in my rear-view mirror; Gammie was looking out of the car window, apparently in deep thought.

'Yes, I'm very sure. I consider you both very close friends and I'd like to show you where we all lived.'

'No problem at all. I'm right by your side,' said Gammie, softly placing a hand on John's right shoulder and affection-ately squeezing it.

'I'm touched that you feel this way and I'm right by your side too,' I added. I was being placed in a ringside position again, and as I followed John's sombrely given directions I surreptitiously eased the pressure on the accelerator to gain just a few extra seconds, a few beautiful extra seconds, to brace myself for where and what I was about to be shown.

Minutes later I brought the car to a halt outside a large

metal 'cow' gate at the entrance of the driveway to John's house, or the shell of his house as it now was.

We got out in silence. As we walked through the gate, the burnt remnants of his home stood in the still aftermath of destruction, just as I had seen it on television. The roof was all but gone, the skeleton of the charred rafters hanging precariously in open space. It was as though I had passed through the television screen, a walk-on part in a disaster movie that provided a brutal and unwelcome close-up of reality. This was sickeningly real and, as my eyes slowly absorbed my surroundings, I could have fallen to my knees and bowed my head in silence, taking a moment to consider the space in which three people had only just died and that I was about to enter. I quickly collected myself, standing firm next to John as he began to show us around his garden; the large, round trampoline was on the right as you went through the gate, the trampoline that Oscar had loved to play on.

'Do you know, every single day without fail he'd ask me to play on it with him. The minute I got home from work he'd be saying "Please, Dad, can we go on the trampoline, now?" and if I said I was busy he wouldn't give up, saying "Pleeease? Come on, Dad," over and over,' said John wistfully as we passed. 'We spent hours jumping on it and fooling around.' There it was in the corner, bleak and silent, no laughing children now.

There, too, was the ride-on lawnmower with which John had allowed Felix to mow the large lawn that circled the house. He told us how Felix had loved sitting on it, despite the fact that he considered the pocket money he earned for doing it wasn't enough: 'Only two pounds? Come on, Dad, it's got to be more than that!'

At the rear of the garden was the wooded area where, John recounted, the weekend before the accident, he, Felix and Oscar had built a den and had played in it all day – a dad with his sons out in the woods, having an adventure together. 'We just stayed there for hours …' he said, lost in the agonising memory of it.

Heather's car, stationary in the driveway, was as she had left it on her final drive home, and a small brick outhouse, hidden behind the house at the end of the garden, contained Felix's and Oscar's bikes and the usual garden paraphernalia. But also in there, sitting on a wooden tabletop, was an old, small, rusted biscuit tin. When John opened it there lay his 'Head Boy' badge from school, glossy dark red, with the words 'HEAD BOY' inscribed diagonally on it in bold, gold lettering. The bright colours were out of place in the bleak day, the badge itself a link to our innocent past. Another reminder of how life had changed for us all, and for John, had changed forever.

As we walked slowly around the garden, I felt like a trespasser, despite having been invited in by John. I had not known Heather, Felix or Oscar and yet here I was in their garden just a few short weeks after their deaths. This was their home, not mine; their private space, their bikes, their trampoline, their car. I walked gently across the grass, as if by treading carefully my presence wouldn't be detected. I could leave and they would never know I had been there, the sanctity and memory of their home, their life and where they had died, intact.

Back in the car, we may have been driving away but the effect of what I had just walked through was still trickling through my veins: simple horror. No words would ever have seemed right at that moment and so the only ones spoken were just a few directions to our next destination: a welcome walk along the top of the coastline.

It was truly exhilarating to be out of the confines of John's flat, away from the remnants of his former home and in the open space and fresh air. At times we all chatted, but in the main John walked ahead in silence, lost in his own thoughts.

We stopped three times as I recall, and each stop seemed to generate a moment of conversational madness and, with it, laughter. These moments were perfect examples of the human effort to keep some sort of normality afloat but failing miserably, as we took to the extreme – the collective propensity to talk about anything no matter how bizarre, so long as it was not the death that was sitting in front of us. It wasn't that Gammie or I had any difficulty talking about the death of John's family with him. The friendship that existed between us, despite the years and the distance, felt like a very relaxed space for it to sit as comfortably as it ever could. However, to release the pressure and attempt to bring some lightness in through the door there had to be some other, healthier, focus, if only for a few brief moments. It was the efforts to fill the space that were questionable.

Our first stop didn't disappoint, as moment of conversational madness number one descended. We sat together at the top of the cliffs on a sloping grass-and-rock bank looking out to sea. Gammie decided he would enlighten us with an embellished description of the masturbatory practices of his grey cockatiel, demonstrating just how the bird completed such an act while perched on his hand.

'Right,' he said. 'I think we need to lighten the mood so I'm going to share with you my cockatiel's most intimate moment.'

'What's he called?' John asked.

'Bob. His name is Bob and this is what he does. Watch closely,' he said excitedly, his voice becoming louder as he held his right arm forward with his forefinger and thumb closed together. 'Now, you see where my thumb meets my finger? He jumps on here, and then he starts thrusting himself repeatedly against the raised edge of the thumb. This bit here,' he continued, pointing to the exact place where Bob apparently pleasured himself.

'Crikey, how can you see a cockatiel's penis to know that's what he's doing?' I asked, laughing.

'He doesn't have a visible penis. He just thrusts his lower body against me. And I always know when he's "come" because he seems to arch his back and stiffen.'

'No way! I don't believe you! How can you be sure that's what he's doing?'

'Because when he's done there's a wet patch on my finger ... now that's what I call clear evidence!'

'Oh, Gammie, that's disgusting! I think you two have become a little too close.'

'Absolutely,' interjected John. 'Bob clearly fancies you. You need to get him a mate, and fast. And you definitely need to get out more, my friend.'

Gammie couldn't have been prouder as he sat basking in the limelight of Bob's sexual adventures. As we laughed loudly together, breathing in the smell of the fresh sea air and with the wind blowing strongly around us, it felt so, so good: mad, but good.

Our second stop was at Ann's Pantry, a small, quaint, double-bay-fronted coffee shop with chintz charm. Wooden chairs with padded seat cushions sat beside small wooden tables covered in red chequered tablecloths. Set back approximately fifty metres from the coast with a view to the sea from inside, it was quiet and unimposing with table areas both inside and out, neither of which were particularly busy at that time. It was just what we needed.

We chose a circular table positioned in one of the front bay windows. John sat on the fixed wooden wall-seat next to the window, and Gammie and I sat on wooden chairs either side of him. As we tucked into our cake, moment of conversational madness number two arrived.

I started to talk about the sale of my last house and the positive subliminal effects of having either the smell of coffee or the comforting sound of the washing machine when viewers were shown around your home. Which would secure the sale?

'No way is it the washing machine. That's ridiculous!' John declared.

'No, I'm sorry, it works. I always used to start the cycle about ten minutes before the viewers were due, so by the time they arrived it was gently turning on its washing cycle. I think there's something reassuring and homely about it. I used to love it as a young girl when the family machine was on at the weekends.'

They both laughed out loud. 'So what happens if the viewers take longer than expected and your washing cycle is now a loud spin?' said John.

'Very funny. It's never happened because it's a well-executed plan – no viewer would be in the house that long. The wash cycle is long enough for me to show them round and then eject them.'

Gammie, unable to conceal his own mirth, intervened. 'No, Jill, I'm sorry, I'm with John on this one – it's definitely the coffee. The smell of fresh coffee is the way to go.'

'Look, I love my coffee but that's just far too obvious. That looks like you're trying too hard, or worse, attempting to hide sinister smells. Trust me, the washing machine is a very subtle approach that has a hypnotic, relaxing effect. You two are looking at this way too literally – very male I might say.'

'You can't be serious?' said John. 'It's absolutely the coffee, and I'm not a coffee drinker. And for goodness sake, who wants to look through the glass door and see your knickers and bra spinning around!'

Who cared whether it was the washing machine or the coffee? At that moment who gave a damn? How ridiculously passionate we were about our respective views, John and Gammie suggesting I was mad for believing it was the comforting sound of the washing cycle that would lure the unsuspecting buyer to sign on the dotted line.

As we sat laughing together again it felt so, so good: mad, but good.

Our third and final stop came after we'd left the coffee

shop and walked back to the top of the cliffs, as the wind and fresh air wrapped themselves around us. Finding a wooden bench, I sat down for a moment facing the sea, while Gammie and John walked off separately down the grass bank for some time alone. Minutes later John returned, and moment of conversational madness number three made its appearance.

I began to talk to him, powerless to stop the words leaving my mouth.

'Do you know, John, years after my father's death I recalled very clearly my mum saying that she had been surrounded by so many people leading up to the funeral but that afterwards, when she truly needed support, they all seemed to disappear and she had few she could call on. Those words have never left me, so I want you to know that you can call me any time. Don't ever be alone.'

'Thanks, that's very kind, but you've got a very busy life and the last thing you need is me calling in the space I'm in.'

'Don't be daft, you really *can* call any time. The offer is a genuine one, so just pick up the phone and ring me if you need to.'

And so I continued. I again insisted he could call me to stave off the madness of silence and loneliness when the bare, cream walls of his deafeningly quiet flat were moving in on him.

'Even if it's just to hear the sound of a friend's voice. You don't need to be like my mum. Just call.'

This would not happen to him because I wouldn't let it. I would always be there for him. Oh yes, I expected him to call me; in fact I insisted he call me every night. Boy oh boy oh boy, what was I thinking?

No laughter now, but still it felt so, so good: mad, but good.

There we were, the three of us, on the windy Welsh coast, all wrapped up in multiple deaths, masturbating cockatiels, house-sale techniques and the offer of daily support. Which had been the maddest moment amongst the madness?

Time would tell.

CHAPTER 7

I turned the key in my ignition and began driving away from John and Gammie, who were standing at the side of the road in front of the modern, flat-roofed, two-storey block of flats where John now lived. It was as though we were parting after a happy family event, all smiles and waves. I didn't hoot my horn to complete this scene of joy.

If ever one event repeatedly showcased how a screenshot of someone's existence can belie its true reality, the deaths of John's family was it. One face, one life story, a million hidden emotions, but with a billion different external interpretations. How easy it is to become seduced by the visual aphrodisiac of others' lives, assuming so much with so little. He looked fine on the outside, didn't he?

I welcomed the journey home. Four hours in which I could reflect on my offer of support. I didn't regret what I'd said, but I could feel my demons circling, quietly waiting to offer a helping hand. *You're different now; you understand yourself and your dynamic in a much deeper way. You have a 'bag of tools', too, remember.* I said this repeatedly to myself, to soothe my anxiety at yet again stepping in and doing what I did best: offering endless support before I'd taken stock. It was all very well having a 'bag of tools', but I'd had no real need to test their effectiveness in the years since my counselling. Well, if John chose to respond they'd certainly be brought out now.

There was no doubting he was a man in need. There was no doubting my very clear and unchecked offer. There was no doubting my propensity to be the only 'prop' in town. And there was no doubting that if he chose to seek out what I had offered, I'd respond. Maybe I needed to place myself in the path of a complete meltdown to see if I could offer the support needed, without yet again becoming a martyr to someone else's cause.

There was no doubting that my ability to separate my own needs from his was untested and, as yet, unclear.

There was, however, one thing that I did feel clear about: it wasn't just my previous counselling that had woken my slumbering self. A closer look at how I was living my life two years before the death of John's family, around 2008, had brought about dramatic changes to both my living space and view of the world.

It had hit me by surprise when I was on a two-week summer holiday in Turkey with my son. As I'd sat in the glorious sun in a hotel beachside bar overlooking the Mediterranean Sea, I'd had what I can only describe as a personal awakening. Had the madness of the sun's heat affected me? No, although the sun had certainly been a catalyst, magnifying and bringing my realisation into sharp focus.

I was only a few days into the holiday and surrounded by so many very polite and humble Turkish staff. After years of using au pairs myself, I had experienced numerous times the notable difference between girls from Eastern and Western Europe. The former had generally come from poor countries and poor families, and moved around our home with grace and humility. The latter, in my experience, had not been overtly possessed of these qualities, and generally arrived with lists of expectations and demands.

An Italian girl called Bella was particularly memorable. She and her sister, Luisa, had arrived in the UK at the same time, the latter going to live with a family in Luton. As soon as Bella crossed the threshold of our house she immediately gave me a list of all the food she must have in the house to eat and just how much of it she would need to feed her healthy appetite. This was clearly going to be beyond my single-parent budget, but that was the least of my problems. Within the first week, Luisa had left her family in Luton, as she was not happy, and had gone to live 'in a hostel' somewhere in London. Her parents had, understandably, been worried. I had immediately given shelter to her while she addressed her next move. She arrived at our front door as I was leaving for a late shift at work, which, unfortunately, I wasn't to finish for another fourteen hours. Throughout that evening as I tried to call home the line was permanently engaged. They had called their family in Italy, without my knowledge and at my expense. I got home in the early hours to find my son, who was six at the time, lying on his bed fully clothed, his curtains open and his bedroom door tightly shut; until that time, it had always been left open. My fridge, which had been full of food for the remainder of the week, was virtually empty. I was due at work on an early shift starting at 7.00 a.m., just five hours after I'd arrived home and, as I considered the sleep I wasn't going to get, Bella descended in haste from her loft bedroom, where her sister rested, safe and with a full stomach.

'Jill, Jill,' she said, with the pronunciation of my name softened and sounding more like 'Sheel, Sheel,' in her lilting Italian accent. She raised her arms flamboyantly as if in desperation. 'We have to go home. We must leave immediately.'

'Oh, what's the matter?' I responded in hushed tones, acutely aware of my son's bedroom adjacent to the foot of the stairs. 'I thought Luisa was going to look for another family?'

'No, she does not want to stay any longer and so tonight we have booked the flights to return to Italy in the morning. We have a taxi collecting us at eight thirty.'

I digested the bombshell as she carried on, unfettered and without conscience.

'So, I would like to be paid for the four days I have worked, please.'

'But I've got to go to work in a matter of hours and am relying on you to take Alexander to school and collect him later. If you leave I will have no one to care for him. Can't you stay for a few days until I sort some alternative childcare?'

Despite my son clearly not having been given a great deal of attention the previous evening, at that point I was a woman with few options. She only had to take and collect him from school for just a few measly days, a school that was a five-minute walk from the house. That's all I was asking.

'No, Sheel, this is not possible. This is *not* my responsibility,' she answered, frowning at me with clear disdain.

'Right,' I said, slowly. 'Well now, I've been trying to get through on my home phone all evening, and so when I've received my phone bill and deducted the cost of your calls tonight, I'll forward what I owe you.'

'Sheel, Sheel,' she said in an exasperated tone. 'If you do not give me the money, how am I to pay for the taxi to the airport?'

I looked at her, allowing a moment to pass before I calmly responded.

'Ah, well now, Bella, that's not *my* responsibility.'

She could contain her sense of self-importance no longer.

'This is not good, Sheel. How can you do this to *me*?'

'I'll tell you how, Bella. I've opened my house to your sister, at a cost to me and without any expectation of a contribution from her while she stays in my home. As a single parent this was money I could not afford to spend – and this is how you repay such generosity and kindness?'

As she puffed and spluttered her way back upstairs, a torrent of Italian spewing from her mouth – none of which sounded particularly complimentary – I walked into my son's bedroom, welling up with tears at the sheer pressure I was now under. I could have crumbled and sobbed as I took the full impact of another single-parent blow.

She didn't care one jot. The flights were booked and the decision had been made without one shred of concern for the impact this would have on me and my son. I was unable to go to work the next day. I took Alexander to school in the morning and returned to the house no more than fifteen minutes later to find that the two girls had left. But before doing so, they had emptied a kitchen cupboard of gifts Bella had given me on her arrival and taken them all with them. To have been treated in such a ruthless fashion when I had offered such warmth and concern was very hurtful. And with a job to perform and a son to care for, it was also particularly stressful.

Weeks later, when I'd regrouped sufficiently to find some humour in the episode, I playfully considered whether it had been my son's young and indelicate observation on her first evening with us that had had her running for the door. She had walked into the kitchen and sat next to Alexander at our pine table, and his dark brown eyes had widened as he'd scrutinised her well-fed curves. Sitting in his bright orange pyjamas, his angelic face studying her closely, he had suddenly reached over with his little finger and poked her in her left leg, exclaiming, 'You've got *big* legs,' in clear and innocent astonishment at such a fine figure.

His weren't the only eyes widened. Inwardly cursing him but also quelling my instantaneous desire to inappropriately burst out laughing, I had interjected before he could grace us with any more of his unguarded observations.

'Alexander, you mustn't say things like that to Bella.'

'But she does have *big* legs,' he'd continued.

I had glared across at him as the sound of his nan's subdued sniggers to my left filled the air, not helping matters one bit.

Bella had undoubtedly been a voluptuous girl, but I clearly needed to have a little chat with that sweet boy of mine about how he introduced himself to future au pairs.

Thankfully, over the years I was fortunate to have four

very good, longer-term girls who adored Alexander and who each stayed for between one and four years. One girl stood out for me. She was Romanian, and her family were desperately poor. She sent most of the small wage she earned home to her parents. Our small, three-bedroomed terraced cottage was clearly a palace to her, and she treated the food on the table at mealtimes like caviar. Yes, our home in Surrey was very pretty, but by Western standards, and certainly Surrey's standards, it was far from a mansion. As so often in life, though, as much as I appreciated her at the time, my true appreciation of exactly what she had brought into our home came only once she had left, and over the following years – the wonderful beauty and clarity of retrospect. She was warm, sweet, emotionally generous and so appreciative of the surroundings she found herself in, despite this being the home of a single parent on a limited budget. That mattered not to her as she walked softly through our home without footprint, and left as she had arrived: in peace. She had only a few clothes and even less money, but she taught me an unintentional lesson about what it is to be rich in life.

I'd had similar experiences with Turkish au pairs too, and staying at the hotel in Turkey further confirmed my view of their values and approach to life. It was staffed by people from poor backgrounds, working long hours for small wages and who, despite these challenging circumstances, possessed something that went way beyond the normal civility one would have expected them to convey to guests. As they moved seamlessly around me I was, quite frankly, mesmerised. They had an intangible something that I was intrigued by.

The backdrop to these experiences had been eleven harsh years of raising Alexander alone since he was two years old while I was working in the even harsher environment of policing. Although I valued the fact that my job was secure and provided me with a decent enough salary, our home had only one wage coming in and the money soon disappeared down some bottomless pit. And policing was a job towards which, along the way, I'd had very differing feelings. These had ranged from sheer ambivalence and wanting to leave, to putting my heart and soul into promotion and wanting to progress higher in the organisation.

It was an ongoing rollercoaster of emotions, and underlying them all was the simple and unavoidable fact that it was down to me to bring home the bacon. Regardless of any desire I may have had to leave and do something entirely different, I had bills to pay, food to buy and a son to clothe and support. Additionally, my home and mortgage commitments demanded that I continue to earn at least the same wage, certainly not one that was lower. There was no room for compromise. My life was simple – get up, get out and earn, head down on the unconscious conveyor belt of life, just ploughing through and making ends meet. The pressure and demands were relentless. Controlled by my responsibilities, I had no control. I felt trapped. My mind, no doubt like that of many in the world in which we live today, was full of thoughts of past and future events and oblivious to the actual moment I was in.

As I looked out at the sea in Turkey, the warm sun wrapped itself around me in a protective embrace and, submerged in the atmospheric and ever-gentle way of the

Turkish people, I was suddenly rudely awakened from my bliss. In the middle of such beauty, alive in that very moment, what was it I could feel inside but couldn't find the words to articulate? What was it I could feel in my soul?

Searching hard, I shut my eyes to try and connect and marry this external nirvana with the deeper recesses of my being, but to no avail. I could feel nothing, absolutely nothing. And there it was, right there, staring me in the face: my soul was dead, shut for business. Tired of waiting for the attention it so desperately needed, unloved and neglected, it had long since retreated without notice. I had become a slave to my outside world and was no longer my own master. I was not free, or I did not feel free. I was stranded in a desert wasteland without a compass.

Left behind, my physical body was running blindly through life, and it was a life in which the merciless fast pace and daily repetition merged together like a parasitic beast, feeding its need at the expense of all else. There was this huge cultural expectation that the only light to be valued was the one at the end of the tunnel, where the mortgage was paid off and you had your pension in hand. Forget the ride: it was all about the destination.

And what guarantee did I have that I'd ever get there anyway? There had to be a different way that was far richer than the road I was currently on. Yes, one that was secure, but one that felt a little less determined. I whispered repeatedly to myself, *I want to be free, I want to feel free.*

I spent much of the following few days completely overcome with emotion, telephoning my mum while my tears flowed. I must have spent a small fortune on calls home but I just needed to talk to another adult and try to make further sense of what had emerged from my epiphany. I was surrounded by the stunning Turkish vista and weather – visual and physical sensory delights – and the charming Turkish people, and was away from the demands of work and 'normal' life. I sat crying. I spent the remainder of my holiday absorbing the magnitude of the proverbial light bulb that had just been switched on in my head, considering what I was going to do with it.

I returned home and tried to rationalise my thoughts. What had I meant when I'd said, *I want to be free?* It was certainly not to be free of my son: whatever the inherent difficulties of being a single parent, he was the light and joy in my life. No, I had not wanted to raise him alone. This was not what I had envisaged for either him or myself, but that was how it was and I was strong enough to deal with the responsibility. He enriched my life beyond measure.

As regards the rest of my life I didn't have a defined answer, nor the luxury of taking myself off into some remote cave to ponder just what it was I sought and come to some wise, considered conclusion. What I could still hear very clearly was a powerful voice from within telling me to break free from the invisible chains that bound themselves around me, and for a moment consider some other way of life, one that would release me from the manner in which I was living and which was slowly strangling me. If I was to relight the spirit within me and nurture my soul, I had to find a different path.

Within weeks of my return from Turkey I chose the next best viable alternative to a cave as a means to catapult us into a different space: I put our home on the market. Once sold, I rented another in a nearby town that sat on the bank at the juncture of two rivers. It was a town house with a first floor living room from which three sets of French doors opened onto a veranda overlooking the stunning river view and an old brick bridge. A mix of mature, intertwined trees completed the pretty picture. No longer anchored by the deep roots of a mortgage, the chains began to loosen and the ground beneath me started to shift ever so slowly.

As we unpacked boxes in our new home in the summer of 2009 I could feel something inside me begin to stir, a fluttering in my stomach and a huge excitement at having broken free. The sheer thrill of not knowing what my next step would be was exhilarating. Life had become a little less predictable, and right there, at that moment, I felt that anything was possible. I was on a different ride, one that at some level had given me a sense of the freedom I sought and, although it was a financially expensive one, I hoped it would be spiritually rich too. I was in control, not my mortgage and pension.

If ever there was a move that could provoke in so many others a clear uneasiness and overt expression of concern then this was it. I had come off the valued housing ladder; I was clearly taking a risk and would eventually see the light and buy again. Oh, the ties that bind us. I just had to put these views to one side and not let them affect the choices I was making. Thankfully, my family did not assume this position; they fully supported me. My mum, a lover of taking risks and living life a little, thoroughly encouraged my different approach. She was a great believer in throwing yourself off a proverbial cliff to see where you landed.

Well, I had certainly thrown myself off the cliff and for the time being I was just going to sit on my veranda, coffee or wine in hand, and watch the boats, ducks and people as they passed by and absorb the simple but beautiful nature that surrounded me. I was in a different space and boy did it feel good. We were very happy.

Perhaps it was the emerging sense of freedom and peace I felt that had emboldened me to step forward. It was a space into which I felt able to welcome John.

Perhaps – I smiled inwardly – he wouldn't seek out my support after all and so the challenge of his presence would never materialise, leaving my peace and freedom to continue to grow and meander softly through my life, unaffected by his.

I drove into my driveway, exhausted, four long hours after leaving Wales, and turned the engine off. It had been a journey during which the previous decisions I'd made to change my life all fell into place.

None of us knew what our next day would bring. None of us knew when our own end would come. But what I did know, in the shadow of a funeral for three, was that there were no yesterdays or tomorrows; we only had our todays. I got out of my car and made my way to the front door with a huge sense of relief. As I faced three deaths, the previous big decisions to sell my house and throw caution to the wind to seek some other path in life seemed infinitely small. As I faced three deaths, none of it mattered at all. I knew I was on the right path.

CHAPTER 8

'Hi, I'm back,' I shouted as I opened the front door. My relief at returning to Alexander and the sanctuary of our safe world added greater volume than normal to my voice. Was I shrieking, I wondered, or did I just sound naturally effervescent. It mattered not; moments later he was running down the stairs to meet me with a welcome hug.

'It's lovely to see you, Mum.'

'And it's wonderful to see you too.' I held him tightly before pulling back and cupping his face in my hands. 'Boy, it's good to be home. Come on, let's get something to eat and you can tell me what's been happening during the last few days.'

He put his arm around my shoulders as we walked up the stairs to the living room, and with every small step, I breathed in the sweetness of his presence, wallowing in my good fortune.

I slipped back into my life effortlessly, and it was as though

I'd not been absent for the last thirty-six hours – everything was reassuringly the same. But as I sat on our balcony later, drinking a chilled glass of white wine and watching the calm river water in the fading light, I knew that nothing could possibly be the same again. The ripple effect of this tragedy reached far beyond one funeral service, far beyond one Welsh community, and extended its reach right into my home as I slowly breathed in the essence of Heather, Felix and Oscar: their lives, their deaths, their tragedy. And the essence of their husband, their father, too.

Within days I had returned to the realities of a full-time job and studying for my Inspectors' exams while Alexander studied for his forthcoming GCSE exams – a pressured environment, to say the least. Throw into the mix trying to make sure I had one night out a week, generally Friday, when I could relax with a girlfriend, attempting to get to the gym at least twice a week, a food shop to feed my son's enormous appetite – *Where do teenagers put their food?* – plus the ironing, plus the housework, plus, plus, plus … oh yes, the inherent mother's premium taxi service extraordinaire … Thank goodness the twice weekly, late night and weekend early morning ice hockey training and matches across the country were having a summer break. Even so, I had no time to sit still, take a deep breath and scream. Sometimes it felt like I had no time to sleep.

There are doubtless lots of men and women out there in the same space. The single-handed provision of every aspect of your child's well-being – emotional, physical and mental – is carried on your shoulders. No mutual sharing and supporting with a partner: just you alone. This was the reason why I had waited until Alexander was older to study for promotion; I just couldn't give fully to both, and so he came first. Looking at him now, such a well-balanced and happy young man, I knew it had been worth every moment. We had a great relationship, full of humour.

'Mum, I know you're in the police but you don't have to conduct a security review every time I go out. I mean, why do you need the postcode of my friend's addresses and their family make-up? None of my friends' mums ask them this sort of stuff.'

The postcode request had become his party piece as he mercilessly mimicked my efforts to patrol his life. This, and all his observations, were always offered in the over-embellished tones of a character called Mandy, the mother of Brian, played by Terry Jones in the film *Monty Python's Life of Brian*:

'Now, make sure you send me his shoe size, his sister's middle name and while I'm at it could you ask his mum if she's happy ... and as soon as you arrive send me the grid reference.'

We would fall about laughing, which only encouraged him to carry on and on and on.

But, of course, our relationship could also be full of the usual frustrations and arguments:

'No, you haven't done enough study yet.' ... 'Yes, I know you love your sleep, we all do, but that's just not going to get you through these exams.'

'Mum, just let me do it myself. The more you go on, the less I want to do,' he would counter, in an exasperated tone.

And in equal measure we had exchanges filled with bucketloads of love:

'Go on, give me one of those big hugs of yours,' I would say. And he would come towards me with a beaming smile, wrapping his tall body and big arms around me and hug me tightly as he lifted me off the ground.

'I love you, Mum.'

'I love you too, darling. You do know you can't ever leave home?'

He'd laugh, tilting his head towards me in humorous disbelief. 'It's going to happen one day. You've got to start getting used to it,' he'd say before sensitively adding, 'but home will always be where you are,' to soften the eventual blow.

However, even now he was fifteen, focusing on my own goals was a strain. Did promotion really mean that much to me? The train ride to and from work was a welcome space to lose myself in – well, almost. My study books a constant reminder not to fall asleep before I got home. Ironically, reading *The Police and Criminal Evidence Act* (PACE) was enough to put the liveliest of individuals into an immediate coma, and so I was caught, it would seem, between a rock and a hard place. I existed in a complete mix of pressure, hope and an overall buzz that life was good and, despite the daily madness, I was happy. I had much to be thankful for, and in keeping with my recent approach to life I was trying to 'live in the now' and appreciate the moment, however crazy the moment may have seemed.

In the middle of the tightly packed can of my life sat John. Well, the truth is that he was the lid pressing down on all the other contents, squeezing them, if it were possible, even closer together. I had returned to London mindful of my offer of support to him, which had been a genuine one. I was aware there were plenty of others offering him support too: his elder sister, his mum, Ellen, and his mother-in-law, Barbara, all of whom he had a close relationship with. He also had numerous male friends, and although they were not all within a physical proximity, they were there to be called on if needed. But I was a friend too, and regardless of my accompanying dynamic, he had just lost his whole family. It was in this spirit that a few days after my return I decided to send him a text; non-intrusive, supportive and requiring no response, something I would have done for any of my other friends in the same circumstances. Whether he called or not was a matter for him:

John, Just wanted to say you are a man amongst men and it has been my absolute privilege to share the last few days with you. You have shown huge dignity, grace and sensitivity to others, while coping with your tremendous loss. Just amazing. Keep strong. Jill x

A day later he responded with a text of his own. Remarkable, considering this was a man that had previously rarely sent text messages – he could barely put one together. Ironically, one of the few physical memories of his sons he now possessed was a brief text sent from Felix. How cherished that had become, a simple line from his son, asking: *Wots my number*? He'd been given a second-hand phone, and had sent John that message.

Brace yourself, incoming text from John. You have been bloody fantastic these last few days. Thanks for everything. Love John.

And a few days after that he telephoned. It was early evening and still light outside.

'Hi Jill, hope you don't mind me calling. I thought I'd take you up on your offer, you know, just to ring for a chat now and then.'

'Of course I don't mind. It's lovely to hear you and you're a good excuse to put down my study books.'

'I can call back another time if that's better? I understand you have lots going on with Alex too.'

'No, now's fine, really. Study rules my life at the minute and so it's no bad thing to break it up like this occasionally, and Alexander has just gone for a run. He's trying to keep his fitness up while the hockey season is out.'

'He sounds very committed.'

'Yes, he is, though running isn't his favourite pastime – more necessity than desire. We go together sometimes, and he certainly gives me a run for my money as I try to keep up with his long legs. But I had knee surgery many years ago and so road running is becoming a thing of the past. Sadly, the gym treadmill is kinder.'

'Knee surgery – why was that?'

'I blame the army – endurance runs in boots,' I laughed. 'I had to have the area behind the kneecap hoovered out. I won't bore you with the detail. Anyway, enough about me, how are you doing now the focus of the funeral is over?' I asked, as I pushed the chair away from my desk and started walking to the living room, seeking a comfier seat to relax in.

My dodgy knees had eased us gently forward, without jumping head first into his post-funeral existence.

'Well, I'm still off work. I've got lots of paperwork and admin to sort out, so I'm keeping myself busy with that. I've just got to keep busy. But honestly, I just take a moment at a time. I can't see beyond that at the minute. It's all I'm capable of.'

'Of course, but what about contact with others so you're not alone in your flat? You must feel pretty lonely in there.'

'To be honest, I don't want to see other people, which sounds awful doesn't it. They're all very concerned and want to help and I know that's lovely, but I just can't cope talking with others. I break down when they start asking if I'm okay and hugging me, and I don't want to keep doing that. It's not helpful.'

'But staying in the flat on your own all the time can't be good for you either, surely?'

'No, I know. It's very quiet, but at least I'm not at risk of having to talk to other people. It's a safe place. Only yesterday I had to go to the bank, and as I was being served my wallet dropped open. I've got a picture of Felix and Oscar in there and the bank lady saw it and started asking me about them. She didn't know they'd died so it wasn't her fault, but I can't risk that sort of thing happening. I'm just too raw.'

'Oh my goodness, that must have been awful. What did you do?'

'I said they were my sons, but then got so upset I had to stop what I was doing and quickly leave. But it's not just there, it's everywhere I go. The other day I deliberately drove to a supermarket in a different town, and would you believe three separate people I know started coming towards me in three different aisles, all wanting to speak to me.'

'They just want to show their compassion and kindness I'm sure – and isn't it lovely you're surrounded by people that feel able to do that? There are many that wouldn't – they'd be avoiding you at all costs.'

'I know, I don't mean to sound unappreciative, but I'm simply not capable of speaking to anyone like this right now. It takes all my strength to walk into a shop and buy some food, but despite keeping my head down to try and avoid this sort of contact I keep failing miserably. I can't bear it. So even though my flat is a world away from my noisy home with the boys, it protects me from too much contact.'

'What did you do at the supermarket?'

'I just put my arm out to stop them approaching, dropped my basket and left. It floors me. Their kindness floors me.'

He was a cup full to the brim and ready to erupt like a volcano at any moment. He didn't know how to deal with his loss around others – both those who wanted to come close, and those who didn't know how. But regardless, he was in no fit state to even try.

'But you don't have to worry,' he continued. 'I speak to my mum and sister, and Heather's mum rings me every day, so I'm not alone.'

'Have you given any further thought to what you're going to do yet?'

'Well, I haven't changed my view about staying here. I simply can't. We've lived here for over twenty years. There are far too many memories, and everywhere I go is just another painful reminder of them all – the school, the people, the beaches. It's a beautiful place but it's full of them, and it always will be. Everywhere I turn is just more pain, there's no escape.'

His voice sounded fragile and without energy, talking in monochrome: deadpan and shutdown. He was traumatised and in shock still, floundering around looking for direction and some place to ground himself. Understandably, that place was not going to be Anglesey.

'I understand, I do. But where will you go?'

'I've decided to get as far away as possible and go travelling. Gammie's invited me to go and stay with him and his family in Australia over Christmas, so I'm going to do that. And then Heather's sister who lives in New Zealand has also invited me over, so I'll probably go on to hers for a while too. Beyond that, I don't know at the minute. I just know I've got to move away from Anglesey. I need to be in places where I can be anonymous. I can't walk down the road here without seeing someone who knows me.'

'Well, these are big decisions and you're not in a great space. I understand going off travelling, but maybe when you've been away for a few months you might want to come back to Wales to feel close to them.'

'No, that's not going to happen, I just can't live here. No amount of travelling will change my mind about that.'

'So, have you decided when you're going?'

'I think I'll be leaving around December. It's going to take me until then to sort everything out here – the house, the business with Micky – and that gives me a few months to do it.'

'These are huge changes for Micky, too. How does he feel about it all?'

'He completely understands me needing to get away from Anglesey and has been a huge support, just like you've been. Thanks so much for everything, I really do appreciate it.'

'Don't be daft, it's nothing. A phone call is the least I can do.'

'No, it's much more than that. You don't have to offer me this after all these years. I do understand that, and I want you to know that I do.'

'Stop getting soppy,' I said. 'You might regret calling me at all soon. I always could talk and talk and talk – don't say I didn't warn you!'

He laughed, and it sounded lovely; a natural response, and one that I hoped would bring him some relief, if only for the few seconds it had lasted.

It felt odd, but at the same time the most natural thing in the world. I was having a conversation with a man I'd barely spoken to over the years whose life had existed, it seemed, a million miles away from my own but who was now calling me and sharing personal details of his day and how he was feeling. It had always been a breeze being around him, but it would take some time to adjust to this sudden change and renewed contact. I just hadn't realised how much contact that would be: a call the next night and the next and the next. Or how long they would be: thirty minutes to two hours. Or how intense and how distressing.

Small, constant raindrops of pain falling onto my shoulders and into my life; a sudden window into a dark world – one only he could inhabit. Alone he may have been, but as he retreated we circled patiently around him, ensuring he was not isolated when he eventually emerged into whatever colour he now saw the world. I raised this with him during one of our subsequent phone calls.

'I think that if I lost my son, the world would lose all its colour, it would just become a bleak black-and-white version. Is that how you see life now?'

'No, it's not black and white. I still see the colour,' he replied.

'Well that's remarkable, I can't imagine finding joy in anything. It would become a colourless existence for me, I'm sure.'

'No, it's not the outside that's changed for me – it's the inside. My heart feels dead, black – I feel nothing inside.'

CHAPTER 9

I was listening to his voice. He was talking about his sons.

'He was so sweet,' he said, as he spoke about Oscar. 'I would take him and Felix on bike rides. We'd go for miles and he'd be trailing behind us, but his little legs would be pedalling away, determined to keep up. He must have been so tired but he never complained, not once, because it was all so much fun to him. He really was the sweetest little boy.'

'Were they similar personalities?'

'Oh no, very different. Oscar was calmer, and could sit and concentrate for hours drawing, and playing with his Lego. He loved school and so it was easy to get him to do his home-work. Felix was more energetic and sporty. Homework was a distraction, so trying to get him to sit down and do it was much harder. He absolutely loved football, though, and one day I took him out of school to go and see a Liverpool match. I'm so glad I did that now.' He paused. 'I'm sorry, I think I'm repeating myself. I already told this story during the eulogy.'

'That doesn't matter. It would be lovely to hear it again.'

'Well, the match was in the evening so I decided we would make a day of it. We set off early, had lunch out together in Manchester, went to see *Avatar* at the cinema, and last of all watched the football – just the two of us having lots of fun. It was only the second match he'd been to and I'll never forget how excited he was. The next morning he came into our bedroom and whispered in my ear, "Dad, yesterday was the best day of my life".'

As he shared anecdotes of his life with his family I would visualise them from the pictures I had seen, and they changed from people I had never known, to individuals with personalities and full lives, their still images awakening before my very eyes and becoming colourful, vibrant and warm. He would mistakenly talk in the present tense as though they were still here, and then suddenly become aware of what he was doing and stop in his tracks. Silence.

Some days it was too much for me to comprehend; the intensity of his emotions was quite something to absorb, and as I listened to his voice, thick with grief and desperation, I would give in to my own overwhelming sadness. Tears would roll down my face and trickle onto the side of my neck, silently at first and then, as I could contain my emotion no longer, my crying would become louder, and he would stop and say, 'Oh, Jill, I'm so sorry. Are you okay? I didn't mean to upset you. I'll stop talking about them.'

'No, really, you've nothing to be sorry for. It's just incomprehensible to me how you're coping. Listening to you describe them so vividly … you bring them to life. I'm sorry to say it, I don't want to distress you, but you do. I want to know about them, but the more you tell me, the closer they become and the harder it is to hear.'

We would cry together. I would cry for them, for him and for myself – tears of sadness, and tears of relief that my son was moments away from me. I could reach out and touch him, call to him and know he was there. It was exhausting.

I was listening to his voice. He was describing his desperate search through the rubble of his former home. He said he wanted to find an intact tangible object – a toy, a book, a picture, clothing, anything would do – something to hold, keep and cherish in the years to come. These were the physical memories he now craved. Not for him a retreat into either son's bedroom to lie on their beds, to hold their toys, to smell their clothes – the ferocity of the fire had destroyed most of the house, and nearly everything in it.

'I went back to the house today. I wanted to see if I could find some of their possessions, things I might have missed previously.'

'Did you go with someone else for support?'

'No, I went alone. I wanted to be alone. But I couldn't find anything else.'

'How painful that must be for you. What do you have?'

'Well, I've got a couple of the boys' red school jumpers which I found in Heather's car boot, and thankfully some old family videos that were in the garage and have footage of the boys on them. And then there's their bikes that you saw in the shed.'

'So not a lot then. But the boys' jumpers must be lovely to hold and smell – things they wore and that were close to them?'

'Yes, but unfortunately I can't smell them. They've been in the car, so maybe that's why their scent isn't there.'

On the one hand, he said, the possessions he sought were comparatively unimportant and relative to his memories, but on the other hand, their very existence was crucial in helping him cling on to those memories. As time progressed, and these naturally started to insidiously diminish, this became more and more important. He described it as 'lost proof' of his history and life, as though it had never existed. Another layer of pain.

I was listening to his voice. He was talking about his wife.

'She did it all, absolutely everything. She planned so many holidays and fun activities for us. Did I tell you we went to Florida four times? That it was our favourite place?'

'No, you hadn't mentioned that. Was that with the boys?'

'Believe it or not, the first two times it was just us. We were like a pair of big kids.'

'I think you mentioned in your eulogy that you met in a nightclub.'

'Yes, in Manchester. And we instantly clicked. We went back there for our first date, and the first dance we had was to "Don't Leave Me This Way" by The Communards, and so that became "our" song.'

'I remember the letter you sent me when I was in the army saying you'd met – we were in our early twenties, I think?'

'Yes, we were twenty-four and married three years later on a beach in St Lucia. We had such a great life together, living in Jersey before moving to Wales and having Felix and Oscar, and had lots of fun before we became parents. Jersey was like one long amazing party, which meant we were very ready to have children when we did. We'd lived a life without responsibility and wanted a family by then.'

'How lovely that you found such long-term happiness together. Tell me something else about Heather … as long as that's okay with you?'

'Of course it is, but are you sure you want to listen to me talk about my family again? It's lovely that you ask, but please don't feel you have to.'

'Now, let's get one thing straight – I'm not asking because I feel any obligation to. I'm asking because I'd like to know more about them and your life together. Yes, it's distressing – how could it not be – but it would seem very odd not to talk, or want to talk, about them. They were your life, John, and they lost theirs.'

'Well, that's where you're different to others. You just jump right in without any fear and don't mind chatting about them or what happened. I don't think you realise that others aren't like that. You make it very easy and comfortable to be open. Do you think your police training has helped?'

'I'm sure both my nursing and policing experiences, particularly my Family Liaison Officer training, have influenced that. But it's also just who I am, and like all of us, my life experiences have shaped that. Fear isn't something I feel at these moments. Do you know, my stepbrother took his own life while I was training to be a psychiatric nurse, and I was shocked to discover that even in that environment there were many who clearly didn't feel able to come to me and acknowledge what had happened – not even a simple hug without words. It's not a criticism of them, just an observation of how even medical professionals, actively engaged in the nursing of those experiencing mental health problems, couldn't take themselves into that space. That's never left me. So if you want to talk about Heather, Felix and Oscar then it would be lovely to hear about them.'

'You're very kind to show this genuine interest and to give me this time. It's not something I take for granted. Just so you know.'

'I'm just being a friend. Now come on, tell me something I don't know about her,' I said, gently.

'Well, she adored Christmas, which for her always started after her birthday, at the end of November. She'd fill the house with tinsel and lights and spoil the boys rotten, creating a magical home for us all. She came alive with the thrill of it all.' Silence.

Listen to the silence, Jill … say nothing right now … just listen to the silence.

Moments later, he continued.

'Do you know the tree and decorations would still be up at the end of January, when I'd insist that they had to be taken down. If Heather had had her way they'd have been up all year.'

∽

My life had taken on extremes: one minute a call with John and talk of death, the next, traffic law. My Inspectors' exam was rapidly approaching and I was sitting at my pine desk in our spare bedroom staring at the arid, black words as they stared resolutely back. Death, traffic law, death, traffic law. Study was a relief from John's world, I told myself, requiring not one shred of emotion, just mental focus. No emotion at all. This should be a comparative breeze.

The telephone rang, and I saw it was John's number. I answered. I wasn't listening to his voice because he could barely talk.

'John, are you okay?' I was trying to sound calm but could hear my immediate concern echoing back to me as the words left my mouth.

He was trying to clear his throat, to bury his distress, but he wasn't succeeding. I was back at the funeral, where I had willed him to start a sentence and speak. Nothing.

'John, talk to me. Are you okay? I know it's a ridiculous thing to ask, you're clearly not okay but – you know what I mean.'

'I'm sorry,' he eventually managed to utter. 'I shouldn't have called. I thought I would be able to talk but I can't. I'll have to go. I'm sorry.' His voice sounded weak and was trembling.

'Please don't apologise. If you want to call later I'll be here, so just pick up the phone and ring.'

His throat cleared again. 'Thanks, but I'm going to go to

bed now. I need to go to bed. I'll call tomorrow.' The line went dead.

I wasn't listening to his voice because he hadn't called.

He was a creature of habit; he'd said he'd call but he hadn't.

I was calling him repeatedly; the ringing tone becoming longer and longer with each attempt as I silently pleaded with him to answer, pleaded with him to breathe. My anxiety was rising rapidly.

Pick up the phone, John. Please pick up the phone and let me know you're alive.

No answer.

Maybe he's in the shower, I reasoned. Try again in fifteen minutes.

Pick up the phone, John. Please pick up the phone and let me know you're alive.

No answer.

Maybe he's having a long soak in the bath, I reasoned. Try again in fifteen minutes.

Pick up the phone, John. Please. Pick up the phone and let me know you're alive.

Maybe he's gone for a run, an extra one to fill his day, I reasoned. Try again in thirty minutes.

Pick up the phone, John. Please. Pick up the phone and let me know you're alive.

No answer.

Shower, bath, run ... there were only so many reasons why

he would not be in possession of his phone. As my mind started taking me to places I was trying not to visit, I began questioning my own attempts at reason and rationale, began punishing myself for not calling earlier.

He always took his phone on his run; he took it for music, didn't he?

Just a shower or bath, then; well, he's had long enough for both now, and didn't everyone take their phone into the bathroom anyway?

He was in such a bad way last night. I should have called him back; for goodness sake, I should have called him back last night, to check he was okay.

He always answered.

I didn't have the telephone numbers for his sister or mum, but even if I'd had them they didn't live close by. They were probably calling and getting no reply too, and were probably just as worried. He'd gone to ground, and with every passing silent moment I began to consider the possibility that he'd decided enough was enough and was dead somewhere. As quickly as I tried to empty my mind of images of his lifeless body – in his bed, in his bathroom, on the living room floor – they bounced back in. Maybe he wasn't even in his flat. Maybe he'd decided to go elsewhere to take his own life; my desperate mind took me to desperate places.

Despite his assurance to me that suicide was not an option for him, I wasn't feeling very reassured right now. Three hundred frustrating miles sat between us.

The silence was deafening.

~

He was listening to my voice and I was not happy. He had eventually called, hours later.

'Where have you been? I've been trying to get through to you all day. I thought you'd gone and done what you said you wouldn't do. I've been worried sick.'

'I'm sorry, I'm really sorry. And I've told you before that suicide isn't an option for me. You must believe that.'

'Well, lots of people say that and then go and do exactly that, so forgive me for having viewed that asserted position with some scepticism – particularly when I couldn't get hold of you for hours. What was I supposed to think? And where *have* you been all this time?'

I was sounding intense and critical. I could hear my voice and the urgency of my words as they flew out of my mouth on a bed of barely concealed, gritted anger and frustration wrapped up in genuine concern. I sounded selfish, I'm sure; I was in the company of a man who was bereft and I was considering my own needs, if not before his then certainly as of equal importance.

But I did feel angry and frustrated at having been left for so long in the dark, and the irony of that wasn't lost on me: he was in a dark space and had left the rest of us in one too, as we'd paced around waiting and hoping for contact.

'I've been in bed – I couldn't face the day. I've been in a … no, I mean, I *am* in a really … a very dark space, and when it smothers me like this I've got to retreat. You're not the only one who's been trying to get through. My mum, sister and Barbara have all been calling too. I'm so sorry, I really am.'

'You know, I truly understand your need to remove your-self from the world, I do. But please, next time can you let me know before you disappear? I'm sorry to go on, but I can't tell you how awful it's been not knowing where or how you were, and now this huge relief that you're okay and alive. It's like some huge rollercoaster that I got onto and now can't control. I want to support you, but can I ask that in future you let me know when you need space and don't want any contact?'

'I'll try, but when I'm really bad I'm just not capable of thinking rationally like that. My mind shuts down. But you must believe me when I say that I have no intention of taking my own life.'

'I care about you, John. Just let me know you're alive and breathing somewhere, if you can.'

I was drained.

He said his body felt leaden and slow-moving. He would get out of bed and force himself to walk through his day in some sort of semi-conscious daze because for him there was no alternative. When he woke in the morning he would wish he had not woken, not because he wanted to die, but simply because he didn't want to face the day – a vast, empty and directionless no man's land. The daily horror of realising that the nightmare was in fact the inescapable and cruel reality of his life immediately gave him a metaphorical beating. Repeated blows rained down on his already shattered being, their sustained power and arrival without notice able to bring him instantly to his knees, reducing him to a distressed, mute ball as he struggled to field them.

I sat at my bedroom desk, head in my hands as the tears

dropped onto my open traffic law study book, the words a blur and the page now wet. Traffic study was not the relief from John's world I had hoped; it was not a comparative breeze, requiring not one shred of emotion. It was a strong and painful link to my past. My father had been a traffic sergeant at the time of his death.

Get a grip, I told myself. *You've studied this subject before for your Sergeants' exam.* But my internal lecture failed to stem my distress. The daily injection of John's family, with its cocktail of death and loss and life's injustice, had raised my father from his ashes, reopening the door of my own pain and bringing my study to a thundering halt. It was now my father's death, not those of Heather, Felix or Oscar, that tormented my thoughts. It was now my loss, not John's. And it was now the injustice of *my* life. I laid my thumping head on the table, on top of my traffic study book, and closed my tired, tear-stained eyes.

I was listening to his voice. He was talking about his need to fill every minute of his day, and how he was running every morning and evening for forty minutes or more. This was not for any release it gave him, but to get himself out of the flat and to keep moving. It was essential to keep moving, not so much to keep the pain and grief at bay, but to make them manageable. They remained close, but the running gave him enough space to breathe and live.

'If I'm occupied at some level, I can just about function. It's when I stop that it hits me, so I make sure I'm busy. Running keeps me moving.'

'Right, okay, well that sounds good. Does the exercise help?'

'I don't know that anything helps, but I put my headphones on and lose myself for a while, which is a distraction. The runs are only thirty or forty minutes, so nothing too long, but enough to fill some time and they give my day some structure too. Strange really – the music is on but I don't hear it, if that makes sense? It gives me a rhythm to run to, but the music that's playing doesn't interest me any more. It was something that brought me so much joy throughout my life and it's like it just died with my family.'

'I'm sure it'll come back in time,' I said gently. 'You've just lost your wife and sons. It must be difficult enough getting out of bed and facing the day, so be kind to yourself and take it easy.'

Silence at the end of the phone.

Music had been his lifelong love, carried in his blood and played daily and loudly. It had now become a tasteless reminder of happier times. It was supposed to be joyous, and there was no joy. Other than on his runs, where it served a function to provide rhythm, music had been cast aside.

The silent flat, his apparent safe-haven, became a double-edged sword. Returning home after his evening run, he said he would eat food, make phone calls and, with the walls creeping slowly in towards him, retreat to bed where the daily battle to function was lost. Lying on his mattress on the floor, exhausted from the day, no strength left to fight his circling omnipotent demons, he would relinquish control and let them descend. He would curl in a foetal ball with a blanket on his head, while the grief coursed through his body, catapulting him into a black hole of despair. It was a hole where he would cry loudly and uncontrollably, his body in spasm with the wrenching emotion, pain and distress, his eyes sore with tears. He had no light or hope, he said, just the cold, bleak blackness, and what he described to me as his 'black heart'.

These were the worst moments of his day, the worst moments of his life, and he would wake the next day to begin the cycle of survival again. He was living a life on permanent, debilitating repeat.

His loss was everywhere he looked, but worst of all it was the clothes he now wore, the eyes he looked through, the food he ate, the wind, the rain, the sun. Unshakeable, it was here to stay, wrapping its suffocating pressure around him.

He did not want to be defined by this, but there was no escaping it: he was a prisoner in his own life, a prisoner of himself.

I was listening to his voice. He was talking about his return to work approximately six weeks after the funeral.

'I need to keep occupied, and so being back should be a good thing.'

'What have you been doing?'

'I've been working in the office. I won't be going out on any jobs but I can do the admin and that sort of thing. And it's nice to see more of Micky and Elwyn.'

'So will you work until you leave to go travelling?'

'Yes, probably. I'll just see how it goes. The first day back was very difficult, though, as the school Felix and Oscar went to is literally next door to our premises. When I'm sitting in the office I can hear the children playing in the playground throughout the day.'

'Oh my goodness! Why subject yourself to that? How can you bear to listen to them?'

'Well, I've got to come to work – I need it for my own sanity – and Micky and Elwyn need my help. It'll be better in the colder months, when I can close the windows. There's no escaping it, so what can I do?'

He had thought going back would occupy his mind, but he disclosed, months later, that it didn't. He would sit in the office unable to concentrate, and he estimated that in the four months he was there he produced about two weeks' work. Micky and Elwyn undoubtedly shouldered the fallout and shielded him from its impact – true friends who stood close by and protected him while he tried to keep afloat, wrapping him up without the need for words, and standing guard around him.

I was listening to his distressed voice. He was crying. 'They keep bringing me more photographs of the boys,' he said, his harrowing sobs engulfing the air. I closed my eyes as the weight of his grief rendered me speechless. To hear such anguished, primal cries, cries that came from the depths of darkness, was paralysing. Sometimes there are no words;

sometimes there is nothing that can be said; sometimes the pain demands a space of its own.

I didn't go to my father's very large, police funeral. I didn't get a chance to say my seven-year-old goodbye. I didn't get a chance to build some sort of bridge from his vibrant presence to his disturbing absence. Our mother decided to take only my eldest eleven-year-old sister. It was to her I would turn years later, enviously digesting her clear memory of being driven in a vehicle behind the hearse, as four police outriders – two to the rear and two to the front of the hearse – escorted our father's coffin to the church.

My own clear memories were of my maternal grandmother making egg, tomato and mayonnaise sandwiches for the wake, held at our home later, and of my paternal uncle playing games with us on the front lawn as he attempted to distract us from the distress of the mourners inside.

My father – some sort of disappearing act, not connected to the events playing out.

As I sat at my desk, attempting to absorb firearms law (having decided to put traffic study to one side in an effort to create some space from my re-emerging personal grief), my father clearly had other ideas. My mind was repeatedly inter-rupted by the image my sister had described: police outriders taking my father on his final journey to his final resting place.

Police outriders, firearms law. Police outriders, firearms law.

Damn John. Damn his grief reopening my own. I shut my

study book in frustration, grabbed my running gear and left for the gym. A run would help clear my mind.

I had to return my father to a place of peace. To a place of comfort, not distress.

Around the interminable darkness lay the wonderful kindness and love of so many: his family, his friends, the childminders who had cared for his sons after school, parents from school and the school itself. So many who had known Heather, Felix and Oscar, and who were also reeling from their deaths. The ripple effect of death had left a community in collective shock and sadness.

As John walked amongst them, realising what little he had left, they dug deep, searched, and found more precious pictures of his wife and sons – pictures taken at school, pictures taken by the childminders, pictures taken by friends – and they came and they gave in his hour of need. These were, he said, pictures he would treasure for the rest of his life. True gifts in the darkness: the gift of more pictures, but also the gifts of kindness and compassion from those who surrounded him. Quietly they walked, their presence, despite his inability to embrace everyone, providing a silent air of care and concern around him.

As he struggled to exist in a life that bore no resemblance to his erstwhile lifelong 'life's dandy' attitude and mentality, I believe it was this dormant spirit that lay beating deep down under all the layers of grief that he somehow managed, through the sound of his tears, to hear. Clearly, life would never be dandy again, but the positive platform that he had always sprung from was undoubtedly instrumental in his early survival. His upbeat, energetic persona, his starting point for all, was now a lever on which he could keep a tight grip to help him steer a course down the grim road ahead.

While we talked endlessly about all sorts – no holds barred – I recall listening to his voice and wondering just how long I would be able to support him in that way. To be so closely exposed to a man who had always been unavailable to me and for whom I felt great affection was difficult. As I struggled to manage the conflict bubbling away just beneath the surface regarding my feelings for him and the role I was playing out, at times it felt like my head was about to explode. I knew it would become increasingly difficult for me to walk alongside him in this way, and I made a conscious decision that at some point down the road, at a natural rather than a prescribed point, I would just have to be honest and distance myself from him at some level. But for now it was simple: he needed friends and I was one of them. I would continue to do what we did best: talk.

I sat at my bedroom desk, invigorated from another run earlier that evening. I looked down, opened my traffic study book and began to read. My father's presence sat quietly and reassuringly by my side. My mobile signalled an incoming text:

Don't expect you'll read this until the morning, but I'd just like to say thank you for all the phone calls and texts over the last few weeks. The care and companionship you have given me goes further than you know in my battle to understand and rationalise what's happened.

You have become my most trusted friend. I will never forget your kindness and hope I can return that kindness someday. Love John.

Tears welled up in my eyes as I read his beautiful words. Damn John. Just as I'd steered myself back on track, I came to another grinding halt. Damn his beautiful words; damn the intensity of my emotion; damn my Inspectors' exam. I surrendered, exhaled slowly, relaxed back into my chair and compiled a response:

For a man who doesn't use texts you say the loveliest things via them. Our friendship has become equally important to me. I genuinely hope that you're able to find light in your life again in the face of such tremendous loss, and can only hope our friendship helps you in some small way to do that. I will always be here for you. Jill x

CHAPTER 10

He was listening to my voice. He was digging for the specifics in my romantic history.

'Enough about me. You're always listening to me. We need to lighten the mood, so tell me about your romantic history,' he said, laughing.

'Now look, I may not have found the same long-term happiness as you with one partner, but I've had my fun along the way and I have a gorgeous son. So I'm not a complete lost cause.'

'I'm sorry, I don't mean to mock.'

It was his way, of course. Outside of very personal and emotive talk about his family, generally elicited by my direct line of questioning, he cloaked his communications with humour and jest. This was the invisible boundary I'd always felt he'd kept, and which I'd also seen in others – questions asked to which the enquirer doesn't actually want an answer, or certainly not one that is in-depth. They become apparent at those moments in life when you start to genuinely respond to such an enquiry, and realise instantly the other person's immediate disinterest in what you're saying: dead eyes, blank expression, a complete lack of encouraging noises in the form of 'Really? Tell me more', or 'Gosh, how interesting!' None of that. Just a passive white wall and a crystal-clear communication that the enquirer is not remotely interested in you or your response.

As he wasn't standing in front of me, I couldn't read those signals. Did he truly want to know the detail or was he feigning interest? I called it 'communication surfing'. There was only one way to find out.

'Okay, if you really want to know. I was married at twenty-four and that relationship lasted about five years. About six months after that I met my son's father, and that lasted five years too. But during the last ten years the longest relationship I've had has been one year.'

'It surprises me,' he said in a serious tone, 'how you've not managed to meet someone and stay with them long-term.'

I registered his 'encouraging noises' and decided to continue.

'I suppose it's a mix of not meeting the right person and not actually wanting to. I've been very happily single with Alexander, and with every passing year the wall around us has become higher and higher. We live in a very private cocoon and, for me, that's as it should be. I want him to feel safe and secure, so gallivanting around looking for men isn't my focus. Now that's a potted history, some of which I'm sure I told you years ago. You can't have been listening.' I was laughing now.

'I understand you want to protect your son, but I'm still surprised.'

'It's not that simple. Relationships are not that simple – though you make them sound like they are. Life's not that simple.'

'For me it is,' he quickly responded. 'Don't make life any more difficult than it has to be.'

'That's easy for you to say. My father's death impacted me in many ways, most of which I was unaware of until I was almost forty. Did I tell you I went to counselling then?'

'No, I don't think you did. Why was that?'

More encouraging noises. I took the decision to expose myself to him, risking his judgement. I knew the benefits of counselling, but he might not see it the same way, as so many others I'd encountered hadn't.

'It's been a great thing in my life, examining and under-standing my own dynamic – or at least attempting to under-stand it. And not just in romantic relationships, platonic ones too.'

I began to explain that a consequence of my father's death had been to unwittingly become a responsible person.

I desperately wanted him to understand.

I desperately wanted him to empathise.

I desperately wanted him to embrace the wonders of coun-selling.

I clearly needed to be less desperate. It shouldn't matter what he thought. But it did matter.

'It all sounds very complex. You know me, I don't look at things too deeply, but if it's worked for you then that's great,' he said nonchalantly.

My heart sank. How could I convey months of counselling and understanding in quick, simplistic terms? Answer: I couldn't. Here was a man who looked at life as it stood before him. There were no unconscious layers – or ones that he was prepared to delve into anyway. He didn't feel the need to. I was the polar-opposite: I delved deeply, I analysed. My life experiences and subsequent quest to understand myself at a deeper level lent themselves to that position, and so did my personality and temperament. John clearly wasn't about to be sucked in too deeply, for now anyway. I hurriedly brought that particular discussion to a close.

'Well, suffice to say I'm conscious of being drawn into relationships where I'm the strength, where there's an unhealthy dynamic that generally only serves one person. I think they're referred to as "co-dependant". I've got an emotional boundary around myself now that I didn't have as a younger woman, and I'm much happier for it.'

'You seem very happy, too.'

'But please don't get the wrong impression. I've had lots of good times and I like a balanced perspective. For all my appreciation of the counselling process, I look back at all my relationships and know why, on the face of it, I was drawn in and attracted. I don't view them as failures, John, rather as the collective value of my life and experiences. It's just a different experience to yours.'

He was silent. I continued to fill the space but moved away from the subject of me and the deep waters we were getting into.

'Anyway, surely counselling is something you should be considering to help you cope with the loss of your family?'

'Crikey, no,' he immediately responded. 'It's not for me. I'll manage on my own.'

'Really?' I said. 'Don't you think you should at least consider that sort of support?'

'No, absolutely not,' he replied emphatically.

I had to say something, just a little something that would push the door into my world slightly ajar, and delicately convey some of what I was feeling.

'I've got to be honest with you: sometimes I feel out of my depth. For all my nursing and policing experience, my own losses were as a young child and a young woman. Yes, my father's death was devastating, but to bridge the gap between that and the loss of all your family and to try and support you in that … well, I'm not sure I can.'

I could sense it briefly settling on his shoulders before he quickly answered – far too quickly for the message to have been absorbed.

'I know you're concerned, but honestly, all that analysis and deep delving, I'm not sure it's going to help and it certainly won't bring my family back.'

'No, I know it won't,' I said gently, 'but don't dismiss it just yet. It's very early days.'

He hadn't heard what I was trying to say. Next time I would have to speak louder.

He was listening to my voice. It was a couple of weeks later.

'Have you thought any more about the counselling?'

'You and I are going to fall out if you keep harassing me about this,' he said light-heartedly.

'I'll have you converted yet,' I continued, unwilling to be blocked. 'Blimey, whoever it is will have their work cut out with you in the room,' I said provocatively.

'What do you mean by that?' He sounded surprised and intrigued at the same time.

I was getting braver, stepping into territory where I had not ventured before, my central role in his life bolstering my confidence.

'Oh, come on, you know you give nothing away to others.'

'I keep my own counsel, if that's what you mean.'

'No. I'm talking about …' I faltered. 'I'm not sure I should be making these observations.'

'Oh, you can't say something like that and not elaborate. Come on, get it off your chest. I'm all ears.'

'Okay then, I'll use a few analogies to help me … I like analogies. Now, are you sitting comfortably?' I said, in a mock-important tone.

'I may live to regret this,' he laughed.

'Well, I've always seen you as an island, with a moat and drawbridge, perhaps. You keep your distance from others … or possibly that's just been from me.' As my words floated in front of me I realised what I'd inadvertently put out there and, not wanting any space for a response, I quickly carried on.

'Or another one would be the "shopfront" scenario.'

'The what?'

'The shopfront – you know, the image we all project to the outside world, what we want others to see. But what we really have to get to are the goods in the shop. They're where the truth lies.'

'This is all getting a bit technical for me. And just how is that relevant, dare I ask?'

I was on a roll. I blame his encouraging noises. I had been given a platform to be honest about how I perceived him. *Sink or swim girl*, I muttered inwardly. *It's now or never.*

'I've just always felt that you let few people beyond your shopfront in through the front door. I'm talking emotionally here. You keep people at bay. Am I wrong?'

'I have to say, I've never given it any thought. No one's ever asked me such a question, but now that you are, yes, I suppose I do keep a distance from others in that way.'

'I think it's quite remarkable actually. I don't think I've ever known anyone so well defended. Not only is your shop door closed, but your shopfront is presented as perpetually happy to the outside world. Whatever goes on inside you, no one else would know. Even now, after all your loss, it remains the same.'

I stopped talking, suddenly aware of the sound of my own voice, suddenly aware of the freedom of my tongue, suddenly aware I needed to rein myself in. Rapidly.

The silence fell between us. Had he been listening to my voice? Had I overstepped the mark and taken him to a place he didn't want to be?

Suddenly he spoke. I could have heard a pin drop.

'No one else needs to see it, Jill. No one else needs to see my distress, my pain, and just what a mess I am in and what my life has become. Why would I begin to burden others with all of that? Why would I want to welcome anyone into my shop right now?'

He was listening to my voice. Those encouraging noises again.

'Tell me something I don't know about you,' he asked. 'Let's keep it light. No requests for counselling, no shopfront analysis – just silly stuff.'

'Are you sure?'

'Yes, absolutely.'

'Okay, now let me think.' I pondered momentarily. 'Well, I did ballet and tap when I was a young girl, but was far too self-conscious to be any good. I passed a Level 1 British Sign Language course years ago, but then didn't have the time to start Level 2, so eventually forgot all I'd learnt at Level 1. I'm halfway through a degree in Psychology with the Open University, which I've put on hold to study for promotion, and I suspect that if I ever try and finish it I won't remember what I've learnt on that either. You can see there's a theme here.' I was enjoying playfully dissecting my life. I took a breath, so my mind could catch up as it decided what other snippets to offer.

'Don't stop. This is very entertaining,' he interjected warmly.

I was on a roll in the face of his encouragement.

'Hmm. I'm quite a good cook, love Italian food – well, just love food actually. Carrot cake is a love of mine, which is why I'll never be stick thin. I'm constantly trying to maintain a size ten bottom. I'm a size six shoe, and once I had a boyfriend who I didn't realise wore a wig. My sister delighted in pointing this out, sniggering as she said, "Jilly, Jilly, don't you realise he's wearing a toupee!" It was clearly a good make. And just to be clear, this is not the same boyfriend who – in a very subtle seduction technique – dropped his trousers and underpants in my kitchen one evening. He clearly thought I'd be unable to turn him down. Oh, maybe that was too much information. Yes, definitely *way* too much information.'

He was laughing out loud. No tears, just laughter. Pure, unadulterated laughter and unrestrained joy, which gushed down the phone all frothy and light. I smiled a huge smile, and laughed too. It was a welcome relief.

We eventually calmed.

'I've been thinking about what you mentioned the other day,' he suddenly said. 'You know, the shopfront thing. Well, it's my boys, my sons – they're in my shop. I let them in from the moment they were born.'

He was listening to my voice. I was inviting him down to London for a few days and ironing out a few details. It was now about two months after the loss of his family.

'You don't have to meet Alexander. I understand that may be too difficult. But just so you know, he's more than happy to meet you. There are a few local bed and breakfasts you could stay at. I can inflict some of my home cooking on you. We can go into London to see the sights. The world awaits.'

'Can I just say that Alex is much older than my boys, so I'm cool with meeting him if that happens. Are you sure he's fine with it?'

'Absolutely. If he didn't want to he'd say, trust me. He loves meeting people.'

'Okay, so long as you're sure.'

'Well, if that's the case, we could go and watch him play an ice hockey match if there's one on. The season's just started again so we're back in the thick of it.'

'It sounds great, but please understand that I'm not the best of company.'

'Just come and be yourself. You don't have to pretend with me. It'll be good for you to get away for a few days. You can be anonymous in London.'

'I like the sound of that. To be anonymous – just another face in the crowd. Yes, that's just what I need.'

'Brilliant, I look forward to it.'

The deal was done and he was coming. It wasn't an invite I'd made lightly; Alexander was just fifteen and, regardless of whether their paths crossed, I had now edged him a little closer into John's world. Was it the right thing to be doing? I wasn't sure. It was one thing to be a young adult getting to grips with the real world, it was another to be faced with a man who had just lost his whole family. Many battle-weary adults struggled to walk the precarious conversational bridge to John, and I was acutely aware that on my son's young shoulders this could be fraught with difficulty. I'd sought his views and feelings before calling John, and had very firmly been put in my place.

'I wondered whether to invite John down for a few days. What do you think?'

'Sounds like a nice thing to do.'

'You don't have to meet him if he does come, as he wouldn't be staying with us. I understand you may find it uncomfortable.'

'What do you mean?'

'Because he's just lost his family, and many people – most who are much older than you – find it difficult being in his company right now.'

'Stop fussing. I don't see the problem.'

'I'm not fussing. I'm being sensitive to your feelings.'

'I think you're making this into some big issue, when for me it's not.'

'I was just checking how you felt about it, that's all ... so I know how to manage it myself.'

'That's lovely of you, but ...' He shrugged his shoulders as though it all rested on one thing. 'More importantly, would he like to meet me?'

'Yes, he's mentioned before that he would. I'm sure that hasn't changed.'

'Well, I'd like to meet him too. So it's sorted. If there's a match on maybe he could come and watch.'

'That's a great idea. But we'll have to tread softly around him.'

'Enough!' he exclaimed. 'He wants to meet me and I want to meet him, so that's all there is to it.'

Pragmatic, uncomplicated and a breath of fresh air. I could

only hope he would be able to embrace the reality of John's company as easily.

As I approached the front door a few weeks later, I looked in the hallway mirror for one final check. Hair loose, mascara and brown eyeshadow neatly applied, but definitely no lipstick. It had to be a relaxed, laid-back impression I gave, not all Marilyn Monroe. I doubt he'd have noticed if I'd answered the door in a sack, quite frankly, but I'd opted for three-quarter length tight jeans and a white T-shirt. Casual was good. It was the end of August and the weather was still warm and sunny. I was anxious. Our previous contact had been for a very specific reason. This visit had no such central focus.

How strange it was to see him standing before me. No funeral suit now, but still very pale and hollow-cheeked with his weight loss. He was wearing jeans and a T-shirt too. But best of all, as he stepped in through the door, he wore the widest of smiles.

Without the need for words he wrapped his arms around me and we shared another big and hearty hug. Boy, we were good at hugs. Hugs negated the need to speak when sometimes there were no words; they simply conveyed warmth and affection between two friends who were pleased to see each other.

We stood and embraced silently. A million unspoken words were shared, and what seemed like a million minutes passed as we held each other close. When he eventually let loose his arms and pulled back, I saw his eyes were glazed and tears were falling down his cheeks.

I gently placed my hands around his face and with my thumbs I wiped them away.

'Oh John, I'm so sorry. I wish there was something I could do to take away your pain,' I said, pulling him back towards me and hugging him again.

He didn't respond. He couldn't respond.

Had I done the right thing in inviting him down?

Had I done the right thing in inviting his pain down?

Had I done the right thing in inviting his wife and children down?

It was too late. They were all standing expectantly in my hallway. I had welcomed them all into my home.

CHAPTER 11

It's funny how the small things in life can unexpectedly illumi-
nate the large things, the small things in this instance being the
ginormous pieces of carrot cake sitting on our respective
plates. We had just arrived in London and were in a cafe,
sitting on tall stools at a round table positioned by the
window. John was directly opposite me and neither of us had
taken a bite.

I was about to pontificate about the calorific price I would
pay in eating such a delicious mouthful and whether I should
be doing such a thing when in pursuit of a smaller bottom,
when it struck me how shallow I would sound. How ridiculously unimportant it would seem in John's world. We had
talked for hours during the last few months about allsorts, but
his physical presence had brought his loss infinitely closer,
immediately magnifying the minutiae of my intended words,
which rapidly shrank in value. All the small and inconsequential irritations in life crowded my mind, parading gleefully in

front of me – a list of Very Important Issues, which now had no importance at all. As John answered his mobile, I began silently to reflect on my specific pet hates.

There's the individual at the supermarket checkout who, in their efforts to move you out of the way, rams their shopping trolley slap bang against your bottom or, worse still, is so close you can feel their warm breath on your neck. One of these days, oh yes, one of these days I'm going to turn and ask them whether, as we're clearly shopping together, they would like to pay my food bill and transport *our* food to *our* car. Oh, the sweet joy that assertion would bring. For the time being, I opt for the snail response: the more you push, the slower I am going to go. Doesn't anyone understand that?

And then there's the individual who, on the early morning supermarket run, decides to park their car right next to me in a car park that's virtually empty. Of the hundreds of empty spaces they decide to park right next to me. *Really*? Just what possesses people to do this?

And the train passenger on the early morning commute who opens their paper wide and directly into your space, while at the same time holding fast their elbow on the middle armrest. This specific offence is more often than not committed by the male gender and is one I've always likened to a cat spraying urine to mark its territory.

And the person who, in the middle of a packed train, loads up the seat next to them with coats and bags and food and, when politely asked to remove said items so you can sit down, huffs and puffs indignantly.

And then there are those who speak with their mouths full, or don't say thank you when a door has been politely held for them; cafe attendants who put cold milk in your coffee when you've asked nicely for hot; drivers who spectacularly fail to acknowledge you giving way to them. Would they want to be treated like that? I doubt it.

All Very Important Issues, and worthy of hours of my time spent expressing my exasperation at such irritating human behaviour.

I felt small, so very small, as he and his life loomed in front of me. He looked huge and indifferent to it all. He *was* indifferent to it all. The prism through which I had sometimes allowed myself to view life now felt narrow, self-absorbed and blinkered. The prism through which he viewed his life stared back at me, powerful and silent. His was a kind perspective, without judgement, without vanity, without ego, coming from a place in which all morally superior people existed. I could only aspire to walk in such a world and try harder to be a better person.

As I checked myself, distracted by my thoughts, he suddenly enquired, 'Are you okay, you seem very distant?'

'It's difficult.'

'What's difficult?'

'The calories in my carrot cake, the importance of the calories in that huge piece of cake ... that's what's difficult. I was about to debate the pros and cons of succumbing to such a treat when I suddenly felt like a fool with nothing very important to say, or certainly nothing you'd be interested in. The small talk of life that right here with you, in the face of your loss, doesn't seem to have any relevance or importance. Do you understand what I'm saying?'

'Yes, I do. I do get it, Jill. I'm aware people struggle in my company because of it.'

'I just suddenly felt buried by it – by you. The cake, the rude barista, every goddamn minor irritation in life that I might want to let off steam about. And then I look at you today and none of it seems to have any place, and I'm struggling right now to find anything important to say. None of it sits comfortably alongside you.'

'You're right, I don't care about any of the small stuff any more, but I don't want you to feel like this when you're with me. I do understand life goes on and that we can all get bothered by things that, on reflection, we should have been bigger than. But we're all human. It's life.'

I looked across at him as he generously permitted me the space to be human. *I might have to save my humanness for when you're not around,* I thought, as I poured the bloody cold milk into my coffee.

'But let me make one thing very clear,' he joked. 'I seriously don't give a damn about the calories in that cake, or any cake for that matter. I'm going to enjoy every last crumb and not give a second thought to how fattening it is. As far as I'm concerned, carrot cake is one of my five a day,' he laughed. 'And I know it's your favourite, so tuck in and savour the moment, and then we can go and explore this big city. Now, do you know the name of the group that's playing here right now?'

'Of course I don't. I haven't a clue, as I'm sure you know only too well.'

'They're called Morcheeba and they're one of my

favourites, so it's lovely to be able to listen to them in the background.'

The buzz of London was just the ticket. Our first stop was St Paul's Cathedral, where we sat on wooden chairs in the back row of the central seating area. Despite the noise of many other sightseers milling around, the powerful solemn atmosphere enabled even those easily distracted to sit in quiet contemplation should they wish to.

'It's beautiful, isn't it?' said John quietly, leaning in towards me to ensure he was not overheard. 'I'm talking about the actual building, the architecture.'

'Yes, quite breathtaking. Does its atmosphere affect you spiritually though – you know, move or strengthen you in some way?'

'No, not one bit,' he answered decidedly. 'I can appreciate how stunning it is, but it's just a building to me and so it doesn't change my atheist beliefs at all. I gain nothing emotionally from being here.'

No point attempting to tread any further down that road, I thought.

'What about you?' he asked.

'I find it very powerful, actually. But then, I don't believe that death is the end. I think my soul will leave my body and return to its source. Not quite a single God at the gates of heaven, more a universal energy. I believe that one day I'll meet my father again too.'

'I hope you're right, Jill. I don't think you are, but if it gives you comfort then that's okay for you, isn't it. It's far too romantic an idea for me though. If I thought once I'd died I'd be with my family again ...' The conversation had come to a natural end, and we sat silently for another ten minutes before climbing to the highest point of the cathedral, under the central dome, the Whispering Gallery. It felt good to explore and to be in a space where we could talk with more ease. Standing on the circular perimeter walkway, we leant against the banister rails watching the ground-floor activity below, as other tourists mingled behind us. A mezzanine floor, one level down and on the opposite side, was full of what I thought looked like folded tables, but I wasn't sure. Straining my eyes, in the hope of discerning exactly what they were, I pointed towards the area and asked John. Light conversation was needed.

'What's all the stuff piled up down there? Can you see?'

His gaze followed the direction of my pointing arm. He peered slowly forward, feigning great interest not only in what they were, but also in such banal chat, and a matter of seconds later he turned towards me.

'Don't you know?' he asked confidently, as though it was ridiculous I didn't know, and conveying clearly that he did.

'No, what are they then?'

'For goodness sake, you daft thing, can't you see they're the table-tennis tables that the clergy have some fun with on their lunch breaks?' he said convincingly. 'Apparently, they like to knock a few balls about, and so they take them down to the ground floor for matches. Bizarre to think of that happening, isn't it, but I've read it does.'

'*Really?* Are you sure?' I responded with a quizzical expression, completely taken in, oblivious to his tall tale. I strained my eyes and looked across again. 'They don't look like table-tennis tables to me.'

My ditzy side was unwittingly making an appearance.

'Yes, absolutely. Keeps them fit,' he continued in a serious tone but, unable to keep up the pretence, he had started to shake with laughter and I instantly realised I'd been fooled.

'Oh, Jill, you're the funniest thing at times. I was jesting. Do you seriously believe they play table tennis in the middle of St Paul's?'

He was laughing uncontrollably, clearly tickled pink at my gullible nature.

'Well, I have to admit, for a moment you had me thinking … but I was struggling with the thought of them lugging the tables to the ground floor and setting them up for a match.'

We were both now crying with laughter at my ridiculous belief that this activity took place; my stomach ached with pain and I was unable to talk. How good it felt to laugh like that. How good it felt to see him laugh like that too. Being ditzy was a small price to pay.

As we left, the sun was shining and we took pictures on the steps outside, the bright day highlighting John's pale complexion and drawn face. He wore a pained and dark expression. His eyes were distant. He was here but looked like he was existing in some sort of hell at the same time, one I wasn't privy to.

A visit to the Victoria and Albert Museum followed, with dinner after and then a stroll around the busy streets of Soho where, to my delight, John decided to buy some music CDs.

'It's great you want to seek out new music, and it was lovely to see you sit and enjoy Morcheeba playing earlier too.'

'Well, buying CDs isn't something I'm doing regularly, but music is where I'm trying to find my solace – not religion. If I can start taking small steps back and try and enjoy it, then that's an achievement.'

An evening at Ronnie Scott's Jazz Club was our final stop.

Neither of us had been before. What a fantastic place. From the minute we entered we were transported in Tardis-like fashion from the frenetic street outside into a seductive, mysterious, low-ceilinged world, where gangsters sitting in the murky corners cutting deals would not have been out of place. The walls were adorned with black-and-white pictures of jazz greats from the past. A central seating area full of small round tables and chairs was positioned in front of the stage, with further oblong tables on both side walls along the whole length of the room, tiered from top to bottom, ensuring a view of the stage for all. The delicious low lighting of the small red table lamps only just filtered softly through the darkness, casting red shadows that sexily outlined sitting customers, dark mysterious figures speaking with muted voices around the music. Discreet table service added further mystery and excitement to the whole place. It felt like we were doing something we shouldn't have been doing. Strangely illicit.

We chose a table along one of the walls and disappeared into the darkness, sitting closely side by side and looking out to the stage as we listened to the house band. We were anonymous amongst the crowds, just as John wanted to be. I ordered a large wine and John a Diet Coke with ice, just as we did seven years earlier when we'd met in the London pub. Snippets of the past were filtering through and catching me by surprise.

As we slowly relaxed and absorbed the hypnotic atmosphere, John leant in to me, whispering in my ear, 'Just close your eyes and soak up the music, really appreciate the music.'

I did as I was told and sat momentarily in the darkness, drowning in the sexy atmosphere and the thorn-in-my-side, sexy man sitting next to me. I could feel the same chemistry between us that had always existed: a natural frisson. He was so, so close and yet so far away. Snippets of the past filtering through.

The fact I was allowing myself these thoughts did not sit comfortably with me. At a time like this how could I allow them to permeate my mind? It would be a long time before he was ever going to contemplate another relationship, and if he ever did reach that point I'd have long since removed myself from the role of perpetual rejectee-in-the-wings. I wasn't his type, remember. A friend I could be, but I was not going to forever expose myself, up close and personal, to the fruit I could not eat.

'Do you know,' he said as we left at the end of the evening, 'that's the first time since my family died that I've truly felt alive with the music. What a place! What a great night! Thanks so much.'

An ice hockey match the next day, with all its speed, aggression and sheer life force soon shocked us out of such sublime reverie. The ice-cold rink and air, bright lights and booming music between goals and breaks were a stark contrast, but another exciting venue for different reasons. The air was alive with the sound and exuberance of screaming parents as the puck and players hurtled around the rink with astonishing speed, desperate to seal a win and, of course, with the vocal expressions of injustice at the referee calls when we failed to secure it. A tremendously exciting sport.

Alexander rolled along in John's presence with consummate ease, fully embracing this new friend and thoroughly enjoying John's desire to understand the sport with his excited questioning.

'Alex, I know nothing about ice hockey, so tell me the rules so I can understand what's going on. Your mum says you play in defence?'

'Alex, what about the offside rule – is it the same as in football?'

'Alex, are there different hockey sticks for the forward and defence positions?'

'Blimey, you look like Michelin Man in all that gear. How do you move around the rink so fast?'

John was simply lovely with him. How could my son not respond to such genuine warmth and interest? But as I stood by and watched them interact, for all John's assertions that, at fifteen, Alexander's age was not a problem, this was, for me, a first outing in these circumstances and I personally found it very difficult. Standing on the perimeter wall seats with John by my side, shouting at my son in support and with overwhelming maternal pride, I was painfully aware that John could no longer do the same with his sons. I felt guilty for being inadvertently and naturally exuberant in the face of my son's achievements. It didn't feel right to be enjoying myself. His loss only served to magnify my joy. His sons were standing right by my side.

'Are you okay?' I said, cupping my hands around his ear in my efforts to be heard above the din of the match.

'I'm fine. Now stop worrying and watch the game.'

As we waited for Alexander to emerge sweating from the changing room, I introduced John to some other parents standing close by.

'So, do you have children yourself?' one of the dads asked John.

I was completely unprepared for the question and the answer.

There was a brief pause.

'I had two sons,' he responded, his voice wavering, 'but they both died in a house fire.'

Shocked silence descended.

The weekend had come to an abrupt and very painful end.

CHAPTER 12

It had felt like the ground was falling from beneath my feet, a cavernous hole appearing below, and as my body floated downwards I tried without success to reorientate myself. I was surrounded by other ice hockey parents in free fall too, our mutual discomfort a life force of its own set in a slow-motion movie. How long would it take for us all to sink to the bottom of the pit and kindly remove ourselves from what he'd just said?

I was stunned by his direct and honest answer. I had thought he wanted to be anonymous in the crowd, that he didn't want to be defined by the loss of his family, but he had placed himself in the centre of the ring with a Belisha beacon flashing on his head:

My sons died in a house fire.

My sons died in a house fire.

Wow. The man asking, to his credit, had remained and offered quiet condolences, but there was no doubting the immediate look of pale horror on his face as he rapidly computed what had been said, no doubting he was eternally grateful for the sounds of his own sons' vibrant, loud voices returning minutes after, allowing him to make his excuses and rapidly leave.

John sounded bewildered and fragile when he called me later from his flat, his voice quiet and delicate. He had left London following the match and we'd not had an opportunity to speak alone, as Alexander had been with us.

'It's the first time anyone's asked me. You know, someone I didn't know. I was as shocked as you, and right there, at that moment, to say I didn't have sons would have been to deny they existed and I couldn't do it.'

'I understand, I do. I just wasn't prepared, if I'm honest.'

He carried on, slowly.

'I already feel like my past has been wiped out … like it didn't happen … it frightens me … and if I'd said no it would have reinforced that feeling.'

I was walking on broken eggshells, already fragile ground that had been further shattered by the brutal blow received the day before, and I was acutely aware of the impact the intensely private and distressing issue that created it must have had on John. It was a scenario that could appear at any given time for the rest of his life. It was perhaps beyond anyone's control, but at the very least I wanted to try and protect him from it happening again in my company.

'Please don't feel I'm judging you. I just feel awful that you walked into that situation and that it could have been avoided. I could have spoken to the other parents beforehand and told them about your background. Then you wouldn't have been faced with the question and they wouldn't have been faced with the answer.'

'No, no, absolutely not,' he interjected. 'It's not something I know how to deal with myself at the minute, let alone anyone else, and I don't want others knowing my background unnecessarily, if that's okay with you.'

'You have to do what's right for you, John, and I really do appreciate you can only take it a moment at a time. I'm just trying to understand and do the right thing too.'

'I thought I knew how I wanted to respond. I thought I'd say no to an enquiry like that, and that I *could* say no … but it floored me. They lived, they were full of life. To have answered no would have seemed like a betrayal.'

'I understand, but don't punish yourself. This is all very new to you. What feels okay one day might not feel okay the next.'

'I know, but I don't want to make anyone uncomfortable. It was completely unintentional, but it was a natural answer. It wasn't a choice I was aware I was making.'

'And I've no doubt everyone will understand that – or at the very least sympathise with such a predicament.'

'Do you know, saying those words out loud earlier, acknowledging their deaths like that … it made it very real and definite, which sounds crazy, doesn't it?'

'No, not at all,' I said, softly. 'It's not crazy. It's a cruel reflection back that their deaths are a reality. Saying it reinforces it I suppose. The fact you could say it may be a positive thing.'

A positive thing? Had I just said that? In my efforts to console and support him I had now made the death of his family sound like some sort of beneficial and helpful experience. Those bloody eggshells.

It was an impossible situation. My overriding concern was for John's feelings. How could any discomfort that I or anyone else felt at such a moment compare to his loss, his feelings?

But I was human. I didn't want to bear witness again to that sort of exchange anytime soon. I didn't want to bear witness to the clear and understandable discomfort of others who had inadvertently punched John in the face, discomfort so tangible I could touch and smell it.

Our lives were normal.

We'd been having a normal day.

We'd been enjoying an ice hockey match, drinking coffee, eating hot dogs, talking about normal things.

But in the middle of our normality, we'd been given our own punch in the face, one that could never compare to John's, but in that moment had felt very painful.

I had to be honest with myself: I was conflicted.

The minutiae of life were raising their ugly and selfish heads again, their narrow-lensed prism becoming spectacularly large.

Me, me, me ... what about poor me?

What about all the others who may unwittingly ask John that same question in the future?

What about *our* feelings when faced with that situation?

Fuck the bigger picture. Right now I wanted to wallow in the glorious minutiae of life, and for a moment permit myself a different conversation with John, one in which I would firmly place on the table how crushing the experience had been, not just for me, but no doubt also for the father asking the question and the others who'd stood listening. I wanted to remind John that we all had our needs, too.

How quickly one can be forced to refocus, to switch back to the wider-lensed prism of life. A few days later I was listening to his voice again, his daily moral sermon. He didn't realise the irony of an atheist unwittingly delivering sermons, but this is how I saw them. The simple act of talking about his life could have been delivered at any church pulpit, as a wise guide to life and what was to be valued.

'I've got to decide what to do with the urns,' he said.

'What do you mean, you've got to decide what to do with them?'

Admittedly I hadn't given his family's ashes any great thought. My father had been cremated too, and the urn containing his ashes had been placed under a square sandstone slab positioned along the perimeter of the church front garden. It wasn't sandstone any more, of course; it was now more mottled green-and-brown following the natural discoloration caused by many years of weathering. But you could still see his name and date of death inscribed and, no less painful year after year when I visited on the anniversary of his death, the words: 'Aged 36 years'. I could stand and stare at 'Aged 36 years' for hours, willing his life story to be different, willing my life story to be different. But the cold sandstone slab always stares back at me, unchanging and cruel. I do wish his ashes weren't under the ground and that they had been scattered to set him free.

'I have their urns here at the flat with me,' he continued, 'and I don't know what to do with them yet. I'm looking at them now.'

'Oh my goodness, how distressing! I didn't realise they were with you. I just assumed they were at the church while you sorted out a headstone or something similar.'

'No, they're here with me. They're on the living room floor against the wall. Don't worry, they're not huge things, just three, small, rectangular plastic boxes. They're only about twelve inches tall.'

I had read accounts of others keeping the ashes of deceased loved ones at home in various parts of the house, but I wasn't sure how healthy that was. As my father's ashes were under the ground this had never been something I'd had to consider. Perhaps it made people feel close to those they had lost and negated the need for a final goodbye. I wasn't an expert, but I wasn't sure it would be for me.

'It wasn't the size of them that concerned me, but the emotional impact that they must be having on you. Wouldn't it be better to put them somewhere that isn't directly in front of you? It can't be easy looking at them every time you're in the room?'

'Actually, I don't see my family when I look at them. I've opened them all and it's just a pile of dust in each, and not a lot at that.' I drew a silent, shocked breath as he continued. 'Heather, Felix and Oscar were larger than life only a matter of months ago, with so much energy and full of fun ...' His speech slowed down as he recalled them, and his voice became quieter. He paused, collecting his thoughts and composing himself before continuing. 'And so I can't get my head around the fact that the dust is them, I really can't. I simply see three, mud-brown plastic boxes, and I don't feel any emotional connection whatsoever. Those boxes are not my family.'

I could feel my emotions welling up and my breathing becoming shallower as I visualised him staring at what was left of his wife and sons: mini towers of death, starkly outlined against the cream walls of his flat, sitting without voice on his cream carpet. I remained silent. Sometimes it smothered me, and I couldn't find words or a voice to respond. Sometimes I wanted to talk about something light, but what I was eating for dinner or how my boring day had gone didn't fit neatly around conversations about his family's urns. I just had to put my 'sometimes' to one side.

'Do you know what they do though?' he added. 'They reaffirm my belief that once you die, that's the end. The urns represent their physical remains, that's all. Their personalities, their love, their laughter ... all the many wonderful things about them, well, they're definitely not in the urns. Those things have gone.'

'I don't know what to say, John. It's so desperately sad. I don't know how you're going to find ways to feel close to them. It's such a personal matter and one only you can find the answer to.' I broke momentarily, before adding, 'And perhaps not for some time.'

'You don't have to say anything. I just need a listening ear to stop myself going mad and to help me keep a firm grip on the reality of my life. Three urns in my living room is my new normal, so it feels crazy sometimes. But to know I can call you and talk about how that feels, and about so many other things, has made such a difference. Honestly, in my lifetime I'll truly never be able to repay the incredible kindness you've shown me, or convey the gratitude I feel.'

'I'm very touched you feel that way, but you've no need to repay anything.'

'It's heartfelt. I don't know where I'd be without you.'

I felt a warm glow descend, his welcome, affectionate words gently resting on my death-weary shoulders. 'You'd be surviving, I'm sure. I'm not the only one supporting you. But do you mind if we keep our call short tonight? I've got lots of study I still need to do and my exam's fast approaching.' I hoped he didn't sense my own need to withdraw and take a breath as I absorbed what he had just divulged.

'Of course not. But before you go, I wanted to say that for all my feelings about the urns I decided to put something personal inside each one, to try and make them human, things that they each loved.'

I was quietly taken aback.

'Is the opening big enough?'

'Yeah, they've got circular, plastic screw caps that sit on the top just inside the edges, large enough for my hand to reach in.'

'Oh, I hadn't realised they'd be so big.' I said, as though this was something I'd recently given a lot of thought to, my own normality rapidly blurring at the edges.

'Anyway, in Felix's urn I put his dark blue *Power Rangers* figure. In Oscar's I put a miniature Lego figure – a little man coloured red, white and blue, and in Heather's I put a picture of her and Felix. It was her favourite.'

Sometimes I had to pinch myself to make sure his reality

was actually *a* reality, one I was sitting listening to, albeit from a safe, cosy space, but one that had the capacity to instantly stun.

I put the phone down and cried as I pictured him holding the small mementos his family had also held and cherished, depositing them into their respective plastic mud-brown urns. Urns he had said were devoid of any emotion for him, but into which he had gently and lovingly placed these treasured possessions as he attempted to bridge the gap between life and death.

I filed into the large hall alongside hundreds of others, the atmosphere hushed and formal. Perfect columns of identical, square, wooden-topped, metal-legged desks filled the room from the front to the rear. A single chair was tucked under each, empty and menacing, gleefully waiting for its next victim. Bland, cream painted walls surrounded us. It was like being back at school again, only this time it was my third attempt at the Inspectors' exam.

As I reached and sat at my allotted desk, the authoritative tones of the male invigilator echoed around the room. He stood on a raised stage area at the front and began to advise us of the administrative procedures. With minutes to spare, I looked upwards to some celestial space where I imagined my father to be. *Come on, daddy,* I said, inwardly. *Send me some divine inspiration. Put a good word in for me upstairs. I'm trying, I really am, and I don't think I could face this for a fourth time.* He was my unseen mascot and it was about time he brought the goods home, I thought, smiling. And of course, if I failed again, I could lay the responsibility at his door!

The invigilator's voice filled the room once more: 'It's nine o'clock. You may open your paper and begin. You have three hours to complete the exam.'

As I turned the front sheet and looked down, the eloquent words of the instructor from the study support group I had enrolled in shouted repeatedly at me: 'Before you do anything, read the fucking question. Just read the fucking question.'

Or RTFQ in polite circles.

Quite.

Beyond John's own attempts to find solace and some sort of emotional and lasting connection to his family, there were many others attempting to do the same. Felix's and Oscar's school was understandably a central focus, as they addressed the sensitive and incomprehensible subject of death with such young children, and so many of them too. John said they were at pains to include him at every step, seeking his views to ensure he felt part of their own efforts.

They had apparently been gifted money collected in the aftermath of Felix's and Oscar's deaths and had decided to use this to create four planting areas in the school grounds where the children could grow flowers, and to commission an artist to complete a mural in the school foyer. It was a copy of a beautiful picture of a sunflower that Oscar had drawn, and it included a football too, acknowledging Felix's love of that sport. One child's parents had also generously donated four benches for the school playing field. Their son had been friends with Oscar.

Beyond the garden and mural, the school had decided to hold a remembrance lunch two weeks after the boys' deaths, the menu including the favourite foods of Felix and Oscar: beefburger, chunky chips, carrot batons, chocolate muffin and chocolate milkshake. A little something nice in the midst of young confusion.

In the following months, after much painful deliberation, John had decided on his own contribution: an annual trophy for the 'Sportsperson of the Year', to be awarded at each school sports day with a small monetary gift to the winner – something beyond the inscribed trophy they could go and have fun spending. His sons had loved sport and it seemed the right way in which to celebrate them each year. The thought that a small child would enjoy being the recipient of both the trophy and the money, something his sons would have relished competing for, gave him some comfort.

Perhaps most poignant of all were the quiet voices and actions of the children themselves as they slowly emerged into the darkness that now surrounded them. Firstly, there was a Memorial Wall, something the school had decided on immediately after the fire, on which posters the children had completed in memory of Felix and Oscar were fixed. When it was eventually taken down the posters were placed in a folder and handed to John. As I leafed through them, all A3 in size, one hit my chest sharply and caused me to draw breath, to put my hand to my mouth and close my eyes in sorrow. It was written in pencil, filling the right side of the paper only, in the hand of a very young child. It said:

To Oscer and filix.
IM Sory that you Daid I want
you bake
Lots of love from — —
Xxxxxxxxx

On the left side of the paper was a large, lopsided drawing of a heart.

Secondly, John was told about the reaction of one of Felix's close friends, ten-year-old Morgan, when his mum, Jules, told him Felix had died with Oscar and Heather.

He'd just returned from the school trip the day after the fire. Felix should have been with them. We walked to Morgan's friend's house, so me and the other mum could tell them together. It was such a beautiful sunny day and so we all sat on the grass in the back garden … my stomach was churning. I just knew that their lives would be changed forever once we told them … they looked so sweet in their white polo-shirts, full of badges and stickers from their day out. I didn't want that to change. I said, boys, we've got some bad news and then told them. It was just awful.

'Is John okay?' asked Morgan after a moment of shocked silence, his ten-year-old shoulders immediately and sensitively empathising with his friend's father as the innocence of his own life was ripped from his young, small hands.

More silence followed before he continued mournfully. 'I

wondered why Felix's seat on the bus was empty. We tried calling him, but there was no answer.'

An image of a school bus, packed with boisterous and happy children but with one empty seat, filled my mind – the seat Felix always sat on now tragically silent. The loud ringing tone of an unanswered mobile phone in the debris of John's burnt home refused to be silenced as I pictured a young child on a school bus waiting patiently for it to be answered.

I was to learn years later that Morgan still hangs his school polo-shirt, covered in the same badges and stickers, in his wardrobe, together with a bag full of goodies that had been given to the children on that day. They are cared for gently by him and cannot be moved, a silent and painful memory of his friend Felix. A moment when young death could not be prevented from colliding with young life. And when young hearts became indelibly changed.

CHAPTER 13

He was waving vigorously at me, with a larger-than-life smile and a face beaming with enthusiasm, and I stood at the French doors in our living room, waving madly back.

How lucky I am, I thought, that my son should feel and display such open joy upon seeing me. A rush of love filled me as I watched him walk over the bridge in his sky-blue school blazer and blue-and-black tie. His mop of wavy, thick, dark brown hair framed his eager face, hair that one of his teachers during a recent parents' evening had referred to as 'a life form of its own'. We had been sitting directly opposite him – he, mid-fifties, short wavy grey hair and wearing a formal shirt, tie and blazer – at a very small square table, studiously awaiting his views on Alexander's performance. The noise of other chatting parents and teachers sitting at other small and surrounding tables filled the large hall. Looking up from the papers on his desk and solemnly levelling Alexander's gaze, he'd slowly and ever so slightly moved his head forward. It was the subtlest of moves, but sufficient to convey he was about to say something of tremendous importance, something to which a pupil may wish to pay serious attention, and something an anxious mother may not want to hear. There was the briefest, most exquisite, delay before he spoke – his deep, imposing voice immediately commanding attention.

'How's *the hair*, Alex?' he asked, deliberately elongating his words, as he looked towards my son's beautifully coiffured and abundant locks, adding a reverential nod in their direction.

As he registered that he was not about to be admonished, but was instead being mercilessly ribbed, a huge grin slowly crossed Alexander's face and he started to laugh, his head perfectly still lest his crowning glory be dislodged.

'Ah, you *owned* me, sir,' he answered good humouredly in his equally deep voice.

'Owned me' is apparently when one person gets something over another and is the young, hip way to express such a happening. My son told me later that this teacher was much admired by many students due to his brilliance at putting them in their place with his witty comments. He'd apparently 'owned' many of them, much to their amused chagrin.

As I warmly recalled such a funny encounter, he disappeared from view, minutes later stepping through the front door, his deep voice shouting to me as I went to meet him.

'How was it, Mum? How did you do?' he asked eagerly, searching my face for his answer.

'I think it went well, but you can never really tell with multiple choice. I hit lucky on a few subjects I like though, so fingers crossed I fall on the right side of the pass mark this year.'

'Ah, brilliant. I'm sure you've done it this time.'

I hugged him tight. 'You're lovely to be so supportive. Come on, let's go out for a meal and celebrate. Whatever the result, right now it feels fantastic to have some free time at long last.'

'Food out sounds great. You've remembered we've got a match in Sheffield this Sunday, so no lie-in for us?'

'Yes, I know, but after the last six months of study on top of everything else, a four-hundred-mile round trip to Sheffield in one day sounds like a breeze.'

Normal life had resumed, minus one less pressure. I breathed in slowly, savouring the smell of free time.

It was the end of September and John had returned to London for a few days, staying in a local bed and breakfast again.

I just didn't see it coming; or rather, I just didn't see him coming.

It was a crisp, sunny autumnal day. We'd decided to go for a walk, and as we headed off down a pretty, residential road leading to the River Thames, the occasional vehicle driving past, I asked John, who had his hands in the pockets of his bright red ski jacket, if I could link his arm. Other than our hugs we had always kept a dignified distance in this respect, but it just felt like the right thing to do. Two old friends, arm in arm, enjoying each other's company. He seemed affected by this simple gesture but said it was okay, and as I put my arm through his I felt my stomach unexpectedly doing somersaults. I was forty-six; he had always been unavailable to me, and he was grieving. I was taken aback by my own physical response.

Five minutes later, as we approached a wide gravel path to our left, positioned between two houses and leading to the tree-lined river embankment, he stopped abruptly and without warning. The calm backdrop of the Thames was certainly no indicator of what was to come.

'I need to talk to you. I need to get something off my chest,' he said, pulling away from me, clearly troubled and openly agitated.

'What's wrong? What's happened?' I answered, immediately concerned.

'Can you come over here, just for a minute?' he asked, pointing to the river. I followed him forward, moving away from the main pathway and stopping under a nearby tree, adjacent to the river. As I leant calmly against the tree he paced backwards and forwards about a metre in front of me, like a caged lion, trying to find his words. I wondered what he was about to say, what he was struggling to articulate. My mind was racing: was he not coping as well as he said he had been? Was he having suicidal thoughts?

'What is it? What's happened?' I asked, repeatedly.

After a couple of minutes he just blurted it out, and once he'd started I could only stand in shock as he laid bare his emotions in a way I had never heard him do before:

'I'm having feelings for you that I shouldn't be having. I know they're deeply inappropriate only three months after losing Heather ... I don't understand it, I really don't. I know my timing is awful … I've always had these feelings for you from childhood … I'm struggling to make sense of my emotions.'

He's struggling to make sense of his emotions?

He wasn't the only one. I stood rooted to the spot, stunned into silence. Was he really saying what I thought he was saying?

There he was in front of me, the man who for the best part of thirty-three years had remained silent on the subject of me, but who was now gushing forth like a burst dam, his emotions pouring uncontrollably from him. Not once prior to meeting his wife, when he had had so much opportunity to do so, had he entertained discussing whatever it was that had existed between us. What had changed? What had catapulted him from the trenches in which he had so successfully managed to remain in his efforts to keep me at bay?

It was my turn to feel like a rabbit in the headlights now. Here he was acknowledging feelings other than friendship for me, an acknowledgement I had wanted from him for many years and which had never been forthcoming, and which he was choosing to do in the unstable aftermath of his loss. Yes, he was right – his timing was awful.

Before I could manage a response he started talking again.

'I'm sorry. I shouldn't have said anything. I don't want to push you away. I couldn't have got through the last three months without you and … I think we've become much closer. I know my emotions are all over the place, but I need to talk about it. My feelings for you go beyond friendship … and I love my wife very much … and so I'm very confused. I'm sorry if it's the wrong thing to have done. You're not saying anything. I don't want to upset you or ruin our wonderful friendship ...'

'John, stop talking. *Please* stop talking,' I said, my tone quiet but assertive. 'Stop saying you're sorry. You've nothing to apologise for. It's okay to be honest, but could you give me a moment to digest what you've just said? I'm feeling a little off-balance right now.'

'Of course. I understand. Take all the time you need. I know it's a shock.'

He had moved closer to me now and was standing only an arm's-length away, looking towards the river. I looked around and registered that we were still alone. No other Sunday walkers were approaching, thank goodness.

I was unsure how to respond to his specific declarations – and standing on a public pathway I wasn't about to – but my overwhelming feeling right there, at that very moment, was tremendous relief, despite feeling most uncomfortable with the timing. At long last he had given us a voice and released us from the constraints of the past. Should I shut the avenue down or should I join him at the table, if only to exorcise the demon and put it to bed once and for all?

I breathed in the crisp, clear air deeply in the hope that this might help dissipate my immediate confusion.

'Shall we carry on walking? Or how about we go and get some lunch at the pub down the road?' he suddenly suggested.

'Lunch sounds good,' I agreed.

We walked back towards the road. No arms linked now. In a matter of minutes an innocent gesture had become one loaded with intimacy. The landscape had changed and with it my behaviour, and we hadn't even reached the pub.

Five minutes later, and with few words spoken, we arrived. It was a Sunday afternoon and the main bar area was busy. We decided to sit in the rear dining room and were led to a small square table in the centre of the room, covered in a white, starched tablecloth and formally laid. It was surrounded by other diners in a quiet and stuffy atmosphere. I immediately knew we'd made the wrong choice and felt a desperate desire to turn and flee, run from the pub and give myself some thinking space. I let the waiter finish his introductions and glanced at the menu. It was pointless – blinded by my own confusion I couldn't see the words, and food was the last thing I wanted. If I'd ever imagined how this moment would be, it certainly wasn't like this. Minutes later I could bear it no more and, rising from the table, I looked across at John and quietly said, 'I'm sorry, I can't stay here. I need to leave. Do you mind if we go?'

Back outside, we sat at a table at the front of the pub, the cold weather ensuring we were the only customers there. As we looked at each other, stumbling to find the right words – any words – I began to wish he'd not spoken and unleashed us into this alien space. I unexpectedly yearned for the safe confines of our previous boundaries, where the rules were clear.

'Do you mind if we go back home?' I said.

We walked back, again with few words spoken, strangely ill at ease in each other's company. Bizarrely, we were suddenly two strangers sizing each other up. I didn't recognise him, or his outburst.

Once back in the warmth and comfort of home I started to relax and make myself a cup of tea. John was standing outside on the living room balcony, looking out to the river.

As I studied his outline, all our youthful missed opportunities to be honest about our feelings came flooding back and I just knew we couldn't miss another. He turned and saw me watching him, smiling in response and coming back into the living room.

'Are you okay? he said gently as he walked towards me, his face a picture of concern as he took the cup from my hands and placed it on the coffee table.

'I feel much better now we're back here,' I answered.

'Can we hug?' he asked, clearly uncertain whether the one thing we always did with ease and without question was now out of bounds. He was treading carefully around me, treading on the broken eggshells under my feet. A reversal of roles and, for a moment, a delicious irony.

'Of course we can hug,' I said, opening my arms to welcome him in.

He held me tightly, and as he did so he whispered in my ear. 'Do you want to talk about it?'

'Yes,' I answered, 'talking would be good.'

As he pulled away, he held both my hands tightly in his. 'I don't want to lose your friendship, Jill. You're far too dear to me.'

'Don't worry, you're not going to lose it. I won't let it happen either.'

We sat down side by side on a settee facing the French doors. The sunny day added further light to the naturally bright room and brought shafts of warmth through the windows.

He began to talk and, as he did so, gently took hold of my right hand, resting it where our legs touched.

'I loved Heather very much. We were very happy for many years and because of that the feelings I'm having for you are deeply unsettling. I feel pretty confused right now.'

'I know you loved her. I'm not judging you for speaking out. You're grieving and your emotions are all over the place, which can throw up all sorts of reactions. There's no harm in talking. After all these years it might be a good thing for both of us.'

'I'm not asking for anything from you beyond our friend-ship – I'm not capable of offering more than that just yet – but I can't control my feelings. The lines between our friendship and something more have become very blurred for me in recent weeks.'

'I'm offering you lots of support, John, at a very difficult time. That's quite powerful, I would think, so it could be to do with that rather than me.'

'But I've always had feelings for you. You must have known that?'

We were going back in time. He was leading the way to the gates of our history, which stood rusty and unused. I could hear the metal dragging on the floor as we pushed them open.

'We had a childhood kiss …' I began.

'No,' he interjected. 'My feelings go beyond our teenage kiss and holiday romance. That was just the beginning. I'm talking about a lifetime of affection. And all the support you've given me during the last three months and our regular chats has only strengthened that.'

'But you never said anything years ago. What stopped you?' A neatly delivered question but one that carried the weight of years of reflection. Those few words couldn't possibly do justice to my hours of analysis, and neither did his answer.

'A lack of confidence; I was young and didn't have the courage to step forward.'

Boy, I'd spent hours pulling myself apart, examining my defects under a magnifying glass and believing he thought I wasn't good enough for him, but it would seem it hadn't been about me at all.

'But you *did* step forward on our school skiing trip.'

'I know. Maybe it was being in a different environment. But once we returned I couldn't bring myself to ask you out again. Do you know, every day for months after I told myself that the next day was going to be different and that I would have the guts to make a move, and then the next day would come and I'd bottle it again. Pathetic really, now I look back.'

'It's not pathetic. Isn't that youth?'

'Maybe, but I wish I'd managed to overcome my difficulties.'

'I always thought I just wasn't your type, or that I frightened you to death, or that you thought you could do better.'

'Don't be ridiculous. None of that's true. I'm so sorry. I didn't mean to hurt you like that.'

'Oh, yes,' I said, laughing to lighten the mood a little, 'your rejection has taken me a lifetime to overcome.' I paused. I felt more composed and ready to expose myself a little. 'But you must have known that I've always had feelings for you too, a lifelong soft spot that I still carry today?'

'Yes, I suppose I've always known deep down that you felt the same way. And that you still feel affection for me today is lovely.'

'Well, when I think of the conversations we have, the amount of time we spend talking, the laughter – when we can find it in the darkness of your loss – all of it ... of course I feel a great and increasing affection for you.'

The gates stood wide open, beckoning me forward.

'But more than our feelings and our chemistry, I've always felt there's something else that flows between us, John ... a natural connection. Perhaps it's our childhood bond?'

'I've always felt it too – a closeness, despite us leading different lives and barely seeing each other.'

'It feels good to talk and be honest with each other after all these years, doesn't it?' I said.

'Yes, it does.'

'But I'd rather not be having this conversation with you. It's truly bittersweet.'

Our words were not spoken in some celebratory way, but rather we trod ever so softly over what felt like very delicate ground. It was a ground born from death, and a ground on which, despite the fragile surroundings and after a lifetime's inability to speak from the heart, two people managed to do so for the very first time.

Once we'd finished, we sat still in the silence, a beautiful, peaceful thirty-three-year silence. As tranquillity surrounded us, and the hairs on the back of my neck rose I sensed another presence, a separate entity. The atmosphere in my immediate vicinity seemed to thicken, slowly touching my face, and as it became stronger, it stretched its reach as it enveloped our heads and upper bodies as though we were being lovingly bonded.

Its presence was bigger and beyond our own, and its powerful, ethereal quality radiated a tangible and breath-taking energy. I wanted to reach out and caress it gently, fearing it might disappear and become a figment of my imagination. I had never experienced such a thing before and, to check I was in touch with my senses, I whispered, 'Can you feel that?'

'Yes,' John immediately whispered back, clearly also affected by what was happening.

We sat motionless and mesmerised, but as quickly as it had arrived, the presence departed. It had been a silent, inexplicable moment.

John, unlike myself, was not a man given to the idea that there may be some other energy force beyond our physical body. Yet he too was completely convinced that something had been with us.

This was at complete odds with how he saw the world. But it was too powerful to deny: we had not been alone.

'Seriously – what was *that*?' I said, when it had left us. I was stunned.

'I don't know, but it wasn't of this earth.' He looked overawed.

'Well, I don't know about you, but I think that was a spirit of some sort,' I said.

'I hate to say this, but I think you might be right.'

The atheist had been shaken.

I was listening to my own voice. The one on permanent speed dial to my brain which refused to stop whirring with all the many questions I was now posing to myself:

Is John emotionally stable three months after the loss of his family?

Answer: probably not.

When John's emotional boundaries had been intact – as a younger man and prior to his marriage – had he steered a successful course around you?

Answer: yes.

Might John regret his emotional outpouring to you?

Answer: yes.

Was it the right thing to talk with John about our feelings?

Answer: yes.

Did it feel good to talk with John about our feelings?

Answer: yes.

If 'yes' to the last question, does that make it right?

Answer: no.

Why is John, after years of silence, stepping forward now?

Answer: must ask John.

I'll ask again, why is John, after years of silence, stepping forward now?

Answer: because he's fragile, because he's looking for a life raft, because I'm strong.

Are you in dangerous waters?

Answer (honestly): hmm … yes, shark-infested.

How can you be sure you are not slipping back into old habits, your saving habits?

Answer: I can't.

Look at this a different way: do you currently feel a 'high' coursing through your veins?

Answer: of course not.

Do you think John feels a 'high' coursing through his veins?

Answer: yes.

Would your previous counsellor consider this to be your finest moment?

Answer: possibly not.

Life was not simple.

As I lay on the beautician's massage table, my eyes closed. Relaxing, hypnotic music played softly in the background and I could feel my naked body slowly let go. Months of study, months of John's pain and then his full-blown declaration, oozed from my pores as the strong hands of the masseuse pushed and pummelled my taut, tired muscles. I was having a full body scrub, followed by a mud wrap, followed by heavenly oils being gently applied to my skin: a delicious ninety minutes of peace, ninety minutes just for me. I was a single parent and this was a luxury I could ill afford, but for one selfish moment I desperately needed to feel nurtured and nourished, to have *my* needs met and not to meet the needs of others. I would have to manage the self-berating voices that accompanied such a treat – they were a constant on the rare occasions I chose to spend money on myself and not on my son.

If ever there was a time to shed old, tired layers this was it. As I closed the salon door behind me, my skin silky-smooth and smelling of aromatic oils, I felt on top of the world. It had been worth every self-indulgent penny. I felt like a new woman.

CHAPTER 14

He was listening to my voice and not getting much airtime himself. This was our first call following his return home and the ground had shifted. Even though we remained platonic friends, our mutual affection had now been declared and had brought with it something sweet to the table of darkness at which we sat. This tempting food sat between us, untouched and inviting, as I slowly breathed in its heavenly smells. I was at the perfect feast, and pondered my options as he spoke.

'How are you feeling?' he enquired tentatively.

'Well, I'm still reeling a little if I'm honest.'

'I feel awful,' he answered, and my heart plunged before he continued. 'I feel so guilty. Since I left London I've turned it over and over in my mind and I can't equate my love for Heather with my feelings for you so soon after her death. I feel very disloyal to my wife.'

I attempted to ease his overt discomfort.

'It's completely understandable that you should feel that

way, but your emotions are throwing up allsorts right now, so don't be so hard on yourself. I'm not about to hold you to ransom down the road,' I said teasingly, trying to inject a little lightness. It didn't seem to register, as he continued in a sombre tone.

'I don't regret saying what I said. We've become so much closer during the last three months that it became impossible not to be honest with you. I couldn't hide it any more.'

'John, even without our past I'm sure in the same circumstances our feelings would have strengthened.'

'I know, but even so, I'm surprised.'

He sounded perturbed. I ran to his rescue, trying to assuage his troubled mind, and once I'd started I could hardly stop myself charging forth. My own concerns about our growing closeness seized the opportunity of a sudden voice.

'But death strips you bare, exposing all your vulnerability and doesn't do it gently. Crikey, when I went through counselling for the loss of my dad my emotions were untethered. It felt like I was reaching into my soul, where my father's death sat, and boy, the pain … I just had to let him sit with me for a while before I could let him go.' I paused, briefly, to breathe easy a little, to quell my own distress.

He remained silent.

'Look, I know you're not into all that soul stuff, but I'm just using it to illustrate the deeper recesses that death takes us to. I've had a lifetime's difficulty in processing one death. I simply cannot comprehend how you are processing the loss of your whole family. No one, least of all me, expects you to be emotionally clear-headed right now.'

'Blimey, where did all that come from?'

'I'm just trying to alleviate some of the guilt you feel. We're friends, and all we're doing is talking and you know what? I think that being honest is good. We spent our youth not able to talk in this way, and now we have … well, it's a big relief to me. And if we're going to be honest, let's have other conversations, the ones in which I can talk about my concerns about the level of support I'm giving you, and whether it's right to be giving you that much.'

'Go on then, elaborate,' he said inquisitively.

'Well, I've mentioned before about my dynamic – my saving propensity – but until now there's never been space to consider that. Well, I've considered it on my own, but I mean together. If we were to put our scenario on paper and look down from above the only sane thing to do would be to place ourselves as far away as possible from each other, but here we are, magnetically joined. I don't begrudge the support I've given you. I'm just trying to make sure that I'm offering it for the right reasons. Sharing what we feel has only added to my difficulty in trying to sort that out for myself.'

I shut my rambling mouth: an exercise in restraint.

'I know at the minute I'm fragile but I'm *absolutely not* an emotionally weak man. I'm normally very strong. It's just that right now I'm not the man I used to be.'

'I understand that. That you're still standing and choosing to live is testament to your strength. But my support goes way beyond the usual stuff offered. You know it does.'

'I'll never take anything you offer for granted, Jill, but I understand if you don't feel able to offer me any more support.'

'I'm not about to disappear. I didn't plan to say what I've

said, so I'm sorry if I've gone on. I think I just needed to get it off my chest, just like you did.'

'Do you feel better?' he asked softly.

'Yes, much better, though I'm sorry to have burdened you.'

'After all the months of listening to me that you've done, it's the least I owe you. And what you've said needed to be said, so I'm good with that.'

'How about we take one day at a time and see where that takes us?'

'That sounds good. Our friendship's lovely, let's just enjoy that.' He appeared to have relaxed a little.

'Can I ask you one more thing before I go?'

'Yes, of course.'

I let silence descend for a moment before continuing in a delicate tone.

'*How* do you grieve for your wife and two sons at the same time? How can you process the enormity of their collective loss? It's incomprehensible to me.'

A brief silence descended again before he answered.

'It's simple: I don't. In my mind, I've put each of them in a different box or compartment, however you want to describe it, and I bring them out one at a time to be with them and leave the other two tucked away safely until it's their turn. It's the only way I know how to manage it.'

I gulped heavily as I digested his response and the tragic image it had conjured.

'Please don't get cross with me when I ask if you've given any more thought to seeing a counsellor to help you through this, to guide you professionally?'

'Not really, but I'll think about it, just for you.'

'I've said before I feel out of my depth at times. It's just not something I'm qualified to do. And what you're dealing with … I can't imagine being able to manage that alone.'

'Well, if you weren't pushing me I wouldn't be considering it.'

'I can't force you, John. You have to want to do it yourself – otherwise you won't engage with the process.'

'Leave it with me for a few days. Anyway, I'll be off now, but before you go I wanted to tell you that the inquest date has been set. It's on the 19th of October 2010.'

'Isn't Oscar's birthday on the 18th of October?'

'Yes, he'll be seven … he *would* have been seven.'

'And your forty-seventh is on the 17th of October?'

'Yes, but I won't be acknowledging that this year. As far as I'm concerned I don't have a birthday – and I've made that clear to my family and other friends. Please don't send me a card or anything like that. I just want the day to pass quietly.'

'I understand, but that's three very hard days in a row. Are you going to go to the inquest?'

'I wasn't sure at first. I know what caused the fire and so didn't think it was necessary, but on reflection I think I owe it to my family. However difficult it is, I want to know the details of how they died and what they went through. Barbara, my mum, sister and other family members want to go too, so we'll all be together.'

'That's going to be a very distressing day, would you like me to come with you for some extra support?'

'That's kind of you to offer, but my police Family Liaison Officer is coming too, so I'm not alone. Don't worry.'

I put the phone down and the feast at the table didn't look so tempting any more. I had lost my appetite.

It had already been, he told me, on a permanent loop in his head: within hours of his family's death, a menacing voice with the same chilling message and a harrowing truth he knew in his heart. But now it had taken up a lifelong residency and become a torturous regime of self-harm:

If a smoke alarm had been in place they could have survived.

If a smoke alarm had been in place they could have survived.

If a smoke alarm had been in place they could have survived.

This time it was the stern, cold voice of the coroner at the inquest of his family.

It was to prove one of the most harrowing days of his life. The circumstances of how the fire had started and the implications for his family inside the house were examined and blown up in minute and distressing detail. How his family had perished.

The house was detached, with two bedrooms upstairs and one downstairs, Oscar's being the last of these and to the front of the property. Felix's bedroom had been situated above the kitchen. The 'seat' of the fire was established by the fire brigade to be an old refrigerator that, unbeknown to the family, had an electrical fault. It had been situated in the utility room next to the kitchen. They had only moved into the house six months earlier, and the refrigerator had apparently been left by the previous owner. As it had still been in working condition, they had decided to use it.

After moving into the house they had been doing many renovations to update the property. What had not been in place when they moved in, and what they had not installed, was a smoke alarm. Had a smoke alarm been *in situ* the fire would, the fire officer said, have been detected while contained in the utility room, and John's wife and sons may have survived. However, as this was not the case the fire had quickly spread, both upwards into Felix's room and into the kitchen and the rest of the house. It was believed that Heather had gone to investigate but had been overcome with the fumes herself before being able to get her sons or herself out of the house.

John said the coroner had seemingly been immune or indifferent to his presence as he repeated the same excruciating statement, which boomed across the room as if on loudspeaker:

If a smoke alarm had been installed their lives may have been saved.

The coroner had then encouraged the sitting press to report on the inquest findings in order to raise awareness of the tragic consequences of not having a smoke alarm installed in the home.

'He didn't go as far as blaming me, but he might as well have done. He could see I was sat right opposite him, but he didn't care as he went *on* and *on* and *on*. By implication it was my fault,' he said in a distant, wavering voice. 'Just horrendous.'

It was the morning after the inquest and he had phoned to let me know he was still breathing, still functioning, still choosing to face another day.

'It's not your fault, John. Please don't punish yourself in this way,' I said gently.

'But it's the truth, however hard that is. An alarm might have saved them.'

There it sat between us, one small, exquisitely bland smoke-alarm box: one simple, exquisitely bland choice to install and one family made safe; or, one simple, exquisitely bland oversight and one family perished.

Hours and hours of previous conversations about his family, about his new existence, about his survival, about his endless pain, had been reduced to an insignificant pile at the side of the room, a land unnecessarily visited. And atop that pile, glistening in all its untouched possibilities, sat one small, exquisitely bland smoke-alarm box, brutal in its message as it silently emitted its piercing, warning beep.

I could barely breathe as this ruthless fact swirled around us, the smoke alarm becoming louder and louder as the uncomfortable truth screamed out. I would never be able to console him. There was nothing I could say – nothing anyone could say – that would change the distressing reality: Heather, Felix and Oscar may have been saved if a smoke alarm had been installed.

The coroner was doing his job, of course, and wanted to do all he could to prevent any further tragic waste of life in similar circumstances, something he had apparently stated in the court he regularly presided over.

I put the phone down and closed my eyes, breathing in deeply as the brick wall of my father's death returned: cold, hard and fucking unmoving, refusing to topple under my repeated lifetime blows, my knuckles raw with death's finality.

It was too late; he could not be saved. He wasn't coming back. It was too late; they could not be saved. They weren't coming back, either.

As my hand shot from under the snug quilt to quickly turn off my alarm clock's high-pitched bleeping, I groaned at the ridiculous hour. It was four twenty in the morning, still dark outside and a very cold, October Sunday morning. I reluctantly jumped out of bed. There was just enough time for a quick wash, to brush my teeth, throw some clothes on and to make the all-important flask of coffee. Mascara was a luxury for which I was not prepared to rise earlier, and so had long since decided that the au naturel look was less frightening than the prospect of sitting in a freezing cold ice rink at five thirty in the morning without my treasured morning beverage. There were no coffee shops open – at or outside the rink – at that time in the morning, and so if I didn't take one with me I wasn't going to get one.

I was conflicted. On the one hand, the first ice hockey training slot meant we would be back home before most sane people had risen from their lie-in and with the rest of the day ahead of us. But on the other hand, it left me with only Saturday morning each week when I wasn't working *and* could enjoy a more leisurely start to my day off. There just weren't enough days in which I had space to relax in the way I would have liked. *At least you don't have to study any more,* I told myself. The rest of Sunday would be ours to enjoy: I was going to cook us a tasty roast for lunch.

I could hear Alexander already. It was quite remarkable that such a young man – who, like many of his age, could sleep on a washing line – would be at the front door waiting impatiently for me at such an early hour, banana in hand, as I quickly gathered my things. We'd made a deal when he first started playing: he would get up for training without difficulty and without repeated appeals for 'Just another five minutes' so we would be on time. But the reality was that this wasn't the reason he was always ahead of me: he simply loved playing ice hockey. From the moment he'd hit his first puck he had been hooked. I hadn't needed to strike any deal, after all.

As he opened the front door he shouted to me.

'Come on, Mum, it's icy out there so we're going to have to defrost the car first.'

'I know, I know. Two minutes and I'll be ready. Don't worry I'll get you there in time to change. Have you got enough to eat – what about a yoghurt for on the way?'

'No, the banana's enough. Otherwise I'll feel heavy and sick on the ice. I've had some orange juice already, so I'm good.'

Thirty minutes later and I was sitting huddled with other parents on the top tier of the staggered seating that surrounded the ice rink. Wrapped up in various warm under-layers, I was secured in a thick, fleece-lined black jacket, with a black scarf wrapped twice around my neck; a cream woollen hat pulled over my ears completed my ensemble. I didn't know who looked bigger – me or my son in all his hockey padding. Probably me, I thought, smiling inwardly.

Leaning my head back on the wall, I absorbed my surroundings. Sometimes in life, in the midst of the mayhem, small windows of unexpected simplicity descended, sharply focusing the senses and shutting out the rest of the world.

As my son and his teammates bounded onto the rink, the sound of their skates slicing through the freshly cut, virginal ice, I opened my flask and breathed in the aroma of pure, fresh coffee.

As the sharp, piercing cracks of hockey sticks hitting pucks resounded through the air, the steam from my cup swirled hypnotically upwards, unperturbed as it silently dissipated.

As the cold ice rink air smothered my exposed face, the hot coffee slowly slipped down my throat, gently warming my insides as it trickled downwards.

As the silence of my own voice reverberated, I breathed in deeply.

As the silence of John's voice reverberated, I breathed in deeply.

Pure ice, pure coffee and pure joy as I watched my son.

Five thirty in the morning training was, right now, pure escapism. I loved the sound of John's voice, but I didn't always want to listen. As the noise of the training session filled the rink, I soaked up the silence.

Following the inquest, John quickly spiralled back into his black hole, crushed by the burden he would carry forever, the burden he had carried from the moment of his wife and sons' deaths. He had not needed the inquest to point the finger of blame towards him. He was only too aware of the simple fact that if he had installed an alarm, his family could still have been alive. The coroner didn't need to bury him down his dark hole with this fact: he had long since put himself there. Every living moment he had left without his wife and sons would remind him of what he had not done.

It was another of those times in life when you breathe a huge sigh of relief that such an event has escaped you. I had not had an alarm in the house I'd sold, either. It was a high-ceilinged cottage, and I had taken down the alarm in order to decorate. Having finished, I'd been unable to put it back together and so had put it on my list of jobs that were difficult-to-do. This particular task had invariably become pushed down the list by what had seemed at the time to be more important and pressing tasks. It was not some deliberate act on my part, but rather the result of my life's constantly frenetic schedule and the need to prioritise. In retrospect, my priorities were clearly not correct, but in context, the immediate day-to-day tasks were given my time and energy, and the refitting of the alarm became a nagging but manageable voice in the background. Perhaps I subconsciously believed myself to be invulnerable, as many of us do,. These things didn't happen to you. This view is probably an uncomfortable truth that exists in many households.

Since the inquest I have repeatedly attempted, by drawing attention to my own inadvertent failure to reinstall the alarm in my home, to verbalise and normalise the mistakes we all can and do make, and from which many of us walk away unscathed. This, in the hope that John will not continue to punish himself and in time, perhaps, forgive himself a little, too. But he will not be moved. He will carry this burden to his own death. His much-loved wife and his adored, beloved sons lost their lives. In his mind, he will never be released from the responsibility he feels. The coroner need not worry.

A few weeks after the inquest John finally acquiesced and booked an appointment with a female counsellor in a different town. To say I was relieved would be an understatement.

'What brought about the change of heart?'

'The inquest and its aftermath, and our recent chats about our feelings. I thought I'd at least try one session. I'm not quite a convert, so don't get too excited yet, but you've nagged me enough to make the call.'

My relief was to be short-lived, however. Two sessions later and he announced in trumpet-loud triumph that his counsellor had advised him that as far as she was concerned he seemed just fine and there was no further need for him to see her.

'She said what?' I asked incredulously, making no attempt to hide my disbelief at such a rapid and seemingly ridiculous conclusion.

'That she thinks I'm fine.'

'But you know that's not the case.'

'I can only be myself, Jill, and that was her response, so for now I won't be returning to her.'

'I'm sorry, but it's not possible to unravel what's happened to you in two hours. So she was either that bad apple in the cart, or she felt out of her depth, faced with the magnitude of your loss. Or, of course, you did what you do best ... you know, that wonderful shopfront of yours that says every-thing's good in life but which belies the truth.'

He laughed. 'Well, I'm off travelling soon so I couldn't have done many more sessions with her even if she'd asked me to.'

I was extremely disappointed. I'd had such a positive expe-rience with my own counsellor, and having spoken so highly of the process I felt completely let down. I had great faith that in the hands of the right person he would come to understand and realise the priceless gift that counselling offered. He'd just not yet arrived at the right person's door.

CHAPTER 15

The cursor hovered over the email that had just been delivered to my work inbox. It was my Inspectors' exam result. I was one click away from a wonderful high, or a repeat of the devastating low I'd experienced in previous years. Sitting quietly at my corner desk, heart thumping and anxiety levels high, I looked out across the small open-plan office. About eight of my colleagues unknowingly beavered about their work, the radio humming in the background. Large high-rise windows looked out across the town, and as I peered down to the street below from my twelfth-floor viewpoint, delaying the inevitable, life carried on. The morning traffic and pedestrians were oblivious to the act of my life carrying on above them. How I wished I was down there with them and not facing my moment of truth. *This is the last time I'm doing it*, I said to myself. *Enough is enough - you can't keep putting yourself through this.*

I looked back to my computer screen and, taking a deep

breath, clicked the email open. As the page loaded, I winced, my eyes half closed and head tilted downwards, squinting to read the contents, as if this would somehow soften the expected blow. There it was, in unmistakable black lettering, cold and stark against the white background, but delivering an instant shot of blissful, multicoloured warmth:

Detective Sergeant Barnes, We are pleased to inform you …

As I stared at the screen, rereading the words to make sure I wasn't dreaming, overwhelming relief filled me. Three attempts, three consecutive years of study and sacrifice … I could barely breathe, as at long last I realised that I'd nailed the goddamn thing. Yes, the hard way – but I'd nailed it.

Taking a moment, I relaxed back into my chair, once more looking upwards to some imagined celestial space, silently hugging my father and whispering, *We did it, Daddy, we did it.*

We were dancing in the hall, arms in the air one minute, hugging the next, and skipping around crazily in circles without a care in the world. Simple, crazy joy. Alexander had just got home and we were celebrating as we shouted loudly at each other in excitement.

'I'm so proud of you, Mum. I knew you'd do it this time. I just had a feeling.'

'I couldn't have done it without you, darling – all your support along the way. It's made such a huge difference, and I'm going to treat you this weekend for being so understanding when I had to study.'

'Don't be daft. You should be treating yourself.'

'No, really. Passing the exam is all I need, so let me show my appreciation.'

'Ooh, alright then, if you must,' he said, a huge grin spreading across his face. 'I could do with some new trainers ... or is that too much money to be spending?'

'No. Trainers it is, and a nice lunch too.'

'I'll go and have a look online to see which ones I like. Are you celebrating with your friends too?'

'Yes, we're going to go out next Friday for a meal and a few drinks, and next time we go home to Nan's I'm going to buy a bottle of champagne to share.'

'I'm so pleased for you,' he said, hugging me tight again. I didn't know who was happier as I lapped up his own unabashed delight at my success.

It was a cold Friday evening in late November in Manchester and I was sitting in a very busy town-centre pub amongst the warmest of company. It was another reunion of old school friends before John went travelling, and all those who had come to the funeral were now seated around a long, oblong wooden table: Colly, John Lyon, Kev, Mel, Amanda, Hutty and his wife Katy, plus a few others we had managed to contact. Sadly, Gammie had since returned home to Australia and so couldn't be with us. The buzz of the bar created a lively atmosphere as we sat and chatted about all things light and unimportant, the narrow prism of life raising its head again, and welcomed with open arms and relief. Talk of death and funerals was not so much forbidden as placed to one side to allow a night of fun and laughter. An outsider looking in would not have suspected that most of us hadn't seen each other for over thirty years, other than at a funeral, as the warmth exuded by our group told a different story. Perhaps the death of John's family had created a closeness between us that was at odds with our lack of lifelong contact, our collective unspoken desire to surround him with a living, breathing, solid history, heightening our appreciation of one another. Or perhaps it was simply a genuine warmth, reignited from our school years. I decided it mattered not: the effect was the same, regardless of its origin.

In an attempt, albeit crude, to create something tangible that harked back to John's past, I had bought a long-sleeved white shirt which we had all secretly signed with affectionate messages. We presented it to him, together with the old pink-and-black high school tie I'd donated. In terms of their relative value to his life these items were small, but as a gesture from old friends, in our effort to show proof of one aspect of his history, they went a long way.

'What a wonderful thing to have done.' he said, as he read the messages and thanked us all, adding, 'Jill, are you sure you want to give me your treasured school tie?'

I laughed, and as I wrapped the tie around his neck and secured it with a knot, I answered. 'Oh, definitely, please have it. Perhaps now it's no longer loitering in my loft I can rid myself of my exam failure demons. A cleansing of my loft will equate to a cleansing of my soul. I'll view it as a cathartic experience – better late than never, I say!'

'Well, you passed your Inspectors' exam, which is fantastic, so I don't know what you're talking about.'

'Yes, but it took me three attempts, just like my Sergeants' exam, and even accepting that multiple choice is fraught with danger, that's quite some achievement. I've failed before I walk through the door, that's my problem.'

'So what happens now at work? Are you promoted straight away?'

'If only. My exam pass is valid for five years and I've got to have passed a second stage within that time frame. So, still more hoops to jump through.'

'Not over yet then.'

'Unfortunately not. But it feels good to have banked the exam, at least.'

'Well, despite being so flippant I know it means a lot to you, and so the gift means so much more to me too,' he said quietly in my ear. 'Thanks for the tie and for thinking about something like the shirt. It's all just lovely, just you.' He put his arm around my back and squeezed, pulling me to him affectionately, before adding, 'I hope you don't mind me asking you this, but I'd like to visit your dad's grave with you while you're here. You've talked a lot about him and I thought you might like to show me where his stone is. What do you think?'

I was taken aback at his sudden and unexpected sugges- tion. 'That's such a sweet thing to offer, but is that really where you want to place yourself right now?'

'Yes,' he answered decidedly. 'I understand it's a very private space and you may not want to, but I'd be honoured if you'd share it with me. Share him with me.'

'That's a beautiful thing to ask and I'm touched. I'd love to show you where he is.'

'Well, how about tomorrow morning? We can buy some flowers on the way.'

'Sounds lovely. I'll buy some yellow roses.'

'Why yellow roses?'

'They were the flowers my dad took to the hospital for my mum when I was born. I love them.'

It felt good to be in a much happier space with everyone, and it felt good to see John surrounded by his childhood friends, some of whom he had kept in closer contact with over the years than he had with me. But it also felt so sad to see Kev, hours later and clearly under the influence of a few beers as we walked to a different pub, draped over John's shoulders and drunkenly and loudly declaring a host of feelings: 'I love you, you know that, don't you? And I know I've had a few beers but it's not the beer talking. We go back a long way, we're mates, and I want you to know I'm here for you. I'm devastated and I wish I could do something to change it all, but I know I can't.'

Despite our laughter-filled evening, death was always only moments away. There were so many people gathered, so many emotions sitting quietly, so much subdued and hidden sadness just waiting for a crack to appear, allowing human frailty to force its way through, alcohol greasing the wheels of darkness.

I brought the car to a halt at the kerbside and turned off the engine. The church, a magnificent sandstone building, was set back from the road on the opposite side, the large expanse of lush green grass to the front shimmering in the morning winter sun. An old, dark brown stone wall approximately one and a half metres high neatly surrounded the grounds in which the church stood and, twenty metres to the right, this turned at a right angle and continued along a grass border, the border where my father's flat, square gravestone was to be found, with perhaps fifteen others all positioned in a long, straight line. An adjacent dirt pathway, accessed via two wide-open black metal gates, led into the graveyard.

'Do you mind if I just have a moment alone first? I've not been in a while, and—'

I didn't get chance to finish.

'You don't have to explain yourself to me. Just give me a wave when it's okay to join you.'

I crossed the road and walked through the gates, sadness engulfing me as I slowly approached my father's gravestone. Leaning forward against the wall, I tenderly brushed away fallen debris, caressing the inscription once more as though gently caressing my father, comforting him in the freezing cold. His ashes must be freezing cold; he must be freezing cold. Closing my eyes, I took in a deep breath and savoured being close to him again. His presence, a comforting illusion perhaps, but it was my illusion and one that softened the four cold, hard edges of his final resting place.

A wave to John and a few seconds later he had joined me.

'Are you okay?' he asked, softly.

'Oh, you know.'

'I think you need a hug,' he said as he wrapped his arms around me.

We embraced momentarily before he pulled away, looking around the nearby grounds.

'Come on, show me where the tap water for the flowers is. I can't see it.'

When we left twenty minutes later, a large and beautiful array of yellow roses danced in the sunlight on my father's grave. I took one last look, one last deep breath in, and reluctantly walked back to the car.

It was a cold, late December evening in London – well in Weybridge, Surrey, to be exact.

I was sitting in another very busy town-centre pub and yet again in the warmest of company, only this time instead of a group warmth it was the glow of one man. Sitting next to me, with his legs touching mine, was John. He was flying to Australia from Heathrow the next day and we were sharing one last evening together. Alexander was staying with a friend overnight.

The low-ceilinged, brick-walled and slate-floored pub was full of Christmas decorations, full of people in Christmas jumpers, full of festive cheer, and packed with standing customers. Tragedy didn't exist here, that was for sure. It was a land of soft hues and glossy lives, happy exchanges and the prospect of Christmas holidays in sight.

We sat huddled together on a cosy, two-seater corner bench, the location of which enabled us to see and absorb our surroundings, but also allowed some privacy and slight distance from the crowd.

He was wearing a black polo neck and jeans, and I'd opted for a black-and-cream miniskirt that sat just above my knees, a fitted, black V-neck jumper and black suede knee-length boots. It had been snowing, and I wasn't about to totter about in high-heeled shoes. We must have been the only two in the pub not dressed in festive colours – though maybe my attention to the detail of others' attire was not so much lacking, as not remotely important. We were engrossed in each other's company, the exciting atmosphere in the background adding a heady and seductive touch. I was drinking a large glass of red wine, something warming for a cold winter's eve, and he was drinking his usual Diet Coke with as much ice as the glass would hold. He was an anomaly: he took the coldest drink on the coldest evening, and had a lifelong dislike of hot drinks. At least I had now persuaded him of the delights of coffee shops. He had been lured by cake and his sweet tooth at first, but latterly he could be seen drinking the occasional cappuccino.

'So how does it feel to be leaving at long last?'

'Well, I'm surrounded by Christmas. Everywhere I look there are families with children, and everywhere I go there are excited children in shops where carols are being played, and so right now it feels great to know that tomorrow I can get on a plane and leave it all behind.' He hesitated. 'But I'll miss you and our ridiculously long calls.'

'Just telephone if you need to talk, but you're going to be spending time with so many others, that it's natural our chats will be put to one side.'

'You know it's not going to be that easy. You've been with me every step of the way during the last six months, and before you say it, it's not about the support and strength you've provided – it's about missing you. Despite all the sadness you've made me laugh. You're a joy to be around.'

'You charmer,' I jested, my eyes welling up with tears unexpectedly at the enormity of his looming departure. I'd given so much of myself to him, so much time and emotion, and despite the fact that I had a very full life he'd somehow found and filled a large space in it. Now he was departing.

'Don't get upset,' he said gently, taking hold of my hand and squeezing it affectionately. 'I'm trying to pay you a compliment and to tell you how much you've meant to me these last few months.'

'Oh, I'm just sad, but it's a good sad. I couldn't be happier that you've got to this point and that you can now get away from it all and be that anonymous person in the crowd. But I'll miss you too.' I leant into him affectionately.

'Oh, you don't get off that easily. I'll be harassing you from across the world – it'll just cost me more,' he joked.

'And you neither,' I responded light-heartedly. 'Your one bad counselling experience won't put me off trying to get you to go to another.'

'Now, now, didn't you say I have to want to go through that process otherwise it's pointless?'

'Yes, but I'll convince you eventually.'

'Maybe travelling is where the answer lies for me. I'll find my answers elsewhere.'

'Maybe. It's a whole new beginning for you, and one which could take you anywhere. Who knows, you might eventually choose to live in Australia, with Gammie close by, and not come back to the UK.'

'I don't see that happening. It'll be great to spend some time with him, and with my sister-in-law in New Zealand, but I'm sure I'll return to this country eventually. I've always fancied living in London so perhaps I'll look to live some-where in the south. What do you think?'

I laughed. 'And there was me thinking I was getting rid of you for good.'

'Well, I'm only going off for about three months, and right now I've every intention of coming back.' He stopped and cleared his throat before continuing. 'I want to be stronger for *you*, so when you look at me you don't just see the weak man I've been since I lost my family, and I can convince you I'm not unhealthily taking your support. I wish you could see that now.'

'You must understand how I feel though?'

'Of course I do. But I'd like more than friendship with you, to at least give it a go, but I understand, after the previous six months, why I'm the last person you should be contemplating a relationship with.'

'You're right. I should be running in the other direction. But I'm not.' I raised my eyes to the ceiling in mock despair. 'And I'm still struggling to find the right answer, so it's a good thing that you're going. We both need the space to think.'

'One of these days I *will* show you that I *am* strong.'

'Maybe there'll never be a right or wrong answer,' I shrugged.

'Look at me,' he said, holding my gaze in his. 'I care about you too much to keep taking all the goodness you offer without looking back at who offers it and at what price, and one day … one day, I'm going to try and give back to you some of the goodness you've so generously given to me.'

'I wouldn't change a minute of it. I love being in your company and I love how we get on so well, our humour – I love it all. I just want to try and clear my head a little, and maybe you've got to do the same. But honestly, you're not like some of the other men I've known in my past, because for starters I never had these types of conversations with them. Either I wasn't aware of the dynamic at the time, or when I became aware I wasn't allowed to speak about it, or to try and change it in the hope of saving the relationship.'

'Give me a hug,' he said and turned his body towards me, opening his arms wide. As we briefly held each other he whispered in my ear, 'We're good, we're very good.' And as he pulled away he said, 'Now, come on, let me buy you another wine, and while I'm at the bar, try and stop that mind of yours. Does it never stop ticking over?'

'No, not really … but I think that's pretty normal.'

'Don't be ridiculous. Mine's empty most of the time,' he laughed. 'You need to try and rest your thoughts a bit more. Trust me, it's a whole lot easier in life when you do.'

He stood at the busy bar only a couple of metres away, and I watched his handsome face as he tried to get the attention of the barmaid. He was as natural to me as myself, an innate presence in my world, and as I soaked up our surroundings and felt the warm glow of one glass of wine smoothly running through my body, I was quite hypnotised.

I had wanted to try and live in the present more and at that very moment that's how it felt. I was alive to him, alive to exactly where we were, and alive to us – our open and honest conversation, our growing closeness and what seemed like our lifetime bond. As I studied the contours of his body along his close-fitting jumper, he turned and saw me and, as he did so, he smiled knowingly. I smiled slowly back and our eyes met.

'What a lovely way to spend our last evening together,' he said when he returned. 'I don't mean the pub environment, although it's a great atmosphere – I mean you and I talking like this in our own little world.'

'Yeah, it's been great.'

'We're good together, Jill … and you know it,' he said, winking.

As we left the pub, he put his arm around me and we walked the short journey back to mine. It was slippery underfoot and I held on to him tightly, enjoying the freshness of the cold night air until we reached the house, opened the front door and walked into the warmth of my home.

We entered the hallway and stood at the foot of the stairs. I opened my arms for one of our hugs, but instead of opening his, he took me by surprise by bringing my arms slowly down to my sides. Taking hold of my hands, he leant in and kissed me gently on the lips.

I savoured his masculine presence and responded. All my previous selves walked towards me, gathering around, looking in. There was no complex dilemma, no unhealthy dynamic, no grief, no pain, no confusion. These had temporarily been replaced by his soft caress across my face, by his increasingly urgent kisses and passion, by his strong body pushing me against the wall. The air was thick with years of desire as he led me to my ground-floor bedroom to the right of the stairs.

CHAPTER 16

I woke before him and, turning on my side, studied his naked, sleeping body. Lying next to me on his back, with the white bedding loosely covering the lower part of his body, his chest rising and falling gently as he breathed, he looked serene, his calm exterior a lie to the bed of complexity upon which we now lay.

I couldn't blame the wine. I'd had two glasses – hardly the stuff of drunken, blurred lines.

I couldn't blame the Diet Coke. He'd had two glasses – caffeine overload was certainly not the stuff of drunken, blurred lines.

I couldn't blame our youthful lack of wisdom. There was no denying, I was *definitely* forty-six years of age, and he just forty-seven … and there was no denying he was *definitely* in my bed.

He woke and caught me secretly watching him. He turned towards me and kissed me softly on the lips.

'Jill Barnes, you're simply gorgeous, and to wake and find myself next to you is … well, unexpected, that's for sure … but no less wonderful for it. You look beautiful.'

'Well, I'm not so sure my morning look is my best,' I laughed, suddenly feeling self-conscious in the cold light of day, as his eyes travelled over me.

'I'm being serious, so stop pushing me away. I'm trying to pay you a compliment.'

'I'm sorry, I didn't mean to be dismissive. It just feels quite strange to wake with someone in my bed. I've been single a long time and grown used to having the space to myself. It's quite a leap I've taken.'

'Someone? I'm not just a *someone*,' he ribbed. 'I'm your childhood sweetheart.'

'Oh, no. A few youthful kisses doesn't make us sweethearts. You were my unrequited love, bringing nothing but anguish to my door!' I said in an embellished tone.

He was now lying on his side, propping himself up with his arm. He affectionately tucked strands of my hair behind my ears, gently stroking the side of my cheek, then pulled away, his face serious.

'Please don't say things like that. If it wasn't for our history and the connection we have, I wouldn't be here in your bed now.'

'I know that, and despite it feeling strange to wake with someone, it also feels incredibly special that it's you. I can't quite believe we're here in this way – thirty-three years after our first kiss.'

'I know, and that's why it's so special. That's why it *feels* that way too.' He paused before adding softly, 'I'll come back to you, trust me. I'll come back.'

I placed my forefinger on his lips. 'No … please, I don't need to hear you make promises like that. I wouldn't change last night for the world, but right now you've just got to put that backpack of yours over your shoulders and start walking and keep going until you've found the place you want to be. You've got to be free to do that.'

'I don't *want* to be free from you, Heather. I need …'

His wife's name tumbled effortlessly onto the bedsheets between us, and his immense discomfort was immediate. The colour drained instantly from his face and his eyes widened, looking towards me, as he placed a hand over his mouth. It was too late: two had suddenly become three as Heather loomed between us. Twenty-three years of love, twenty-three years of life, twenty-three years of walking together – she was vibrant, colourful and very present.

As she calmly took her place and I naturally recoiled at his mistake, the moment passed – it was probably only a matter of seconds but seemed infinitely frozen in time. In muffled tones from his covered mouth, he poured forth his embarrassed apologies.

'I'm so sorry, Jill, I …I *know* I'm with you. Of course I *know* I'm with *you*. It's … years of being with Heather … it's habit. I can't believe I …' His hand fell from his mouth dejectedly.

I quickly moved to alleviate his obvious distress.

'There's no need to apologise, honestly. You were together for a long time and it's a natural mistake to have made. Don't be so hard on yourself.'

'But I don't want to upset you. And after last night …

and … I've ruined the moment now. This wonderful moment and I've ruined it. I'm truly sorry.'

'Please, listen to me. You haven't ruined anything.' I paused before continuing, marshalling my thoughts. 'I mean, a psychologist might have a field day with that Freudian slip … but as I'm no psychologist …' I laughed, poking him playfully in his stomach to lighten the mood.

'You're very generous to react in this way. I'll make sure it doesn't happen again.'

'You can't make promises like that, and I wouldn't want you to. Now come on, where were we?'

'Come and lie with me,' he said, rolling onto his back and opening his arm to welcome me in. I snuggled in closely and rested my head on his shoulder, running my hand slowly through the dark, curly hair on his chest.

He let a minute pass before answering.

'I was saying that I need to go off and have some space, but I don't need space from you, you fool.' He squeezed my arm as if to reinforce his words. 'For goodness sake, we've just made love. We've finally got it together and now you want to send me packing. What sort of logic is that?'

'Because I seek my own freedom. Perhaps in offering you the same, I'm asking for it to be returned.'

'I'll be back,' he said assuredly, then added light-heartedly, 'and you're not free!'

We lay together in silence, our newly encountered bodies entwined, savouring our last intimate moments together.

∽

As I looked out of the kitchen window later that afternoon, I watched my son and John building a large igloo together at the front of the house, the snow falling heavily and settling on their thick winter jackets, woollen hats and gloves. We were second in a row of nine townhouses which curved gently round in an arch, forming a circular courtyard approximately twenty metres in diameter. The perimeter wall that contained additional parking bays for visitors was empty of cars, covered in snow, and it was here that the emerging igloo took centre stage – much to the amusement of passing neighbours.

John had been adamant he wanted to share some time alone with Alexander before he left. 'He's been so welcoming to me during the last few months and it can't have been easy sharing you, so I just want to make sure he knows it's not just about spending time with you. I love hanging around with him too.'

'He knows that already. You couldn't have been nicer with him, that's why he really loves it when you're here. Honestly, you've been so sensitive to him and his needs.'

'Stop getting all sentimental. I'm sure I get more from it than he does, and let's face it, I can't talk about football and music with you, can I?' he laughed.

Clearly the igloo was finished, as a snowball fight had ensued, shrieks of laughter lifting through the air as they hit one another repeatedly, skidding and falling to the ground as they frantically tried to gather snow. They looked like they'd known each other for years. In the few months that John had walked through our lives, and while he battled with the loss of his own sons, he'd shown nothing but respect, tremendous warmth and acknowledgement to Alexander. Throwing snowballs with my son, not his, as life painfully marched on.

Hours later I drove into the drop-off point at Heathrow airport and managed, amongst the mayhem, to find a vacant bay. It was dark and the heavy snow had brought chaos to the rush hour traffic. John was not sure whether his flight to Australia would even depart amongst the many cancellations, but it hadn't been called off yet, so fingers were crossed he would manage to escape the country on schedule.

His leaving was understandably symbolic, drawing a line under his previous life and attempting to move forward. He was emotional and visibly distressed as we hugged at the side of the car.

'I'm going to miss you,' he said.

'I'll miss you too, but this is the right thing to be doing. It's good for us both to have some space.'

'I know it is and I'm ready to go, but I'll be back. I don't feel the need to disappear without trace. I just want to go walkabout for a while.'

'Well go, then,' I said, smiling as I released my arms and touched his right cheek with my hand affectionately, 'and take care of yourself.'

'Thanks – for everything,' he said, then stooped and kissed my lips softly, before picking up his bag and, with tear-filled eyes, walked towards the terminal.

I was calm, not without emotion, but as his figure slowly disappeared into the crowd I felt a surprising sense of relief and, in the face of his emotion, guilty that I felt that way. Maybe it was also symbolic for me, a setting adrift of the life raft I suspected I may have become. I had supported him a lot and, although I didn't regret a moment of it, our time apart would provide me with some distance and rest from bearing close witness to the intensity and complexities of his loss, and give me space to simply focus on myself and my son for a while. And beyond that, too, it would offer a period during which I could attempt *not* to think about it all, to achieve some purity of thought.

Purity of thought? Who was I kidding. After the previous night that might prove more difficult than I'd hoped. I'd made the waters muddier. We'd made the waters muddier.

I would have to try and take a leaf out of John's book. 'Life doesn't have to be difficult. Keep it simple,' I could hear him saying. Yes, I would try and keep my overactive mind and view of life 'simple'. I laughed to myself at the sudden irony of my intended future efforts: if only it *were* that 'simple.'

As I made my way home through the treacherous weather, the solitude of the car and the hum of the wipers occasionally cleaning the snow from the windscreen were a welcome haven. I reflected proudly on my wiser self.

One of the things I had learnt from counselling was that my disproportionate reactions to the ends of some of my previous relationships had been rooted in my father's death. This was referred to as 'convoluted grief': my childhood loss manifested as the demise of a relationship unwittingly became an outlet for my unresolved grief. One experience in particular stands out – a relationship with a man who pursued me with a passion and, five months later, having secured my love and full attention, ruthlessly dispensed with me, without notice, without explanation and without a shred of feeling. He simply disappeared, as my father had done. His behaviour was undoubtedly cruel and I was clearly better off without him, but the emotional impact of his instant departure was far more painful than it should have been. He wasn't worth shedding tears for but, it transpired, most of my tears weren't for him after all – they were the childhood tears for my father. The end of this relationship, and that of many others, represented a loss I hadn't come to terms with: all loss equated to colossal pain. It was another huge awakening.

As the distance between John and myself grew with every passing mile I drove, I felt none of my old desperation to hang on at whatever cost. I felt none of the familiar overwhelming distress as someone I cared for hugely started to walk in the other direction. And although this was not a relationship of any length, I was definitely invested. I didn't view our night together in some loose, disconnected manner. On the contrary, I felt nothing but a wonderful closeness. Yet, as I'd stood before him as he stepped off into an unknown future, I'd known I needed no more from him. He was leaving and he was free to do so. He was also free not to return to my arms. To find myself in such an effortless space, after years of love's confusion, felt like the sun had risen and I'd come home.

Some forty-five minutes after leaving his side I walked through my front door, welcoming my new-found and much-needed space. I had presents to wrap and a bag to pack for our Christmas getaway. Only ten minutes later my phone rang. I saw John's name flashing on the screen.

'It's me,' he said. 'The flight's been cancelled because of the snow. It's absolute mayhem here.'

My heart sank.

'Oh no, that's awful! Have they any idea when it might be rescheduled?'

'Well, it's certainly not going to be tonight and right now no one seems to know much at all.'

He sounded unsure and distant, his voice breaking as he spoke. I was acutely aware it would have been Felix's eleventh birthday, and sensed one small thing would push him into a meltdown – the conditions were ripe. Jostling fellow passengers, queues for information and the frustration of being stuck in the middle of a cast of thousands – all at a time when he wanted to flee and be alone. It was surely some sort of living hell for him.

'I'll come back and collect you,' I immediately offered, making no mention of Felix.

'No, no … thanks for the offer, but I'm going to stay here. The staff at the check-in desk said to come back early in the morning to see if there are any seats on any other flights. So, I need to be here.'

'But where will you stay?'

'I'm lucky enough to have found myself a bit of floor space against a wall, so I'll sleep there. Everyone else is doing the same.'

He'd mentioned previously that airports transported him back to happy times when his family had been flying off on various holidays. He now found the physical effects of being in them quite dramatic: an aching chest, a shrinking throat, soreness at the back of his eyes and a general bucketload of misery. Add this very painful day into the equation, and the thought of him lying on a cold, hard airport floor without his son was not one I was going to accommodate with ease. Kindness was needed. A friend was needed.

'Please let me come back and pick you up,' I said, my tone gentle and concerned. 'I can't bear to think of you on your own, stuck in a departure terminal on Felix's birthday. I can drop you back early tomorrow. It's no problem at all.' I silently chastised myself: I had spoken in the present tense, as though his son were still alive. *It 'would' have been his eleventh birthday, you fool,* I repeated to myself. It was too late; the words, the suggestion, were out there. I decided not to draw attention to my mistake and he didn't correct me. Perhaps his distress rendered him incapable, or perhaps on today of all days to talk about Felix in the present tense was a small comfort. It wasn't the time to start analysing the detail.

'You're very sweet to care in this way, but you're not going to change my mind. If I'm to stand any chance of getting on a plane in the next twenty-four hours I've got to be here very early tomorrow morning.'

'How are you, John … honestly? Tell me how you are.'

He cleared his throat but didn't speak. He was, understandably, struggling.

'Are you going to be okay?'

'Yes,' he eventually answered, vaguely. 'But I can't talk any more. I just need to go and lie down and be with my own thoughts.'

'Promise me you'll call if you change your mind.'

'Stop worrying. I'll be fine. And this way I can be at the check-in desk at five tomorrow morning. They said to come back then.'

I put the phone down, cursing under my breath, appealing to some unseen entity to *Give the man a break, will you.*

Mercifully, I'd been heard, and the next day Mother Nature momentarily calmed, allowing a sufficient window for a few flights to leave. Some sort of order had apparently been restored at the airport and John was Australia-bound before lunch, released from his temporary prison, his spiralling emotions salvaged in the nick of time.

From one check-in desk to another, this time at Perth airport where, before he'd even stepped on Australian soil, he had been dealt a welcoming slap in the face. Calling briefly the next day to tell me he'd arrived safely, he was describing what had happened.

'I stood in a massive queue for "International Visitors", and when I eventually got to the check-in desk, the security man said I was in the wrong place because I was recorded as an Australian citizen. I'd completely forgotten about the visas we'd been issued last year to come and live in the country.'

'How distressing. What did you say?'

'I asked to speak somewhere private and they took me to a side-room, where I told them what had happened. They were very kind and generously said they'd give me a six-month visitor's visa.'

'Well, it's lovely they treated you sensitively but what a very painful reminder of your family.'

'A painful reminder of the road we didn't take. The road that would have made them all safe.'

I suspected he was never going to forgive himself for not taking his family to some remote Australian outpost, an outpost that prior to their deaths had been sufficiently unappealing for them to change their minds at the last minute. It was an outpost that would now forever be some utopian dream, a perfect land untouched by tragedy, reached by a glistening road of happy-ever-afters – a shimmering mirage of a missed yesterday and a yearned for tomorrow.

CHAPTER 17

It was Christmas morning and I had just woken. I would shortly descend the stairs to open presents with my son and my sister's family. We were staying with them over the festive season.

As I lay in bed enjoying a quiet moment, I leant across to my bedside cabinet and lifted a small box John had left me, neatly wrapped in shiny red Christmas paper and tied with a red velvet band. I gently unwrapped the paper and opened the small dark blue box inside; there sat John's Head Boy badge and a shiny gold locket on a delicate chain. As I lifted them both from the box I noticed the badge had been engraved on the rear with the words: TO THE BEST HEAD GIRL. I welled up with tears immediately. I had lost my Head Girl badge at a party many years before.

The image of myself at this event came flooding back. I'd been about nineteen years old and at a fancy-dress party dressed as a schoolgirl from St Trinian's, with my old pink-and-black-striped school tie hanging loosely around my neck and my Head Girl badge clipped to a white short-sleeved shirt I was wearing. Pigtails finished the look, along with drawn-on freckles. I have a picture of myself trying to hug a man who had gone as an Oxo cube and who was paying me lots of welcome attention. Somewhere between me, his bulky outfit, the dance floor and the drink, my badge fell from my shirt and was lost forever. I rued the day I had been foolish enough to take it out and risk the loss of this small but valued token of my past. As I held John's badge in my hand, I rubbed the glossy front and considered the enormity of the gift; this was one of the few possessions he had left from his previous life and he was now generously offering it to me in the hope of assuaging my own regret. A tear rolled down my cheek as I closed my hand and held it close.

As I put the badge and locket back in the box a few minutes later, my phone rang. I was surprised to see it was John.

'Happy Christmas,' he said. He was trying hard to sound upbeat, but I immediately sensed he was struggling.

'Oh my goodness! You're calling all the way from Australia, you mad fool. It must be costing a fortune'

'The cost isn't important. It's Christmas Day and I wanted to say happy Christmas to you and Alex and your family.'

'What a lovely surprise to hear your voice. I've just opened your present and the badge – what a truly thoughtful thing to have done. I'm so touched. Are you sure you want to give me this?'

'Absolutely. After everything you've done for me, it's a little something to show my appreciation.' His voice was wavering, and he was clearing his throat, something he was prone to do when he was trying to quell his surfacing emotions.

'I can't tell you how much this means to me. Thank you so much – for the badge, the locket, and the thoughtful engraving too. They're both very special. But come on, enough about me. How has your day been so far? And I don't want you to tell me it's all been fine and you're good, because it's me you're talking to and I know you too well.'

'I'm not going to pretend that it's all okay, not with you. It's been awful. I had to leave the table halfway through Christmas lunch because it was too distressing. Gammie and his family have invited friends who have two children, and together with their own two young boys ... it all became too much. I feel awful that they're all treading around me so carefully. I'm sure it's ruining their day.'

'I'm sure that's not how they see it. Gammie just wants to be a good friend and support you. I don't imagine for one minute they thought you were going to be the life and soul of the party. It's your first Christmas without Heather and the boys. It was always going to be the most painful of times.'

I could hear him sniffling as he cried.

'I thought I'd be able to cope better once I was out of the UK. I was trying to be strong.'

'I think you're expecting far too much of yourself. No one expects you to sit in the middle of a family home full of children with some fixed smile, John. Stop being so harsh on yourself. You need to take soft steps right now, not almighty lunges. Gammie will understand if you need to withdraw and be on your own for the rest of the day.'

'I think I'll maybe go for a walk for a few hours to get some space and to give them some too.'

'That sounds like a good idea.' My voice was deliberately gentle. I was acutely aware that with every word I spoke I was treading on incredibly sensitive ground. I tentatively took another step forward. 'Perhaps you need the time to be alone with your wife and sons, however painful that is. I know you like to keep moving so you don't get buried in the emotion, but maybe today you need to sit still and let them sit with you. They're right by your side, not back in Anglesey.'

His cries had become louder and my own tears now ran, unchecked, down my cheeks. There was nothing I could say to fill the chasm in front of us. It was Christmas. He should have been opening presents and playing with his sons, watching their excitement and watching his wife fill the house with tinsel and food and festive spirit. But he wasn't. He was playing a walk-on part in a scene in someone else's life. Nothing I could say would change that; nothing I could say would ease his pain. My tears would not be stopped as I listened to his cries. I had absolutely nothing left. I was beaten.

'Happy Christmas,' I shouted joyfully as I pushed Alexander's bedroom door open, my phone still warm from John's call. For him, at the age of fifteen, Christmas morning would have been a much more leisurely affair had it not been for my nephew and niece – five and two respectively – who I could already hear shouting with excitement downstairs.

I was straddling two worlds, separated by the mere few seconds it took to terminate a call. One minute, invited into John's dark existence, the next, thankfully, smack bang back in the middle of my own. I inhaled the sweet air of my own life, the sweet presence of my son and the gloriously sweet taste of relief as I gently but firmly put John to one side and looked forward to the exciting few days ahead with my family.

'Happy Christmas, Mum. What time is it?' he responded sleepily.

'Time to get up and see what Father Christmas has brought you,' I joked. 'Come on, everyone else is already downstairs.'

'Okay,' he yawned. 'Give me five minutes. Any chance of a nice coffee?'

'Of course. I'll be making myself one.' I leant down and kissed his head affectionately. 'It's wonderful to be with you. We're going to have a fantastic day.'

'I've got some great presents for you, Mum. I can't wait until you see them.'

'Neither can I!' I laughed. 'But remember, your cousins think Father Christmas came down the chimney last night.'

Of course,' he said, as numerous voices, adult and child, shouted up from downstairs.

'Aunty Jill, Alexander, are you coming? Father Christmas has been and left lots of presents under the tree. Hurry!'

The sweetness of innocence surrounded me as I walked down the stairs.

Beyond the Christmas Day celebrations, the general Australian environment and climate were thankfully what John had expected and hoped for. The beaches, the sun and the relaxed way of life were far more sensitive to his emotionally fragile state, and so a little gentler for him to walk through. He called me again a few days later.

'I took your advice and I've been going out each night for walks to the harbour to have some space.'

'Is that helping?'

'It gives me time alone to cry if I need to, and it removes me from the whole family-scenario for a while. It sounds awful, doesn't it? Gammies so kind to me and his children are lovely, but it's very difficult being this close to another family … under the same roof. I'm having feelings that are unlike me.'

'What do you mean?'

'Jealousy. Envy. I watch Gammie's sons and I can feel it rising inside me, and I don't like it. I'm not the jealous type, so it's taken me by surprise.'

'It's understandable, though. Are you managing to enjoy the days at some level, and being anonymous in the crowd?'

'I feel numb if I'm honest. I can enjoy outings, but I don't feel any great emotion. I'm relieved to have got through Christmas and so now I can focus on all the activities I've got planned. And yes, it feels good not to be recognised everywhere I go. We're all flying to Exmouth for New Year, and Gammie and I are going to go off and do a few things together, which I'm looking forward to. We're starting with a swim to look for sharks.'

'You want to find sharks? Blimey, most people just want to avoid them, me included. I could think of saner things to do, but if you've decided then I'm sure there'll be no changing your mind.'

'No, you won't change my mind, so don't try to.'

It was the during the first few weeks of John's walkabout that it struck me. He'd mentioned on a few different occasions prior to leaving that he would be participating in numerous sporting activities while he was away. I suppose I'd considered them individually at the time and, although I saw them as extreme sports, I hadn't grasped their collective impression nor been sufficiently distant from him for the penny to drop. But as he rushed from one to another with increasing determination, calling to update me with the details, they suddenly merged together and I saw it clearly: he was deliberately placing himself in danger, deliberately challenging life – his life – and pushing himself to the edge of darkness. He said that his sister-in-law in New Zealand had suggested a few of the activities, but he had no need to agree to them all. From where I was sitting, this was in keeping with his prevailing need to throw himself blindly forward.

I suspected this was probably an unconscious mechanism operating deep within him, but I had become the unwitting observer of his dance with death as he crossed from Australia to New Zealand and finally to America.

I was listening to his voice. He sounded alive and energetic. It was the second week of his Australia visit, and he was now in Exmouth.

'Oh boy, you should have seen them. They've got to have been seven feet long and we were right behind them, snorkelling. Gammie knew exactly where to go to find them. My heart was pumping through my chest with the adrenalin when I saw them emerge from the coral and swim in front of us. Absolutely exhilarating. We followed them to get some pictures.'

'That sounds terrifying to me. I don't understand why you'd want to place yourself in such danger. It's the last place I'd want to be.'

'Ah, well that's because you risk-assess everything. Sometimes it's good to live on the edge.' He sounded cavalier, enthused with bravado.

I laughed. 'Well, on this occasion that's okay with me. I value my life, and following sharks around? That's just plain mad. But help me out here: I can understand Gammie doing something like that – he's a live-on-the-edge type of guy – but you? Why do you suddenly feel the need to start partaking in this sort of crazy, dangerous stuff? It isn't something you've wanted to do before, is it, so why now?'

'No, you're right. I did a three-thousand-foot parachute jump when I was twenty-one, and some white-water rafting a few years later, but since then, nothing.'

'Madness, that's what it is.'

'No, Jill, it was a thrill, a massive thrill. I could do it all over again.'

I was listening to his voice. He sounded alive and energetic. He was still in Exmouth and it was only a few days after our last call. He was describing his flight in a two-seater microlight plane, one seat in the front for the pilot and one at the rear for John. It sounded like some crude tin-can mode of travel. It was supposed to have been a two-hour journey, but it had been rudely interrupted.

'Oh, you wouldn't have liked it,' he said. I could see him silently beating his chest, as though he'd accomplished another challenge that most would avoid. 'It was so basic I could see the engine blades, and I was sitting in a little uncovered pod. The noise of the wind and engine was deafening, and then, as we reached two thousand feet, the engine started to splutter and cough and just cut out.'

'You're joking. What did he do?'

'Honestly, this guy was so cool even I couldn't believe it. He just calmly told me through my earpiece that the engine had packed up and he was going to attempt an emergency landing.'

'You must have been petrified?'

'No, not at all. In fact, I felt pretty calm.'

'Oh yeah, sure,' I said, sarcastically. 'You can't tell me that as the plane's about to drop out of the sky and you're looking possible death in the face that you didn't feel remotely bothered?'

'Well, you can believe it or not. I didn't.'

'What happened then?'

'He managed to land on a deserted beach somewhere, fiddled around in the engine for a few minutes and then said he had to take it on a ten-minute test run and he'd be back. Sure enough he returned.'

'And you got back in with him?'

'Yes, of course,' he laughed.

'Madness, that's what it is. Sheer madness. You just don't have to be placing yourself in such vulnerable positions.'

'No, Jill, it was a thrill, another massive thrill. I could do it all over again.'

This was becoming a theme.

A few days later and he called again. I had now returned home from my sister's. As I picked up the phone and spoke, I wondered what was in store. What other pursuit had he engaged in that he was about to share with me. Thankfully, I'd been given a respite, albeit a sad one. A few days before, he and Gammie had gone to a New Year's Eve party. John had left early and headed to the beach for some time alone. It was the early hours of the morning, and a very calm and balmy atmosphere. He was describing a strange occurrence that had unnerved him.

'You know me, I don't believe in anything beyond death, but this really made me think. I was lying on my back on the beach looking at the sky and listening to my music when suddenly I felt a gust of wind. The night was so calm, it came out of nowhere. That bit alone was strange enough, but at the exact same time a shooting star flew across the sky and Kid Creole and the Coconuts started playing 'Don't Take My Coconuts' on my iPod. I was spooked – I used to play this song whenever I drove Felix and Oscar anywhere in my work van and they both loved it. The strangest thing was that my iPod was on random shuffle. I hadn't chosen it.'

'Oh, how weird.'

'It sent a shiver down my spine. It was a similar sort of thing to the night at yours when we felt that energy around us.'

'Did it make you feel that, in that moment, they were close to you?'

'Yes, I actually thought they might be looking down and were telling me they were there. In that fleeting moment, I could feel them all with me.'

I was listening to his voice. He had left Gammie's and was now in Sydney, and apart from lunch with an old friend one day, he was, for the first time, alone.

'I think being here alone for a week has been a waste.'

'Why do you say that?'

'Well, just sauntering around on my own doesn't seem to have any purpose.'

'But isn't that why you've gone off travelling – to be alone?'

'Well yes, but I'm finding it very difficult.' Silence.

'Are you okay? What's wrong?'

'I'm in a place I've never been to before, seeing all these wonderful new sights, and the only thing I feel is dead inside because my family aren't here to share it. It's all just one cruel reminder of the massive hole they've left. The only thing I see when I look at anything new is their reflection. I'm struggling with it.'

'It was never going to be easy, John. You must have had moments like this when you were with Gammie?'

'That was different, because I had others around me a lot of the time and the pace was faster. I know you think I was nuts looking for sharks and getting in that microlight, but you know, in those moments I was so focused on what I was doing that it took me to another world where I could escape the pain.'

'But you eventually have to come back to this world. You can't live the rest of your life on some crazy mission so you don't have to stand still.'

'Why can't I, if that's the only way I can cope?' He sounded like a petulant child who was being told something they didn't want to hear.

'I'm not trying to tell you how to live your life, you know that. But you don't need me to tell you that if you keep running at that sort of pace, eventually you'll run out of steam. It's not the physical energy required, it's the emotional.'

'I know what you're saying, but right now that feels better than uneventful days. I'm sorry, I don't mean to take it out on you.'

'You don't need to apologise. Talking, no holds barred, is good. As for uneventful days, I'm not sure I'd call them that.

You're constantly on the move. It's exhausting just to listen to your daily schedule.'

'I'm keeping busy, that's all. I forgot to tell you – the other day I went to Bondi Beach and there, larger than life on the shore wall, was a painting of the cartoon character Felix the Cat. Out of all the thousands of cartoon characters. I mean, what are the odds of that happening? He was from the 1920s and I think quite obscure. I remember Heather and I bought Felix a DVD of Felix the Cat when he was about five or six so he could see the cartoon character of his namesake. Boy, it was dated.'

'How painful.'

'Yes, but it was a bit like the night on the beach in Exmouth – it made me feel like he was around me and wanted me to know. Strange, isn't it? Me, the lone atheist taking comfort from random happenings in the belief they may be caused by my family communicating in some way.'

'There's nothing strange about it. If your religious beliefs were ever going to be examined, then it was going to be at a time like this.'

'But I don't believe in God, and I don't believe in any existence after death.'

'You know, for once I'm going to give you some of your own type of advice. Right now, try and keep it simple. If these happenings have given you some sort of comfort, then don't over analyse them. Just keep hold of how they made you feel.'

He was clearly living on auto pilot. This was not a man sauntering around the globe in some chilled-out state; this was a man on the move, continuing the race that had begun the moment his family had died. The race to keep ahead of the demons behind him. He was surrounded, being chased from behind, and enduring the self-imposed chase to the front as he pushed himself to previously unknown limits. Every which way there was a challenge, one he had to win if he were to survive. He would not be thwarted, and so with dogged determination he continued: another thrill, another packed day, followed by another thrill.

Another call, another update.

'I'm leaving for New Zealand tomorrow. It'll be lovely to see my sister-in-law, her husband and my niece and nephew. We've got lots planned. First up, a three-hundred-and-eighty-metre bungee jump, then I'm going to do the world's highest bungee swing and, last but by no means least, a fifteen-thousand-foot skydive, and all in just four days,' he said, triumphantly.

I had allowed myself to move in closer. I had allowed myself to become intimate and in so doing my emotions had deepened. Perhaps I was falling in love with him; perhaps I was falling in love with being responsible for him, falling in love with my own unconscious needy bones once more. The nuances of the situation mattered not: I was struggling as I listened to him march forward, displaying an overt disregard for life and his own safety.

His next text didn't alleviate my concerns:

You are the reason I get up in the morning. You are the reason I'm

still alive. You are my reason to live for. Because sometimes there is
no other reason. My love, John xxx

I was touched. How could I not be? Poignant, melancholic
sentiments conveying heartfelt gratitude for breathing life into
his life. And yet they also gleefully confirmed I could now take
full responsibility for saving him ... apparently from death
itself. Boy, I'd come a long way. I reread the words again and
again and, as they sank in, I shuddered. Whether he was
aware of it or not, he had just placed the baton of responsibility for his life very firmly in my hand. I clasped it loosely,
lest I assume the mantle.

Alongside this long-distance emotional juggling act sat the
actual responsibility of my life – my son – and he was clearly
not very happy – with the pressure of study, the sacrifices of
study, just plain hard study, in fact. A position that was
proving difficult in the face of twelve looming GCSE exams.
His laid-back demeanour, as far as I could see, was now a
spanner in the works. Discipline and commitment were saved
for ice hockey training, ice hockey matches, the right fuel to
eat to ensure his energy on the ice and, of course, the specific
discipline and commitment to bunker down in his bed at each
and every available opportunity – something at which he
excelled.

It was a late Saturday morning and he was still to be found
hidden under his quilt, the day galloping away as piles of

books sat gathering dust on his bedroom desk. I was standing at his doorway trying hard to stir him, and he was having none of it.

'Come on, Alexander, it's midday already. You can't afford to spend any more time in bed when you have so much study to do.'

'Mum, *please* let me get up in my own time. Just a few minutes more, that's all,' he groaned, frustration at my apparently unwarranted intervention hanging off his every word.

'You said that one hour ago and you're still not up. Your exams are only a few months away. Once they're done, you can stay in bed all day, but right now you don't have that luxury.'

'I've got *ages* until my exams, and you're just piling more pressure on me by standing at my bedroom door. Don't you see that?'

'Please don't make this difficult. Don't make me the bad person here. I'm just trying to support you.'

'Five more minutes. *Please*, just five more minutes and I'll be up.'

This was going to be a long few months. I'd only just got rid of the pressure of my own study and now I was carrying the burden of his.

Thirty minutes later and he emerged into the kitchen like a large bear after months of hibernation, yawning loudly, stretching and looking for food. Perhaps, I considered wryly, I could bargain my way to exam success via his stomach. A sliding scale of culinary offerings: focused and committed study would bring home his favourite chicken enchiladas; on less productive days, the threat of a plate of steamed vegetables.

'What's for dinner tonight,' he asked on cue.

'Nothing,' I joked, 'if you don't get some study done.'

'You do know that if you keep going on at me I'm only going to do less. I've said it before, and it's *so* true.'

I laughed. 'Well, that's a logic I don't understand, but I see where you're going with this – it'll be my fault if you fail.'

'I don't mean that. I just don't like you pressuring me.'

'Very few people like the pressure of study and exams – I do understand how it feels. You have to try and find a way of managing it, and I'm trying to help you, believe it or not.'

'I know you are, but can you try and give me some space?'

'I'll try, but I'm not going to sit back silently – it's too important. You know my exam failure at school is my lifetime regret, but it doesn't have to be like that for you. You're very bright, you're in the best school in the area and you have so much support around you. Don't take it for granted.'

'I know, I know. But please, some space, okay?'

'Okay.'

As I stuck large sheets of white paper to his bedroom wall later that afternoon and helped him draw a massive study timetable for the forthcoming months, with an array of different coloured markers, I was like a woman possessed. Visual! He loved visual and now he could see exactly how little time he had left before those exams were upon him.

I knew what it was about of course, and it went way beyond my motherly desire to support him and see him succeed. I had to be brutally honest with myself: any school exam failure for him would mean me reliving my own, a prospect I simply couldn't face. His success would become my success, wouldn't it? All my demons sitting on his young shoulders. Through the mist of my own regret I knew I had to give him the space he'd asked for, the space to take responsibility for himself, the space to walk his own path and face his own successes and failures. This was his life not mine. Well … it would be after his exams.

No one ever said it was going to be easy.

CHAPTER 18

I was at the gym, running on the treadmill and sweating profusely, music playing loudly in my ears as I pushed myself forward. During the last five weeks, while John trotted had the globe, I'd told myself this was the place to clear my head, blow the cobwebs away and rest my constantly busy mind. But my thoughts refused to give up residency:

Was it right to have become lovers?

Answer: no answer. That was clearly going to take more than one run.

If you were ever going to become lovers, was it too early to have crossed that line?

Answer: probably, possibly, maybe not, of course not.

Will you ever be able to state categorically that you were drawn to John for the right reasons? A youthful attraction doesn't always manifest as an adult one, and if you and John had met as free adults in other, less tragic circumstances, would you have still found him attractive?

Answer: that's a ridiculous question and one which you know you'll never have the answer to, so focus on questions you may be able to find the answer for.

Are you falling in love with John?

Answer: possibly, probably, possibly, probably.

Did you mean what you said when you told him you were setting him free?

Answer: yes.

So, John may never return to the UK, or to you?

Answer: no.

So, this whole internal conversation with yourself could be a pointless exercise?

Answer: yes.

Better to stop thinking and just run, then?

Answer: yes, but easier said than done.

As I increased the treadmill speed I could picture, standing beside me, a staff sergeant from my six months' training as a military policewoman: shaved hair, metal-rimmed glasses, six feet four, with long slim legs and broad shoulders. It may have been years since I'd encountered him, but his image never failed to join me if I ever thought I was tired as I ran and needed to feel inspired to keep going. He was a reminder that there was always a reserve in the tank. I just had to dig deep and find it.

'Do. Not. Stop. Barnes,' he would say slowly, as he ran next to me on our regular squad 'endurance' runs, leaning his towering body down towards my ear as he spoke. I say endurance 'runs', but generally at the point he was issuing his menacing words I was just about able to lift one foot in front of the other, exhausted, with sandbags down my back and in the repeat cycle between squad members of either carrying an extra car-tyre around my waist, or assisting others to carry a massive tree trunk. The forces taught me that if I ever thought I'd reached the end of my physical reserves, I should think again. There, I had found a physical and emotional endurance and strength I didn't know I had, reaching the bottom of my empty barrel repeatedly, and still finding some other unidentifiable life-source to keep me going. I had also seen the beauty of true teamwork: you got to the end together or not at all, the men taking one sandbag apiece from each female member and sharing them around, just to lighten our load a little. The best example of this had been when a fellow female squad member, tall and lean, had spectacularly hit her metaphorical wall on one memorable run. As she fell to the ground, groaning 'No more, I can't go on', our staff sergeant had hollered, 'Pick her up now … I said pick her up now, and keep moving!', and she had rapidly been lifted by numerous male colleagues and carried briefly in the air as though she were a stretcher, before demanding to be put down and continuing forward. I had never, and have not since, experienced this type of cohesion and genuine comradeship. I may have been bruised all over, my body aching in parts I didn't know I had, and pushed to my limits, but one thing I knew: I was in the richest of company.

As I heard the staff sergeant's voice telling me to keep running I smiled, as I always did when recalling him. His outer, sterner layer had belied a soft centre, which he had been unable to conceal. No words had been necessary; it was an aura of humility and concern he'd carried, a humanness that some of the other instructors either did not possess or had successfully hidden with stern exteriors that would never be fractured. The physical training instructor had particularly terrified me as she'd shrieked, 'Get over the fucking things, Barnes,' when I'd failed once more to launch myself into a diving forward roll over a high stack of wooden gym benches. I'd run towards them, determined to fly like a bird but, instead, felt my leaden body lurch backwards in contorted horror at what was most definitely an unnatural physical act. Her voice had become increasingly hostile as she'd shouted, 'You should have been a fucking actress, Barnes. Now do it a-fucking-gain, because you're not going anywhere until you're fucking over it.' Different approaches, achieving the same desired result: trained soldiers.

As I considered how much longer I could continue this particular run, my face red with exercise and feeling wistful about my previous youthful fitness levels, my phone conveniently rang. I could see John's name flashing on the mobile screen and I jumped off the whirring treadmill, placing my feet either side as it rotated on without me.

'Hi,' he said, enthusiastically. 'Are you okay to talk?'

'Well, your timing is perfect. I'm sweating on a running machine, in need of oxygen and not looking my best, so you're a good excuse to stop,' I said, out of breath.

'What music are you listening to?' he immediately enquired.

'Oh, Barbara Streisand. You can't beat "Don't Rain On My Parade". I've had a bit of Dolly Parton and Cher too.'

'For goodness sake, woman,' he laughed. 'I'll grant you, Barbara is one of the all-time greats – I went to a concert of hers with Heather years ago – but I'm going to have to take you in hand and move you forward a few years, get you some modern music to listen to.'

'Stop being a music snob. I just happen to like different things to you.'

He quickly changed direction. 'I've had the most exhilarating and, yes, frightening experience of my life this morning. I did the bungee jump.' He was off without pausing. 'This wasn't like your ordinary bungee jump from the edge of land, Jill. There was a metal cable between two mountains and I was taken out to the middle of it in a small metal bucket-like structure that was only big enough for about nine others. To make it scarier, it had a glass floor so you could see the drop beneath you. The feeling as I dropped over the edge and hurtled downwards is indescribable. I wanted to go back to the top and do it all over again.'

'The thought of that makes me physically sick.'

'Well, I've got to admit that as I was winched back up, for once I did feel vulnerable, but that was nothing compared to the euphoria and high it gave me. It's addictive. You've got to try it one day. You don't know what you're missing.'

'No, and I don't want to know either. I'll stick to the treadmill if you don't mind.'

'I thought you were a trained soldier. Where's your sense of adventure, and of joy in facing yourself with a challenge?' He was taking overt pleasure in ribbing me. I wasn't going to be drawn in.

He had banked another one, and no sooner had the adrenalin rush subsided, he had the next one in sight.

'I'm doing the bungee swing next. Can't wait for that.'

'Well, take care with that, but I'm now freezing cold in

sweaty Lycra, so I need to go and warm up under a hot shower.'

'Before you go I wanted to say that I miss you, and to tell you I'll be back. My feelings for you haven't changed since I left.'

As I reflected on John's 'keep running' mentality I smiled wryly. I realised I had unwittingly morphed into him and was now running too: running physically and running to find answers. These were not gentle jaunts which saw me skipping merrily along in some carefree way, but runs that were deliberately long and hard, pushing my own body to its limits. I was generating my own challenge to be conquered, in the frustrated hope that the sheer physical release my body felt during and after would clear my confused brain and create a space into which the right choice could descend and, like a slot machine paying out on a jackpot win, start flashing psychedelic lights to reveal the answer: this way, this way, this way. The irony of this position was not lost on me.

After the gym I would wrap up warm with a steaming cup of coffee and brace the chilly weather on my haven of peace: the living room balcony. As I sat overlooking the pretty river and bridge, listening to the birds sing and watching life pass by, a sense of peace would descend. Away from the busy gym noises, I could allow my thoughts to calm, and I could truly reach within and ask myself some very difficult questions.

The complexities of where I had placed myself were at times

overwhelming and, although I was personally finding the space between us welcome, it hadn't yet provided any greater clarity. My awareness of my own dynamic sat on my shoulder like an irritated teacher giving me a sermon. There was no release from its voice, a permanent fixture played on repeat – the nagging voice of reason, the nagging voice of disapproval, posing relentless questions which demanded clearly defined textbook answers, from which I could make clearly defined textbook choices. My head felt like it was about to explode as I attempted to wade through the treacle at my feet that had now risen to the level of my neck. I had chosen to walk alongside John, to support him, and I had chosen to cross the platonic line. I had no option but to keep afloat and swim in the treacle that now surrounded me. *Simplify this,* I could hear myself saying. *Keep it simple.* I looked at the other choices I now had.

Option one: I could abandon all I had learnt thus far about myself and continue forward in uncertain territory, every step forward dissected to ensure I wasn't getting sucked down the path of my previous self-destructive behaviour.

Option two: I could use the break of John's travels to draw a very strong line under not only my support for him, but also any notion of a future relationship. Remove myself ruthlessly and with military execution from the equation – a move necessary if I were to ensure I no longer swam in such difficult waters. A successful pupil who had applied her learning to optimum effect.

Option three: I could say that crossing the platonic line had been a mistake, and suggest we should revert to a simple friendship where, just as in the years before, we could send each other occasional emails, popping in briefly and from a distance to the other's lives.

The 'simple' problem was that my feelings for him had deepened. I loved his company. I loved his simplistic view of life. I loved our history and how he seemed to 'get' me without explanation. I loved our shared laughter about the silliest of things – table tennis being played in St Paul's for one. I loved how I'd broken his tooth on the first meal I'd cooked him: chicken pie, roast potatoes and green vegetables. He said it was the potatoes that did it and, in keeping with his tendency to rib me good-naturedly, often said I still owed him the dental fees for the tooth repair. I loved our ease as we walked together, and how we could talk endlessly about anything. I loved how he would walk through the door of my home and tread softly over the ground, his joy at being in the company of me and my son transparent as he circled the walls around us, understanding he was an outsider. I loved watching him immersed in talks with Alexander about the rules of ice hockey, his respect and acknowledgement of my young son silently standing at his side. I loved watching Alexander's response to his warmth, and seeing their friendship develop. I loved that through the veil of his own dark world he walked into mine and brought sunshine, a radiant, beaming light that was at dramatic odds with his black heart. He was determined to enrich my life and that of my son as he took strength from my support and, with his gentle manner, treated us like delicate and rare gifts in his life that should be handled with the utmost care.

My collective love of all things John created a spaghetti junction of life choices. These were not neat black roads mapped out with a beginning and an end, but disordered ones that ran across each other, blurred and undefined. It was a great grey area of alternatives from which I could discern no particular direction. But perhaps the choice would not be mine at all. I was not the only one empowered and free.

I was listening to his voice. He was telling me about being surrounded by pictures of his wife while he was staying with his sister-in-law, Susan, in New Zealand. As he walked through their home, Heather's pictures adorned the walls and looked over him. He had crashed down from his bungee jump 'high' and was flatlining. His voice was low and his speech slow as he tried to explain his feelings. The exuberant intonation that had accompanied his bungee jump elaborations was glaringly absent.

'Before I arrived here I was focused more on Felix and Oscar. Remember the compartments I mentioned, how I manage my grief by taking them out one at a time?'

'Yes.'

'But here, with Heather's family and being surrounded by her pictures – well, she's taken centre stage. I wasn't even aware I'd consciously taken her out, it's just happened naturally.'

'Can you talk to Heather's sister about how you feel? Are you able to stay with them if it's too painful an environment?'

'I'll be okay. They're lovely people and making huge efforts to make me feel welcome, but I can't talk to them about it.'

'I'm sure Susan would understand if you explained how you felt.'

'No, I can't. It's distressing to me that I can't open up to them, but perhaps it's because they're grieving too and it's all too close. I don't want to upset them by breaking down, so I'm just going to manage it myself.' He was reeling.

'It was always going to happen,' I said gently. 'Eventually Heather would come to you and Felix and Oscar would have to quietly stand to the side. Maybe this is her space, maybe it's time for you to sit with her.' I paused. 'Do you mind me asking ... what do you miss about her the most?'

The silence crackled as he slowly considered his wife. I wondered if I had asked the wrong thing at the wrong time and was about to break the silence when he answered, his voice vulnerable and full of tenderness.

'I miss so many things about her, so that's difficult to answer. But if I were to identify one thing it would be her wonderful calmness. She had this very still quality about her that filled our home and our life.' He cleared his throat before continuing. 'I miss her voice too. It would be so good to hear her voice right now.'

I didn't respond immediately, wanting to give space to his disclosed feelings and to allow myself to digest his response. It must have been a couple of minutes later when I spoke, minutes that were not uncomfortable, but deferential to his wife.

'I'm going to go so you can be alone with Heather, with your thoughts. Call me if you need to talk, and take it easy.'

I had walked into a room marked 'Private', an intruder suddenly aware they had strayed. It was Heather's presence I could feel. It was as though she were alive and very much at my side. This was her husband, the father of her sons. This was her time, not mine. She had come to me also, and I instinctively knew I had to quietly leave.

The phone was uncharacteristically quiet over the following few days, the ebb and flow of John's grief evident. He had withdrawn into his own sanctum accompanied by his wife, and I was about to enter my son's – his bedroom, where he was sitting at his desk, studying – and I suspected I was welcome in neither. Space, at this point, by bizarre coincidence, was required by them both. Risking the wrath of the latter, I knocked on Alexander's bedroom door and pushed it slowly open. It was a Sunday afternoon and I'd just finished reading the papers, in which I'd found a wonderful quote by Michelangelo:

The greater danger for most of us lies not in setting our aim too high and falling short, but in setting our aim too low, and achieving our mark.

I just had to share it with him.

'How's it going?'

'Not bad. I thought you were going to leave me be for a few hours? You're hopeless,' he laughed.

'I come bearing gifts.' I smiled as I placed a bowl of chocolate-chip cookies – my shameless mid-afternoon negotiating chips – on his table.

He peered down, his face a picture of mock disappointment.

'Only six – what about the rest?' he joked. 'I fancy a few Jaffa Cakes too. Have we any left?'

'Nope, you've already hoovered those up. So cookies are as good as it gets right now, and what about a thank you,' I admonished, playfully patting his head.

I placed the quote on his desk in front of him, freshly cut from the magazine.

'Look what I've just found in today's paper supplement.'

'For goodness sake,' he said, raising his eyes to the ceiling as he read the words.

'But it's so true. Aim high, Alexander – don't ever underestimate what you're capable of. You can get through these exams and successfully come out the other side with a fantastic platform to move forward from. Let me stick this at the end of your shelf.'

'*Really?*' he said, as though I'd lost the plot.

I placed my arm across his broad shoulders protectively. 'Come on, give us a break, will you? I'm trying very hard to give you space and support you at the same time. It's not easy. I just want the best for you. You know that, too.'

'I know you do, and I do appreciate everything you do.' He started to laugh as he continued. 'So, here's the thing – if I let you stick that quote on my shelf so I'm forced to read it every day, what's in it for me?'

'What's in it for you? Better exam results hopefully, you mercenary individual.'

'No, come on,' he continued, holding the paper quote high and unreachable in his outstretched arm, still laughing. 'How about making me those delicious enchiladas this week?'

'Oh no, really? They take an absolute age to make.'

'I can taste them already,' he said smacking his lips together. He wasn't daft; he knew exactly what negotiating chips he had. I was most definitely dining at a table with a wily teenager. Lovable – but nonetheless wily.

As I left his room, quote firmly attached to the edge of the shelf just above his desk, I wondered just who was in control of whom. *I* was supposed to be bartering with his favourite food, not him. I smiled as I found my enchilada recipe and began writing a shopping list, the mist of my own regret still circling.

'It's me,' he announced joyfully down the phone. He was back and on another high. 'I'm sorry I haven't called, I just needed some space.'

'Stop apologising. I understand you need to be alone. This was the whole point of you going away, and if I'm honest I didn't expect you to call as often as you do. How are you?'

'I'm good, I'm really good,' he said, his usual buoyant personality screaming at me. I was doubtful of such a vast improvement in his mood but chose to say nothing. He sounded bright. He was breathing. He was choosing to face another day and he was gushing about the fantastic highs of the bungee swing and skydive he'd completed since we last spoke.

'Did I mention it was the world's largest bungee swing?'

I didn't get chance to answer as he continued.

'It was *the* most terrifying of all the things I've done and, as I stood at the edge waiting to fall, the instructors made it a whole lot worse by pushing me backwards and forwards with the harness, pretending to let me go. They were loving it, deliberately heightening my fear. Honestly, you've got to see this thing. It's about a sixty-metre drop, and a two-hundred-metre swing – crazy stuff, but what a massive high it gave me as I fell through the air and started swinging.'

'Yes, crazy stuff. Crazy, crazy stuff.'

My reflection back, unsurprisingly, failed to register as he moved rapidly on to his skydive.

'I've got to tell you, falling backwards out of that plane and then looking at the breathtaking landscape as I descended … I could have stayed up there forever with the peace, the quiet and the stunning views. It was pure escapism and freedom from the world. What surprised me, though, was that being taken up in the plane was worse than dropping out of it. It was this rickety, fragile old thing and very noisy. It climbed up so steeply that I could feel it vibrating. Blimey, my heart was thumping. I thought the engine was going to cut out.'

Small mercies, I thought. We were moving forward slowly: he'd said he hadn't felt frightened at all when the engine of the microlight plane had abruptly stopped. Perhaps this was a sign he was becoming ever so slightly aware of the danger in which he was repeatedly placing himself. I took my opportunity.

'I know you think I risk-assess everything, but honestly, by most people's standards the stuff you're choosing to partake in is dangerous. It's as though you're actively putting yourself in a vulnerable position. Why do you want to keep doing that – pushing yourself to those limits? Do you think, somewhere deep down, after losing your family, you value your life less? That you're testing your own mortality?'

'For goodness sake,' he laughed. 'Don't go analysing me. It's very simple. I'm just finding ways to feel alive and bring some excitement into my days. It's nothing to do with losing my family.'

'*Right,*' I said, elongating my word, making clear I was doubtful about his statement.

After weeks of listening to his colourful descriptions of 'living on the edge', as he put it, I decided to push the door of his world slightly and tentatively open. I had to say something to him about how it was affecting *me*, something, on the face of it, he hadn't considered at all. I spoke slowly and with deliberation in the hope of conveying with greater intensity the place in which I was sitting.

'Have you any idea how it makes me *feel* – to listen to you describe these hair-raising and dangerous activities that you persist in doing? We're friends. We became lovers before you left and I care about you, regardless of whether you return or not. But to stand by and listen to you describe moving from one thing to another, well … it's not been easy. It isn't easy.'

It felt good to have reflected my position calmly back to him in the hope of raising his eyeline and forcing him to see beyond his own narrow, adrenalin-filled tunnel.

Silence.

I wasn't about to fill the space. I wanted him to wake up and see me, standing in the wings.

'I'm so sorry,' he said in a quiet and suddenly muted tone. 'I hadn't realised it was affecting you this way.'

'I understand you must do whatever it is that helps you

find a way forward, but I want you to know how it feels over here too. Just for one moment, I'm asking you to try and see it from my perspective. You can't have it all ways – my support, my concern ... my affection ... and then repeatedly hang yourself over the precipice of life.'

'I've been selfish, haven't I – just focused on myself?'

'I'm not trying to curtail you, John. I'm the one who set you free to go forth, never to be seen again, but do you understand what I'm saying? And please don't tell me I'm risk-assessing in the extreme. The sports you've been doing *are* extreme, and the collective impact of them in such a short space of time has been, for me, very powerful.'

'I feel terrible that I've upset you. I can only say that I've just been absorbed in my world and hadn't got to yours. I'm genuinely sorry. Believe it or not the main reason I called wasn't to tell you about the bungee swing and skydive but to invite you to come and join me for a week. I'm going to Los Angeles and Las Vegas in a few days and I wanted to treat you to a holiday – a few days in each. It's my way of saying thank you for all your support. Will you come? I promise there'll be no bungee jumps involved,' he laughed. 'All you need to do is get yourself to Los Angeles Airport – I'll send you the tickets.'

'Wow, that's very generous of you and a lovely offer. I've never been to America and I've always wanted to go. But you don't need to do something like this.'

'Jill, Jill, Jill. Please. Just say "Thank you, I'd love to come". It's as simple as that. I want to treat you, so let me.'

'Are you sure you're okay with me being in your space? I'm conscious you went off to be alone.'

'I wouldn't be asking if I didn't want you to come. Now

just say "Yes, John," and I can book the flights.

'Yes, John,' I laughed. 'Thank you for such a kind gift.'

A few days later, and with my son safely on his own school skiing trip – the first time he'd been skiing – I found myself in a packed Los Angeles arrivals terminal.

I looked ahead at the long queue in front of me to pass through security and sighed, acutely aware he was on the other side and that I was powerless to cut short the time it was going to take for me to reach him.

Relax, there's nothing you can do about it, I told myself. He'll go out for some fresh air if it all gets too much for him.

As I walked out of the terminal into a sea of faces, I could feel my excitement rising. It felt strange to be meeting up in a different country. A welcome breath of fresh air was blowing through, and with it a sense of freedom. The freedom to be two normal people, anonymous in America.

I quickly scanned the waiting crowd, momentarily unable to find him. Suddenly his face appeared, and he waved as he pushed his way towards me, larger than life and with the biggest of smiles.

'How wonderful to see you,' he said as he opened his arms wide and wrapped me up, hugging me tightly. I wallowed in the warm Los Angeles heat and the warm embrace of my friend. It felt good to be in his arms.

As we left the airport, arms entwined, he turned to me and said, 'Now, let's go and make some memories.' Smiling, he pulled me tightly towards him.

CHAPTER 19

I shouldn't have gone. He was with me, but he wasn't with me. We were two people in the same country, walking the same daily path, sharing the same hotel room and the same bed, but I knew he occupied a different land to mine.

As we took in the Sunset Strip, Rodeo Drive, the Hollywood Walk of Fame and a Beverly Hills' coach tour in the warmth of the sun, I could touch him but I couldn't reach him.

He wrapped his arms around me, held my hand, laughed, shared conversation about the sights and told me it was lovely to spend some time together. Our new-found intimacy was supposed to bring us closer, but I knew I was alone.

Uncharacteristically, I felt unable to probe him in my attempt to gain access to the world he inhabited and elicit a more truthful picture of how he felt. Instinct told me to circle, not to approach, but after a couple of days I could no longer subdue my natural proclivity to dig beneath the surface layer.

'You don't seem yourself,' I said in a concerned, tentative

manner. We were sitting outside a restaurant on the Sunset Strip having dinner. The evening warmth, the dark, night sky and gently burning table-candle blurred the edges of his palpable boundary, baiting me forward.

'Oh, you know,' he answered, bleakly, his blue-green eyes dark with sadness and shut down.

'Well no, I don't – not really. I'm not talking about your loss. It's something else that's different,' I responded quietly and with unease, observing closely every nuance of his body language. As I watched him slowly process his answer, the world around us ceased to exist.

He looked across at me and studied my face before calmly answering.

'Sometimes, we don't need to analyse and dig deep for some meaning that doesn't exist. Sometimes there is nothing deeper going on, not in my world anyway. Can we leave it at that for now?'

'Of course we can. I'm sorry,' I answered hurriedly, immediately sensing his irritation.

'Please don't be sorry, let's just enjoy our food and savour being here without feeling the need to find some meaningful explanation all the time. Life can be taken literally, you know.' He laughed as he made his dig.

I retreated emotionally, making a personal vow to myself not to cross his line again for the duration of our holiday. I developed an alter ego, an internal bystander, invisible but alive to, and confused by, his sudden distance. He had pulled up his drawbridge once more and had left me out in the cold as he did so. My previous selves walked towards me again: I was thirteen; I was twenty; I was a lifetime of John's ambivalence. They stared back at me; he stared back at me, all knowing and wise – dripping with foreboding.

If there was ever a place in the world to take life literally Las Vegas was it. Surely no one who walked through there had the headspace to consider anything other than what was presented before them. I felt like I'd been spun around repeatedly, dizzy with the heady world that engulfed me. This was twenty-four-hour entertainment that smacked you in the face the minute you arrived, hypnotising in its full-frontal assault and designed to lead you into a path of vacuous indulgence.

Standing in the marble-floored, high-ceilinged, opulent reception area of the Venetian Hotel watching the throng of people passing me by, the atmosphere full of anticipation, I was hooked.

In the hotel, a whole floor had been given over to a bright, colourful array of shops, ice-cream parlours selling a multitude of different flavours and cones, food, glorious food everywhere and a river running through it all where you could take a gondola ride. Marrying it all together was an endless supply of enthusiastic and helpful staff with permanent smiles etched on their faces. I half expected a white rabbit to suddenly emerge and hop around – it would not have looked out of place. It was a world within a world, one that felt safe and joyous, and yet moments away there existed its complete antithesis: the downstairs casino, packed with slot machines, card tables, scantily clad women dancing on tables, people haemorrhaging money, sex and drink, bright lights, more money, more sex, more drink. I was on a fast-moving, risky, flirtatious merry-go-round that was alive with excitement and reeking of life on the edge: nothing safe here. John wanted to live on the edge a little – well, hell, he could live on the edge *a lot* in this place and he wouldn't have to step foot beyond the perimeters of the hotel to do so. But step foot we did, and found ourselves surrounded by the same crazy environment, buzzing with people, bright neon lights, noisy traffic and colour everywhere. We were in a mad, mad world – a sensory delight and a complete overload of fun. I submerged myself in it all and washed away his perceived remoteness.

We enjoyed a night out at Caesars Palace seeing Cher, and experienced a truly breathtaking helicopter ride over the Grand Canyon, where we landed and sat drinking champagne as we tried to absorb its vast and magnificent landscape; the stunning views and its calm, radiant beauty, finished the holiday off.

He hid himself well throughout, except for one moment.

When we were on the coach taking us to the airport for the helicopter ride, he'd sat next to me looking out of the window with tears running down his face. He hadn't looked my way: I'd sensed he couldn't, that he wanted to be left alone as darkness descended. I'd placed my hand on his arm affectionately and said nothing.

The whole week felt strange. We had become lovers only recently, creating a space for greater intimacy and openness, but bizarrely we were unable to speak as freely as we had done as friends. I wasn't sure whether this was because of his apparent distance or because our new world had brought with it an acute awareness of ourselves and of each other. We were stark-bollock-naked, both physically and emotionally, in the risky deep abyss of romance, the risk heightening our senses.

It felt strange, too, because I did the trip his way, surfing through the fantasy world we found ourselves in. No open conversations, no sharing of our innermost thoughts and feelings and, above all, no discussion about us. It all lay untouched in the corner. I surfed it all just like he did and had asked me to. We laughed, we held hands, we made love, exploring each other as new lovers do – but only, I felt, touching him physically not emotionally – and I opened my arms to all the wonderful experiences he treated me to in the generosity of his gift. It was light and bright and lots of fun.

It felt strange because we seemed to be having our own mini-fantasy in the Las Vegas fantasy that surrounded us. But fantasies are not real, and I left wanting to return home to my own life and my son. I didn't want to inhabit that strange world any more.

I pulled up outside Alexander's high school, which was positioned at the end of a residential road and set back from the tree-lined, perimeter pathway by approximately fifteen metres. A staff car park filled much of the area to the front, within which a large tarmacked drive, about five metres wide, led up to the modern brick two-storey building and its six glass front doors. On the opposite side of the road, running the length of the school's frontage, were parent or visitor parking bays, into one of which I reversed.

He would be home from his skiing trip in Austria anytime

now and I couldn't wait to see him, to give him an enormous hug and re-enter the world I loved and recognised – the world *we* shared, not the strange worlds of Los Angeles and Las Vegas, which had been successfully navigated, but thankfully left behind. It felt good to be back on terra firma. I relaxed back into my seat and waited, looking admiringly at the building. This was the most sought-after state school in the area. I'd heard it was known as the poor man's private school, though looking at the parents' cars that rolled up outside and having met and mingled with them at numerous school events, it was clear there was nothing poor about most who attended here. I think the description probably referred to the fact that the school's Ofsted results were so good they negated the need to pay for private schooling to secure a decent education, should you be in the luxurious position of having such a choice. Well, I was a struggling single parent; private schooling way beyond my reach, and so throughout the six years Alexander attended the school I felt nothing but joy, and very lucky, that he'd secured a place. Our previous home had originally been just outside the catchment area but, courtesy of an apparently low birth rate in 1995, they had widened the net and caught us in his year of intake. He loved it at the school, too, and after our recent move it was only a ten-minute walk from home, allowing him more precious minutes in bed. What was not to love?

It was a Sunday afternoon and, other than a few cars that had started to appear containing other parents, the road was devoid of the usual mayhem of weekday vehicles.

Ten minutes later and the large packed coach slowly approached, coming to a halt outside the school. Sitting tight in my seat, I muttered to myself. *Try not to look like some overzealous mother. Give him chance to get off the coach and say his goodbyes to his friends.* Two minutes later, I could contain myself no longer as other parents started to surround the alighting throng of pupils and teachers, and the driver quickly began emptying bags from the luggage compartment onto the ground. As I approached the crowd, I suddenly saw him, a huge smile lighting his face and his arm waving excitedly in an effort to get my attention. My heart melted. He was safely home. *We* were safely home. Just the two of us, as it had always been. Watching him make his way towards me, pulling his suitcase, all was well in the world – my boy was home. Moments later, he wrapped his arms around me, hugging me tightly as he uttered the words any mother wants to hear after seven days apart. 'I'm starving, Mum, what's for dinner?'

This was the land I knew and loved. This was the land where I belonged.

Once home, my distance from John gave me the space to reflect on how powerful the emotions raised by childhood memories can be. I began to wonder if our perceived connection had been nothing more than a figment of our young fertile imaginations and had been wrongly accorded greater significance the older we'd grown. Closer inspection was perhaps unravelling us back to that truth.

I recalled that during the counselling process to grieve my father's death, I had decided to return to the house we had been living in when he died to take a closer look, in just the same way.

It was a small, innocuous, semi-detached property, that melted into the landscape of the other small, innocuous, semi-detached properties sitting alongside it, an image that was at odds with the large, dark presence it had occupied in my mind.

I had written to the occupants and explained my dilemma: I just needed to walk inside and face the power and pain it held for me to see if it remained. Thankfully, they were delightful people who were most appreciative of why I wanted to return and generously welcomed me into their home. Their humility and overt sensitivity had allowed me to take a step back in time and briefly immerse myself in a world long since gone, and in so doing face the demons that haunted me.

As I drove down the quiet, residential road it all felt so small: the narrow road, the little houses – like a miniature toytown on a Monopoly board. The inside was just the same: all so much smaller than I remembered, but immediately enveloping me in the trauma of thirty years earlier.

The living room looking onto the back garden, especially, conjured memories of my mother lying on the couch crying after my father's death, the same living room where my father had lain on the floor on a Sunday afternoon as we climbed all over him, playing.

And there were the stairs leading up from the left of the hallway, where I had sat on the bottom step shortly before my father had died, and where he had straightened my knee-length, patterned white socks and told me I had to go to

Brownies that evening to be sworn in – despite my not wanting to. His sweet, supportive, gentle manner had been in perfect contrast to his broad, tall frame and strong presence as he'd knelt closely in front of me.

I climbed upwards and arrived on the landing, where I found the same slat-panelled wood banister securing the area, the banister on which my mother had laid four sets of clothes each night for my siblings and me, ready for the next day.

Then I was in the bedroom I had shared with my sister, where every night our father had come to kiss us goodnight as we lay in our bunk beds. Little did I know how treasured and exquisitely sweet those memories would become.

As I descended the stairs I was transported back to the morning after his death when I had taken the same journey, only to find my mother sitting on the living room couch, surrounded by relatives as she sobbed, and to be told my father had died. Gone, just like that. I was seven and had no real comprehension of what had been tragically ripped from my life.

I sat on a low, brick perimeter wall in the back garden, its layout unchanged, and breathed in every blade of grass, every plant, every flower, hoping to breathe in the essence of my father. The sun took pity on my forlorn figure and emerged, shining down wonderful rays of warmth, gently caressing my fragile self. For all its grief-filled lining, I didn't want to leave this place in which he had once walked, the home we had once shared. I wanted to stay and sit with him forever.

I had chosen to return and walk through it all, my pain palpable as I allowed him to descend and face me, bringing him closer and removing his dark veil. His death was darkness, he was not. The cavernous hole he had left was darkness, he was not. The lifelong want to see him again, to smell him, to touch him, was darkness, he was not. The house was darkness, he was not. He was warmth and fun, a daddy who had brought home sugar mice in white paper bags, a daddy who had driven us the long miles to Cornwall for our annual holidays as we excitedly ate the sweets he had bought us in the back seat. A daddy who showered us with love.

In returning and walking into his shadow I had managed to separate him from the darkness of our childhood home and bring him out into the light to sit closer by my side, loosening the tight grip of painful memories as I did so, reducing their power and hold over me.

Perhaps the distance I perceived in John was his own reaction to our closer inspection of one another: he had decided it had been a mistake but couldn't find the courage to tell me how he felt.

Beyond the possibility of our youthful rose-tinted glasses giving life to some misguided belief that we had some sort of bond there was one other, perhaps more plausible, explanation.

I had known it was never going to be the case that meeting up in America would somehow eradicate the trauma of his loss, and I knew it was undoubtedly early days to have become involved, but perhaps I'd underestimated how this would sit between us.

His wife had arrived without notice in New Zealand,

opening her compartment door and making her presence felt. He had either been unable to place her back inside her compartment as he'd previously described, or she had refused to return, following him to Los Angeles and on to Las Vegas. Grief didn't generally do as it was told. I suspected Heather had been with us throughout the whole week. His life-partner had walked by his side, not me. It was she with whom he'd had intimate conversations, not me. It was her arms he had wanted to feel wrapped around him, not mine. It was her voice he'd wanted to hear, not mine.

I was acutely aware I was walking on Heather's territory, and however delicately I did that the guilt walked with me. I don't know if that would have changed if we had waited a few more months or another year. Perhaps in respecting her memory and the huge part she had played in John's life I was always going to feel this way. Perhaps John would always feel this way too.

It was possible I had been an unwitting observer at a private event. Heather had arrived and, I suspected, was not going to give notice any time soon.

CHAPTER 20

The phone had been eerily silent since my return. It had only been four days, but this was not his normal pattern. He was clearly taking space and I was relieved. John's distance during our trip to Los Angeles and Las Vegas had pushed me into my own wilderness, a place in which, just like him, I was free. He wasn't the only one who needed to be alone for a while; I was remote and unavailable as I took a step back and viewed him quietly. I was resolute: when he eventually emerged, I would make no mention of how I had found him during our holiday. I could surf conversation and feelings too, albeit not in quite the same masterful and persistent way as him, but none-theless, surf them I would.

He had travelled to San Francisco following my departure,

planning to take a coach to Yosemite National Park on his fourth and final day. It was this day on which he burst forth once more into my world, at full throttle, animated, and gushing excitedly about the place in which he was standing. The phone vibrated with his high-octane delivery.

'Wow, I had to call to share this with you. I'm in Yosemite and I've got to say, it's *the most* breathtaking, *most* beautiful place in the world. I'm going to try and describe this to you, but honestly, I know I won't be able to do it justice. Try and picture this: close your eyes … are they closed yet?' he asked, impatiently.

'Yes, yes, they're closed,' I answered, hurriedly.

'I'm surrounded by sheer cliff faces with massive boulders sat on top of them, waterfalls everywhere with the cleanest water cascading down, and you know those beautiful, slender pine trees I love? Well, there's got to be literally thousands here, and they're so tall they seem to disappear into the ether.'

I didn't have the chance to answer in the affirmative as he continued enthusiastically.

'Then there's the icy cold, crystal-clear stream water I've been drinking, and the untouched snow. There are so few people here that it's like some enormous perfect white blanket that I get to walk on for the first time, listening to it crunch loudly under my feet … and the bitingly cold winter air, which just makes everything look and feel so vibrant. And the whole thing is topped with a sky so clear and blue, Jill. It's simply stunning. I only came here for one day and I'm due to get back on the coach soon, but I can't leave. I'm going to stay for a few more days and explore it all.'

'Where will you sleep, though?' I managed to interject.

'There are some small wooden cabins at the base of the valley, so I'm going to book one of those. But time's running out so I'm going to have to dash to make sure they don't close before I speak to them. I also need to let the coach driver know that I'm not returning with him. I'll call you in a few days, but I insist that while I'm in such a beautiful place we can only talk about beautiful things.'

'That sounds like a lovely idea to me. It's great to hear you sounding so uplifted, it really is.'

'It's this place, being here. If there's a heaven this is it. But enough of me. Before I go, are you okay?'

'I'm good, just fine. Enjoy the rest of Yosemite and take care out there,' I said nonchalantly, no deep waters running now; surfing felt good.

The line went dead. As quickly as he'd arrived, he disappeared, his surroundings clearly transporting him to another high.

Cold hard cash. That's what I'd resorted to, as Alexander's exams moved closer and closer and the collective study demands of twelve subjects were forced through the eye of a needle. *Move aside food,* I said to myself, as the bargaining chips at the table moved to a whole new level and I began walking over questionable ground. The stakes were high, I reasoned. Perhaps the added impetus of monetary gain would propel him to the finishing line in one piece and with a handful of good results.

'Okay, I've decided that if you get an A I'll pay you £50, if you get a B I'll pay you £25, and if you get a C I'll pay you £10. Any grade of D or below earns you nothing, not even enchiladas,' I joked, as I put more fuel down on his desk, this time a bowl of nuts and two satsumas.

'What, you'll pay me £50 for every A?'

'Yes.'

'Wow.' His face lit up. 'This could cost you. Are you sure? It's very generous.'

'I'm sure. I know how soul-destroying relentless study can be and so I'm just trying to add some fun to it.'

'So, let me get this right. You're my mum, who's supposed to be guiding me to make the right choices and live by the right standards, but at the same time you're buying my results?' He was clearly enjoying his moment as he leant back in his desk chair, looked towards me and raised his dark brown bushy eyebrows in mock disdain. His dark brown eyes glinted mischievously as he toyed with me. There was nothing worse than a smug teenager holding up a mirror to your own weaknesses.

'Very funny. Don't go there, or you'll prick my moral conscience and I'll retract the offer.'

'Honestly, you don't have to pay me – I want to do well for me, not money.'

'I know, and it's fantastic how you've buckled down to it all.'

'But hey,' he quickly added, 'if it makes you feel better, I'll accept those terms. Very reasonable … yes, very reasonable. Though I do think that an A could be worth £60.'

'Don't push your luck. Crikey, look what you've reduced me to. I'm swimming in a swamp of questionable behaviour.'

'I didn't take you there!' he retaliated quickly.

He was too clever for his own good, that sweet boy of mine.

Five minutes later I left his room. Three more notes now stuck to the edge of his shelf, outlining what was to be paid for each grade – right next to the inspirational quote from Michelangelo, who, I was pretty sure, hadn't envisaged a cash exchange when he wrote such wise words.

Fifty pounds or sixty pounds for an A, I pondered, the mist of my own regret still circling.

A couple of days later John called again, still exuberant about his surroundings, unable to conceal his joy at the apparent nirvana he now found himself in.

'Can you believe, I've walked in complete quiet for nine hours each day without passing a single soul. I don't think I've ever felt more in touch with nature than I do here. You've got to come here, Jill. It's untouched by man, pollution, modernisation and progress, and in today's world that's remarkable. Its vastness is quite something to comprehend and, if I'm honest, completely overwhelming. There've been moments when I've felt alive inside, which I haven't felt since my family died. I wasn't expecting this ...'

I said nothing as his sentence broke away. He was conveying a seismic shift in his emotions. A space was needed for them to emerge.

'I'm going to tell you something now,' he continued after a brief silence. 'I've just returned from a four-hour hike to the top of Yosemite's highest waterfall. It's *nine* times higher than Niagara Falls – can you imagine that? And the waterfall … it was so graceful, narrow and sleek, rolling off the top effortlessly. But as I stood at the top, something inside me decided to move slowly to the edge of the precipice … so I could look down. As I peered over, I moved my right foot forward so it dangled beyond the edge. I must have been a split second from death … I could have been gone in an instant, just like my family. I was absolutely terrified. It was so exposed it made me dizzy. I felt like I was in some sort of trance, but then I suddenly woke and pulled myself back.'

My heart was pumping as I assimilated his words.

I thought we were only allowed to talk about beautiful things. I was supposed to be successfully surfing conversation, keeping it light and not seeking any deeper, meaningful interpretation of what was going on with him or with us. I pictured him standing alone as he pondered whether to step forward and throw himself off, in those few seconds dancing with death again, riddled with pain and disconnected from the world. His grief shimmering malevolently around his desperate form.

I felt a surge of overwhelming, raw sadness rise up within me and was aware my breathing had become shallow and slightly laboured with the distress I felt at his disclosure, my hand clutched against my mouth in silent horror. I wasn't about to surf this one. Every instinctive bone in my body returned to its natural, default position as I tiptoed forward. I didn't know what to say in that instant. I just knew I had to say something.

'Oh, John, that sounds so very sad. To think of you

standing there like that, contemplating taking your own life. I thought you said you would never consider that. I thought you said you were feeling alive for the first time.'

'But that's the point. When I pulled myself back and sat down, despite shaking with the fear and realisation of what I'd just done, I felt huge relief that I was still alive. It's the first time I've felt that since my family died.'

'I don't understand why you would put yourself in such a position. You could have toppled over accidentally. You must have known how dangerous that was?'

'We're all a moment away from death, Jill. I don't fear it, certainly not now. Maybe I just wanted to test how far I would go, to see how much I value my life, because since my family died life itself doesn't seem to matter any more. But Yosemite, surprisingly ...' he broke momentarily while he considered what he was about to say. 'It's challenging that view. Life suddenly feels very powerful. So in this space I was just exploring that.'

'You have lots of people in your life that care about you, John – your mum, sister, Barbara and the rest of Heather's family, me and so many friends. Please don't lose sight of that. You're not alone.'

'I do know that, and I care about all of you too, but it's been a very strange day. I'm exhausted now, so I'm going to get off if you don't mind.'

He wasn't the only one who was exhausted. I felt drained listening to him, vicariously living his experience and unable to field the emotion that came with that. I was blissfully unaware that more was yet to come.

I was back at the hockey rink. It was a Saturday this time, early evening, home match. Not as cold as the early five thirty training slot, but cold enough nonetheless. Hot chocolate and programme in hand, I found myself a seat with the other parents as the players burst onto the newly cut ice and began warming up.

Ice hockey wasn't just a fast sport, it was a pretty brutal one too, as players smacked into each other, battling for control of the puck. But beyond that aspect, I'd been surprised when I first went to a few professional games and watched as grown men took their helmets off and started brawling on the ice, irritated by who'd done what to whom, while the referee looked on and young children, all agog, pushed their faces up against the plastic safety guard circling the rink edge. I wasn't comfortable with it but, apparently, it was all part of the fun.

It was towards the end of the second period when my son was taken out, blindsided, as he manoeuvred the puck. I could see the opposition player hurtling towards him, smacking into his side at speed. He fell to the ground instantly, like a skittle being hit at force, and moments later, when he'd managed to get up, he quickly exited the rink. I looked on, concerned. In all the years he'd been playing I'd seen him take plenty of knocks, but this had seemed a particularly nasty attack. However, as they returned to the ice for the third and final period, he was back playing and so I rested my troubled mother's mind.

As he emerged after the match, though, it was clear he was

in a lot of pain. he provided me with a graphic account of the team coach conducting an examination of his shoulder during the break between the second and third periods, from which he'd apparently determined that Alexander had a dislocated shoulder.

'He lifted my limp arm up first to see where it was most painful, and then without notice just snapped it back in.'

I winced at the thought.

'How did you manage to play in the third period then?'

'I struggled through. I didn't want to let the team down. But it's really hurting now.'

Five hours later – our Saturday evening over – we emerged into the dark from the accident and emergency department of our local hospital with Alexander's arm in a sling. X-rays had revealed that his tendons had been torn across the front of his shoulder. The consultant's instruction that he couldn't play any ice hockey for about another ten weeks was the final straw: he was not a happy young man.

'Well, look on the bright side,' I said teasingly as we drove home, 'just think of all the extra study you'll be able to do now.'

He scowled as he complained loudly and bitterly about the offending player and how, by the time his arm had healed, the season would be all but over.

I gleefully considered all the sudden and unexpected luxurious Sunday morning lie-ins that lay ahead. I would miss the game, but I had to be honest: I'd relish the space too. I'd have to stop myself doing cartwheels in the kitchen when I got home.

It was his last day in Yosemite and John had apparently packed his walking boots ready to leave later. Wearing only his trainers, and determined to make the most of his final moments, he'd set off with snow and ice underfoot, his natural inclination to explore and his wanton disregard for his own safety taking him down a pathway closed to the public in the winter and marked 'Danger'. His voice as he now relayed what happened next was subdued, the buoyancy of previous calls, glaringly absent.

'It was terrifying. My trainers have no grip, and the further up I walked, the worse the terrain and conditions became – steeper and icier. I was walking for about an hour when I realised I was out of my depth and turned back, but going down was even worse. I must have missed the turning for the route I'd walked up, because eventually I came to a sheet of ice about ten metres wide that was blocking the path.'

'I can't believe you ignored the danger sign.' I was quietly incredulous.

'You know me. Sometimes I like to live on the edge. Anyway, the ice stretched from the mountain side to the cliff edge at a forty-five degree angle where there was a two-hundred-foot vertical drop to rocks below. I was trapped from behind and, unless I managed to cross this, trapped from the front.'

I wondered how much longer he would keep placing himself at risk like this, but didn't raise it.

'So what did you do?'

'I lay down, facing forwards, and inch by inch moved

slowly across, knowing that each move could be my last. I thought my heart was going to jump out of my chest it was thumping that strongly. Sweat was running down my back, and the physical and mental strength I needed to try and hold on was exhausting. I started to feel very tired very quickly. I thought it was the end, that I was going to slip off and die ... and that no one would find me because I'd been foolish enough to go into an area marked "No Entry". I couldn't find any grip with my hands or trainers. I was literally sliding across, hoping that my body wouldn't start slipping down and drop over the edge.'

'Honestly, I don't understand you, John.'

'It's shaken me ... I didn't want to die. You'll laugh at this, but I started speaking to some other higher being – if such a presence exists – asking them to let me live. How funny is that?'

He sounded drained.

'I'm not laughing, John. Trust me, I'm not laughing. You keep pushing yourself for reasons only you understand. Maybe you needed this wake-up call. It's one thing actively choosing to take yourself to those extreme spaces, but you weren't in control today, nature was. You can't always dictate the terms.'

'I know, I know, I was stupid. I feel very lucky to be alive. You know, this place has had a profound effect on me. Its exquisite beauty, its stillness – it's all so raw and powerful. Until now, everywhere I've been I've struggled to enjoy myself because my family weren't with me. But here ... well, it's a life-affirming place and I've had moments when I've been completely immersed, when the pain of my family's absence wasn't my overriding feeling.' He paused. 'I'm sorry, too.' His tone had softened.

'Sorry – what for?'

'How I was in Los Angeles and Las Vegas. I was struggling. I'd only just left New Zealand with Heather's family and I could feel her presence strongly. I felt guilty that I was spending time with you. I just couldn't talk about it at the time.'

I was silent, letting him get it all off his chest.

'Talk to me, Jill, say something.'

'You're not alone in feeling guilty. But that's a sensitive subject, and maybe after what you've been through today we should leave that conversation for another time.'

'Of course. I just wanted to apologise and try to explain.'

'Surfing's good right now,' I said light-heartedly. 'Enjoy Washington.' We finished the call and I put the phone down. I sat immobile on my chair, reflecting.

For the first time since he'd lost his family, a small crack of light had emerged from his black heart and the impenetrable numbness within, glinting gently through, trying to find a space in the darkness and, as it did so, awakening his shut-down soul. For all its glorious unyielding power, Yosemite National Park had reached in and ever so softly laid its soothing hands upon him, soothing hands that had given him a glimpse of hope that he might once again find true joy in life and in the world that surrounded him.

But it had done so much more than that too. He said that as he stood at ground level in Yosemite he'd felt insignificant, engulfed by the earthly power of the place. He'd been reduced to a small pebble in the water, a drop of water in a stream, a grain of sand in the desert. And as Yosemite's raw nature had ruthlessly placed him one slip-on-the-ice from death, removing his autonomy and impervious to his insignificant presence, he had finally reconnected with himself and with his own value and desire for life.

CHAPTER 21

I was listening to his voice. He was on top of the Washington Monument having just left the Holocaust Memorial Museum. He sounded sombre, and had clearly been affected.

'It was truly harrowing, but the more I saw the more I became transfixed – the haunting pictures, the inconceivable accounts and the loss of all those lives in such horrifying circumstances.'

'Surely that wasn't the best place for you to be?'

'You're wrong, actually. I was there for four hours, and even then I didn't want to leave. Believe it or not, it's helped me.'

I didn't interject, sensing he needed to talk.

'You know, since I lost my family, I've struggled to … put their deaths in to some sort of perspective. Until now, I've felt like I was in a land that no one else could possibly understand. Here, in the States, I've been able to find some sort of sanity that resonates.'

He stopped talking momentarily. I could hear his mind ticking away as he considered his thoughts.

'But that's understandable … in view of the level of your own loss.'

'But how awful does that sound. I've found sanity in the insanity of the Holocaust museum and the depth of human suffering found within those walls. Its impact has been quite profound. I came away thinking that if all those who survived could carry on, with many, if not all, of their families having died, then I could too. For the first time since my family died, my loss and pain seemed infinitely small by comparison.'

I was listening to his voice, my ear still warm from the call he had just made, no more than one hour earlier.

'It's me,' he said, gleefully, as if we'd not spoken for months. 'Just two minutes more of your time. I forgot to say earlier that when I was standing on top of the Washington Monument the estate agent called to tell me the sale of my house has gone through.'

'Oh my goodness, that's so sad for you.'

'Yes, it's been a very emotional day, but surprisingly, one which has made me feel more positive about the future – not so much the house, but the museum.'

'It's an awful lot to take in, in just a few hours.'

'Well, I wanted to try and end it on a positive note, so I'm also calling to say that I'm going to New York in a couple of days, and wondered if you'd like to come and join me?'

Boy, I felt like I was being bounced off walls in a small

room as I was front-loaded with myriad conflicting images: emaciated, sunken figures standing in lines in concentration camps; the burnt rafters of John's former home; the bright lights of Times Square beckoning ... or not. This wasn't normal.

'Crikey, give me a minute to catch up, you're way down the road ahead of me. *Slow down* a minute ... I can't imagine how awful you must feel right now about the house sale – the home you all shared?'

'I can't look back with any happiness to the memories I have with my family right now. It's too painful. So I just see it as the cutting of one of the last physical ties to Anglesey. I'm not capable of processing anything more than that.'

'But even so, it's quite a moment for you.'

'Well, the distress I do feel is that it's as though a door has closed permanently for me, and there's no turning back. But after the day I've had I'm trying to focus on something that makes me happy, and that's you – being with you. Will you come to New York?'

'It's a lovely invitation, but I'm not sure that's such a good idea after how you were in Los Angeles and Las Vegas. But also ... the image of you standing at that cliff edge in Yosemite was very distressing. Don't you think you need space alone to think about where you're at?'

'I understand, I do. I'm sorry about when you last came out here, but I'm feeling much better now – I wouldn't be asking if I wasn't. As for needing space ... I've had lots of time on my own recently, and so it would be great to share some with you again.'

'It's not as easy as packing a suitcase and jumping on a

plane, John. Last time I came out Alexander was on a school holiday, but that's not the case now.'

'At least think about it. I'll need to know by tomorrow to sort out the plane tickets. Trust me, I'm in a much better space.'

Three days later I was sitting on a plane to New York, Alexander encouraging me to seize the moment, and with my mum and one of her friends, Jenny, safely ensconced in our home for the following week.

'Go, Mum,' Alexander had insisted as he put his arm around me lovingly. 'Me and Nan will be fine together. I'm not a little boy any more, you know,' he said, laughing as he sliced clean through one of my tightly held apron strings. He clearly wasn't going to suffer from separation anxiety in my absence. 'Of course, I'll miss you,' he added sensitively, 'but Jenny has told Nan that she's going to cook lots of lovely meals for me.' Blimey, he'd got it all worked out – a replacement chef *in situ* and I hadn't even left. I smiled as I sat waiting for the plane to take off, imagining the three of them rubbing along together, Alexander completely in charge, of course. Young, handsome and charming – they didn't stand a chance.

Another airport, this time New York's JFK, and another big hug from my friend. I tried to observe him surreptitiously as we made our way to the hotel in a cab in the hope of gauging his emotional state. Did he seem better than when we had last seen each other? Was this the same man who, weeks earlier, had peered over the edge of a cliff and considered death? Were there signs of Heather in the immediate vicinity? I searched his face for the nuances of barely concealed grief – the heavy brow, distant eyes, the pained and fixed expression he wore without effort. I realised I'd outstayed my welcome when I suddenly heard his voice.

'Stop staring at me,' he admonished. 'I'm fine, so don't go looking for something that's not there, okay?' He raised his eyebrows as though I was ridiculous for even considering his emotional or mental state. He took hold of my hand and squeezed it, smiling broadly as he held my gaze, his blue-green eyes twinkling.

'I've got lots planned for us – the Harlem Globetrotters tonight in Madison Square Garden, an evening of jazz at a place overlooking Central Park, a helicopter ride over the Hudson river. A visit to the Empire State Building is a must, and Macy's department store, too, and on a more sombre level I thought we could go to Ground Zero and pay our respects. What do you think?'

'Wow, that all sounds fantastic. But will you be okay visiting another memorial where so many died – that could be very distressing?'

'I couldn't not visit it, so I hope you feel the same way too.'

'Of course. I'm just putting it out there.'

'I'll be okay. Now, enough of the serious stuff. It's *so* good to see you again. We've just got to make the most of this big city. Brace yourself – it's going to be seven action-packed days, so hang on tight.'

For all the joy of seeing the many New York sights and sharing them with John, one activity became our surprising favourite: our daily morning venture to Starbucks in Times Square, conveniently situated just a couple of minutes' walk from our hotel. As we sought refuge there on our first day from the bitterly cold February weather and the knife-sharp wind slicing across our faces, it felt like the whole world had descended upon the same space.

This bustling coffee house was a place that had no time for death, no time to stand still, a place that had to keep moving as life went on – an infinitesimal dot on the world stage, but brilliantly illuminating the billions that stood upon it. Within its walls, John's loss instantly evaporated to a distant yesterday. It was bursting at the seams with noise and people and laptops and phone calls, and endless queues of waiting customers, joyfully embraced by a multitude of smiling, overtly friendly staff who were a tour de force as they stood serving in a single line behind the galley counter with no more than a couple of inches between each of them. Their easy, genuine, infectious banter with customers and each other, and their sheer enthusiasm, created the effortless platform from which this alluring environment sprang.

There was no doubt about it: this was the engine room of New York, and it was in top gear, roaring full throttle ahead and leading the way. We had most definitely arrived in America.

I could have drowned myself in coffee and eaten pastries

all day to stay and be part of that mesmerising place – the comings, the goings and the frenetic collective buzz of it all.

We somehow managed to find two seats at a long, central, oblong table, and squeezed in between other customers. Thick winter coats lay everywhere, ensuring there was little room to manoeuvre, but creating the cosiest of feelings. We were sitting huddled together with our steaming hot coffees. As always, John had bucked the trend on the food front and chosen a cold yoghurt topped with granola and, in keeping with coffee house tradition (and it being a little too early for cake) I had selected a buttery croissant.

'What a place,' said John. 'Shall we cancel the rest of the day and watch the world go by in here?'

'Isn't it funny how we're surrounded by so many people and yet I feel like we're in our very own invisible bubble.'

'We are.' He put his arm around me and, pulling me in towards him, quietly said, 'Thanks for coming. It means the world to me.'

'You don't have to thank me. I wanted to come.'

'I know I've got a long way to go, but since we last saw each other ... since Yosemite and the Holocaust museum, something inside me feels a little lighter. It's a small shift but it makes me feel more hopeful for the future.'

'It's good to hear you talk like this,' I said, squeezing his hand.

'I wanted to say sorry again for how distant I was in Los Angeles and Vegas.'

'Stop apologising. It just threw up lots of issues – whether we should be together, whether we've crossed that platonic line too early, feelings of guilt surrounding Heather ...'

'You don't have anything to feel guilty about. Heather was my wife and the only one who should feel like that is me. And I do. I've said before that if it wasn't for our history, I wouldn't be in this space with you. I know that doesn't make it right, but it helps me to understand myself at some level.'

'But when we were in LA and Vegas I sensed her presence strongly. I felt very uncomfortable – not because Heather was there but because I was. You just needed to be with her. She was in your shop.'

'Yeah, you're right, she was. But she's always been there – not that I understood that analogy until you mentioned it. I can't change the fact we became more than friends only six months after her death. I can only try and explain it. It's like having two tracks. On one is Heather and the boys and our life together, and on the other is you, and they're separate and will never cross.'

'But they did cross in LA. Grief isn't something that can be controlled in that way. You know it isn't.'

'I'm not explaining myself very well here. I'm not talking about my grief, I'm talking about how separate each track feels to me, and this is reinforced by the fact that Heather and I had a different relationship to ours. She didn't delve as deeply as you do, and neither did I when we were together. Honestly, I've never known anyone probe so deeply into someone else's mind.'

I laughed in acknowledgement.

'I think we need to lighten the mood a little, so I'm going to take a leaf out of the John Bickley book of life and attempt to surf the whole subject. It's simply solace you seek – the solace and comfort of sex, nothing more, nothing less. Just a physical release of every conflicting emotion you feel right now. I just happen to be the willing victim. You see – that took me less than a minute to say and could have saved us the last twenty minutes of analysis!'

'It's you I seek,' he said seriously. I could get sex from anywhere, but it's not about that. I love being with you, and I know the timing is awful but please don't diminish our involvement in that way. Don't reduce yourself to that sort of role in my life. It couldn't be further from the truth.'

'Oh my goodness, we've morphed into each other. I didn't mean to offend you, I was just trying to be light. I think we need to clear our heads. Come on, let's go for a walk in the cold.'

He leant in and kissed me softly on the lips. 'You're love-ly – you couldn't possibly offend me. I just want you to know that choosing to be with you, although complex, is easy too. I feel very lucky that you want to be with me – for now anyway.'

'You sweet-talker,' I laughed. 'With compliments like that I'll stay at least another day.'

We returned every morning for the rest of the week. How could we not? It was our own safe world, invisible to all but ourselves and where we lost hours together, our legs entwined under the table, engrossed in each other and alive with the throng of life that surrounded us.

This was a place that had no time for death, no time to stand still, a place that had to keep moving as life went on.

~

He took me by surprise when he said it. We were being taken around Central Park in a horse-drawn carriage on our last day, covered in blankets and huddled together. The weather was still bitingly cold and crisp, but with a stunning, cloudless blue sky.

I didn't need a definition of us, but he offered one anyway.

'It's been such a wonderful week and suddenly it feels like we're more of a couple than we did before, if that makes sense.'

I squeezed his gloved hand and rested my head on his shoulder.

'How would you feel about me renting somewhere near you in the south when I return to the UK? It would give us the chance to spend some time together.'

'A day at a time – no expectations?'

'Yes, as long as you don't start talking about that "being free" malarkey,' he laughed.

I laughed too. 'You'll come around to my way of thinking eventually. But on a more serious note, I can't continue to be your main source of support, John. Will you find a counsellor when you get back and give it another go?'

'Yes, but only for you.'

'Can I say one last thing about it? I'm asking you to try it again, fully appreciative of what a life-changing process it can be. We're okay today, but in time you may want to walk on a different path, and I understand that.'

'And so may you. But for the record, I'm not going anywhere.'

I put my own gloved fingers to his lips. I was determined we would walk together unfettered by such restrictive ties and unnecessary expectations. Experience had taught me it would only create an unhealthy environment in which the blind pursuit of love could mistakenly play hostage to the many ugly and hidden human frailties: jealousy, cruelty, weakness to name but a few, and give them a voice in love's name. I didn't need to create an image of what he, we or love should be. He was free, whether he understood it or not.

He was not so easily silenced. 'I've fallen in love with you, you must be able to see that. I don't want you to set me free. I want you to want to be with me, and to love me too.'

I glowed at his loving words, radiant against the cold spring air.

'Oh John, I've *always* loved you. You must have been able to see that, from when I was thirteen to today at forty-six.'

He laughed. 'Now, that's not fair – you're making your love for me sound greater than mine for you.'

'Well, what can I say – unrequited for so many years.' I nudged him in his side and smiled.

'Let's not revisit that,' he said light-heartedly before continuing in a more serious tone.

'I just want you to know how I feel today, sitting here in this carriage. It's something so simple, but with you next to me it feels like the only place anyone could possibly want to be in the world right now.'

'What a gorgeous thing to say.'

'It's how I feel.'

'I feel the same way too, but can we just—'

'Can we just what? Don't ruin this gorgeous moment. For once, let simple be beautiful.'

'But don't you see, it's because I love you that I can't bear the thought that the love we share for one another is contained. I don't want to crush it with expectation, and all I'm asking is that we give it the space to breathe. Let's not mould it into something we thought was love. It *has* to be free, John, and only then will we know.'

'For goodness sake, know what?' he asked, puzzled.

'That it's pure. That it came to us naturally, and we didn't chase it down, put it in a vice-like grip and refuse to release it, pandering to some other unconscious need of ours that operates at a much deeper level.'

'Oh boy. You and I are so different. I can't say I understand you most of the time,' he laughed. 'I mean, your mind … it takes you to some spaces I don't think exist in mine. I've listened to everything you've said, but right now I insist I have the last word. Do you know what I know?'

'No. What?'

'My love for you *is* pure. I see you clearly, all of you, and I've fallen in love with everything that makes you who you are.' He kissed me softly and pulled the blanket up around us as we held each other close underneath, the sound of horse's hooves signalling our way forward.

Pragmatic, uncomplicated and a breath of fresh air, my son was once more responding to my motherly efforts to ensure he was happy as aspects of my own life changed. I'd just told him John was planning to come and live nearby on his return and that we would be seeing more of him.

'That's fantastic. I think he's great, so I'll enjoy that.'

I continued gingerly. He'd had me to himself for much of his life and I didn't want to upset the equilibrium of our life – his stability and security. He was, and would always be, my priority.

'We've become much closer recently, more than just friends. And so we thought we'd see how we got along once he's back.'

'What, he's your boyfriend now?' he said, smiling warmly at me.

I felt strangely self-conscious. Wasn't it supposed to be the other way around – my son bringing home a girlfriend and seeking *my* approval?'

'Well, I suppose so. I'm not sure I'd describe him as that just yet. We're going to take it a day at a time and see how things go.'

'I'm so pleased for you. It'll be lovely for you to have a nice man in your life. You've been on your own for so long. It's about time you met someone.'

'Oh, I don't need a man in my life, Alexander. I love our life as it is – just you and me together.'

'I know that, and I do too, but I really like John and I'll get to see him more. It'd be great if he could come to more training sessions and matches with us, when my shoulder's better and I'm playing again.'

'I'm sure he'd like that very much.'

'I won't be your only focus then either!' he said, laughing.

'Ah. You won't fall from under my radar that easily,' I said, laughing too.

His full approval was essential. I wouldn't be taking another step with John if he wasn't in step with us too.

CHAPTER 22

He was back, he was in the south, he was staying in a local bed and breakfast, and seven days after his return we were in the middle of a full-blown argument in my living room. The New York bubble had burst with a bang, as two equally determined forces locked horns. For seven days, he'd had to face the reality of engaging in some semblance of a normal life, and from where I was sitting, it had already hit home. Swiftly booking another holiday, this time skiing, he was preparing to leave. His clothes were barely unpacked and now he was departing again.

'What are you talking about – keep running? Running where?' he said, exasperated.

'You have to stand still eventually and face life. Your life.'

'What *are* you talking about? It's one week away for goodness sake. I'm not going on another long-term walkabout. It's seven *days*, not seven *months*.'

He was decidedly animated. I'd easily ruffled his usually

calm feathers, provoking an uncharacteristically angry response. This was new territory: we were normally harmonious and at ease together, not fractious and indignant.

What *was* I so upset about? I believed he was free to walk this world in whatever way he chose. Check. I believed he was free to walk with whomever he chose. Check. We had agreed we were taking one day at a time. Check. On that basis, I should have been packing his suitcase for him, booking a taxi to the airport and waving him a fond farewell at the front door as he disappeared into the distance. Today together, tomorrow in different parts of the world. This was the manner in which we were supposed to be walking together. Check! Check! Check!

As if he could read my mind, and with lightning speed, he seized upon the 'freedom malarkey' (that he'd not long since mocked), positioning himself on the moral high ground of a matter he'd professed not to understand.

'It's *you* who said we were "free", and now you're challenging me about going off on a short break. That's hardly "being free" now, is it?'

The irony of his stance would ordinarily have been funny but was lost as he wafted his barely concealed enjoyment at scoring this easy point in front of my face. Oh, the beauty of words and sentiments, so easily slipped from the tongue without a true and tested value! This was a belief I had asserted with heartfelt conviction and which was now being held up for close examination. Was I falling at the first hurdle, unable to live by my own verbalised beliefs, paying mere lip service to my apparently strongly held views? I didn't think so.

My issue went beyond going travelling again, albeit for just one week. It was the immediacy with which he had suddenly and unexpectedly planned a new holiday. Instinctively, I could see he was struggling with his return. He seemed distracted and restless, and although he had always planned at some point to go skiing, I suspected it suited his need to keep moving. He was now on the run to Italy, and I could see his escape playing out before me in slow motion. Perhaps he would never find that restful space and would be running for the rest of his life.

I *couldn't* keep running with him.

'It's got nothing to do with being free, it's got nothing to do with you going skiing, it's about your inability to sit still, your need to keep on the go all the time. You've only been back seven days and you can't bear it.'

'What's wrong with wanting to be active and fill my days with positive things? It's better than lying in bed depressed every day.'

'That's not fair. I've done nothing but support you for the last eight months and encouraged you to go off travelling, to find a way forward. But this is different.'

'*How*? How is it different?' he said impatiently, as though I was talking a language he didn't understand.

'Because ...' I paused.

'Because *what*, exactly?'

I paused briefly before continuing. I was treading on delicate ground, but if we were to stand any chance of walking a step further together then I had to tell him what I felt.

'Because you can't keep running from your pain like it's

some sort of race that you have to constantly be winning. You can't escape it – it's inside you.'

'That's ridiculous. I've been dealing with my pain every day since my family died. I know exactly where it is.'

'I know that,' I said softly. 'I've seen it, I've heard it and I've felt it acutely. But that's not what I mean. I'm talking about standing still long enough to face the reality of your life without your family. And as much as you say you're dealing with your pain, isn't that just you managing on a day-to-day basis rather than looking at it in a deeper way?'

'Maybe I don't want to look at it in a deeper way. Maybe I deal with things differently. Maybe I'm just going on a one-week skiing holiday. Why does everything have to have some hidden meaning with you?'

'I'm sorry, but you won't change my view. You can keep travelling for the remainder of your days and find yourself in different places, different hotel rooms. But when you look in the mirror it will only reflect the same thing back to you – your life now, without your family.'

'You're wrong. I always intended to go skiing and you're making it into something it's not. I need some space right now, I think we both do. I'm not going skiing for another week, so call me if you want to talk.'

'I won't be needing to talk because you're right, I need space too. I'm not about to change my view either.'

Seconds later, he was gone and I was surprisingly relieved. I didn't feel the need to contain him but I did feel the need to define where I felt he was at.

If he wanted to lead a nomadic life with no ties then that was okay, because he was *free* to do that. And if he wanted to walk with me and attempt to progress our relationship then that was okay too. And while we were together, he was *free* at any time to say he had changed his mind and needed to go it alone or that I wasn't the one for him. But I was adamant I was not going to become stuck in the middle, as he oscillated between the two scenarios.

I was not going to just wave him off again without a challenge, whatever the rights or wrongs of the dispute were.

Day one: silence; no telephone ringing, no texts, no doorbell and no more listening to his voice.

I missed him as I skulked on my veranda. I missed him as I sweated on the gym treadmill, hoping to clear my mind.

This was a defining moment for another reason. I was aware that, from the minute I had started to support John, if he'd disappeared off my radar and his regular contact with me had changed, I would have made tremendous efforts to locate him and ensure he was safe and well, that he was not suicidal and alone. At some level, I had been saving him. I would step in, rush to his side and attempt to make everything in his world okay again. I was aware I had been playing out this role and had consciously allowed myself to – he'd needed support and I had been prepared to give it. But over time I knew this would have to change, and so although I gave it freely, there was always going to come a time when I had to draw a line under the dynamic that existed between us, and for me that time had arrived. One week of skiing had brought us to a junction in our road.

I missed him, but I resisted the temptation to call and make sure he was okay. I had to see if he would come to me instead, to show he was concerned about my welfare and prepared to put my needs before his.

Day two: silence; no telephone ringing, no texts, no doorbell and no more listening to his voice.

I began to imagine him in his bed-and-breakfast room, alone, grief-stricken and spiralling dangerously downwards. My unhealthy needy bones were poised to rush forward and retrieve him from his bleak world, waiting for the worn door of years gone by to open and free them to do their task. *Save him, save him,* they sang seductively.

The skiing holiday was now a distant memory.

I missed him, but I sank my feet deeper and looked towards myself, not him.

I missed him, but resisted the temptation to call to see if he was surviving.

Day three: silence; no telephone ringing, no texts, no doorbell and no more listening to his voice. His silence was booming.

I missed him as the desperate image of his forlorn figure in my imagination became more isolated with every passing silent second: curled up, mute and without hope. I pictured him in the depths of his black hole, alone and unable to face his day, an image of my own creation, but the more powerful for it. Who would run to his aid if not *me*?

The worn doors of my needy bones were now opening. I slowly breathed in the heady anticipation of my imminent rescue of him as it floated towards me, knowing the delectable high it would bring.

I missed him, but resisted the temptation to call to see if he was still breathing. My hands twitched as they hovered over the phone.

Resolute and stubborn, I sat on my peaceful veranda drinking coffee, waiting.

I looked towards myself, not him.

Day four: my phone was ringing, his name was flashing from the screen, and once more I was listening to his voice.

'Are you okay?' he asked tentatively.

'No, not really.' I answered dejectedly. I was depleted after three days of my own mind games.

'I don't want to be in this space with you, Jill. I care about you too much and it's not how we are together. Can we talk about this if I come over?'

'Yes, we can talk, but Alexander is here, so we'll have to meet somewhere else. How about your car?'

Ten minutes later I was sitting in his front seat, his car stationary in a small car park around the corner from my home.

'Can I hug you?' he asked

I nodded and leant forward as he wrapped his arms around me in the confined space and held me for a few minutes in the quiet, whispering in my ear, 'I want to be here with you, don't you understand that?'

I pulled away and looked at him.

'I'm feeling weary with it all if I'm honest. You *are* free to go off and lead some nomadic life if that's what you want, but

I can't get caught up in the middle of you doing that when you're telling me you want to stay put too.'

'You're not in the middle of anything. I've thought about what you said, and I'll accept you're right in that I *am* struggling since I came back. I'm finding it hard to be in one fixed place. But it's only been seven days. I just think I need time to get used to this very different life I've returned to. Maybe I booked the skiing holiday earlier than I might have because of that, to give myself some space to adjust. But I'd always planned to go at some stage. I see it as a last holiday before I come back and rent somewhere. But I'm not aware that I'm running from anything.'

'But that's the point, isn't it – it's not a conscious decision. It's something that operates at a deeper level and I needed to raise that, in view of you leaving the country again so quickly.'

'I'll cancel the holiday rather than upset you, and I've said I'll start looking for a counsellor.'

'I don't need you to cancel the holiday. What I needed was to talk about how this was making me feel. You owe me nothing other than being honest about which path you're on.'

'I'm on the same one as you right now, believe it or not.'

'There's another thing too.'

'Give it to me,' he said, laughing. 'Come on, I've got broad shoulders. What is it?'

'That during the last three days it was very important to me that for once I wasn't chasing after you, making everything right for you, with my needs not considered at all – by you or by me. It's always me that puts it all back together, and it's exhausting to be on constant alert about how you are, when my welfare doesn't seem to feature. You can't say that's not a truth.'

'I know you've been a huge strength to me and I'm going to start returning that, trust me. I do think of you, all the time.'

'I'm not talking about all your generous gifts and holidays, I'm talking about something more subtle than that – the dynamic between us, how much support I give you and how that isn't balanced yet. It's got to start shifting to a healthier middle ground. I can't be that person to you forever. Do you understand what I'm trying to say?'

'Yes, and I know in the past I've not been good, but I telephoned today, didn't I? I know it took me three days, but I did call eventually. I'm trying. I don't want to lose you. I just need some time to find my feet, okay?'

'Yes, okay.'

'Are we good?'

'Yes, we're good. So, how have you been for the last three days?'

'Well, I've kept myself busy with a few games of golf.'

Golf! This was not the desperate image I'd had.

'Oh, charming. I see how it is,' I chided, jokingly. 'Let me get this right – while I've been worried sick about how you are, you've been trundling around a golf course?'

He swiftly brushed aside such a suggestion. 'No way was it like that. It was a release. I needed to get out of the bed-and-breakfast room before I went mad. I was missing you terribly and it was my way of filling the space, but I wanted to talk to you every day. I was just being stubborn.'

'Have a great week skiing.' I placed my hand on the side of his face. 'And take care.'

'I'll be back before you know it,' he said, winking at me as he drove off.

After three days of silence he had emerged, reaching out to me and placing my needs before his own.

I had to see him do it.

I had to see that he was capable of doing it.

I could no longer be the only strength.

The ground beneath us had shifted ever so slightly in my direction.

One week later he returned, and one week after that he had secured a twelve-month rental agreement on a second-floor flat in the nearby village of Hersham. Like my house, it also overlooked a river, with the added beauty of a huge willow tree standing in the surrounding neatly landscaped gardens, and with a little balcony leading off from his living room. He couldn't have hoped for a more serene and peaceful perspective.

In keeping with his promise he was now trying to find a local counsellor.

'You have to want to do this, otherwise it's a pretty point-less venture.'

'Well, I can't say I'm a convert just yet, particularly after my last experience. If you were to ask me what level of belief I had in it as a process, I'd say it's at about ten per cent right now.'

'Ten per cent. What's the point in going, then?'

'Because I'm open to trying it again and because it's important to you – to show you I'm not running away from it all.'

'Okay. Well, I think I may have found the right person for you. There's just one catch.'

'What's that, then?'

'He lives three hundred miles away in the Lake District.'

'Three hundred miles?' he shrieked, incredulous.

'Yes. But I understand from my mum that he's worth every mile to get to.'

'How does she know him?'

'Via her own work as a counsellor. She speaks very highly of him and wouldn't be recommending such a long journey if she didn't think he was worth it.'

'A six-hundred-mile round trip in one day might be a bit much.'

'Well, it'll certainly test your ten per cent commitment,' I laughed. 'You could always stay overnight locally, or with your family, to split the journey.'

'No, if I'm going to go through this, I want to have the space to do it alone, and I won't want to make it a two-day event either.'

'Would you like his number so you can call him?'

'Yes. That'd be great.'

'I'll speak to my mum later. One other thing.'

'What's that?'

'He's called Ray.'

CHAPTER 23

It was a few short weeks later that John found himself in the Lake District, walking down garden steps that led to the glass-panelled back door of a terraced house. It was some ten months after his wife and sons had died. He said later that as he was considering his ambivalent and sceptical position on the merits of counselling, the door had suddenly been opened by a white male who he'd thought was in his early sixties.

The man was about five feet eight inches tall, with short, fine, dark hair and dressed in dark trousers and an open-necked pale-blue shirt.

'Ah, you must be John,' he'd said. 'I'm Ray,' and he'd put his arm out to shake hands.

John was led down a narrow hall and into a small, simply furnished, understated square room; a fawn two-seater sofa sat against one wall with an armchair opposite, and a small, oblong, wooden coffee table was positioned between the two, not directly in between, but to one side and within reach of both the chair and the sofa. A full jug of water and a box of tissues sat on top. Behind the chair was a floor-to-ceiling bookcase filled with what John described as 'spiritual' books, and the walls were adorned with scenic paintings, all apparently by Ray.

It was days later and, unprompted, John was sharing with me his first few moments in the counselling room.

'So how are you?' Ray had asked, after a few administrative matters had been sorted.

'Oh, I'm good. Coping well I think, so yes, I'm fine, thank you,' John had asserted.

There'd been a pause as Ray had steadied his gaze and studied him, before responding slowly and with deliberation.

'That's a very long journey to have travelled to tell me you're fine.'

Oh, the subtleties of counselling.

It was the beginning of a seventeen-month process, one in which Ray slowly seeped into not only John's life, but also mine – counselling doesn't always stop at the counsellor's door; its silent reach cascaded beyond the counselled.

Two weeks later John was talking, unprompted again, having returned from his second session a few days earlier.

'He doesn't say much, you know. A whole ninety minutes and he barely talks.'

'He's not supposed to,' I teased. 'You're paying him to listen to you. It's a good sign.'

'I know, but even so, I thought he might have a bit more to

say. He's very quiet. A bit unnerving if I'm honest, as he sits looking back at me with those steady eyes of his.'

'I'm all ears if you want to elaborate.'

'I thought you weren't supposed to ask me about what went on – you know, start digging.'

'You started talking about him, not me, and I'm not about to ask you the detail of what you spoke about. It's written in the counselling bible somewhere I'm sure – your sessions are sacrosanct and between only you and Ray. I understand that.'

'You can't help yourself,' he began laughing. 'It's an impossibility for you not to be inquisitive. It's who you are.'

'Very funny. But on this issue, you don't have to tell me the boundaries. Honestly, I know where my place is. If you want to share it then that's your decision, but I won't come looking. As for Ray – well now, that's different, so if you want to tell me more about him ...'

'Only that when he does speak, it's gently, and very slow ... and with conviction ... and this all just seems to magnify the meaning of his actual words. Less is certainly more with Ray.' He paused for a few seconds. 'I mean, you could learn a lot from him.'

His observation had clearly tickled him as he chuckled away to himself.

I laughed knowingly. I was a failed work in progress.

'There's something very still and peaceful about him too. I swear he doesn't move at all the whole time I'm in there. For a small man his presence fills the room and feels very powerful.'

'He sounds intriguing.'

'Yep, there's something about him. I can't quite put my finger on it, but I like him a lot.'

'I couldn't be happier for you, particularly after the other lady you went to. It really is key to the whole thing working.'

'Well, it's a start, so we'll see.'

'I'm fascinated by your description – you know, sitting opposite you, all knowing, nodding occasionally, offering few words.' I laughed. 'From now on I'm going to call him 'The Wise Man Of The North.'

'You daft thing. Why do you want to call him that?'

'Oh, just a hunch. I feel his presence and his silence already and I haven't even met him. Maybe you brought him back with you – you know, his energy.'

'You and your funny talk,' he mocked. 'No, I can categorically say he's three hundred miles away, tucked up in the wilds of the Lake District.'

Hmm. I wasn't so sure about that.

I watched from my living room balcony, the early summer sun brushing softly against my face as John's red car drove from the front forecourt below and disappeared from view. He'd just collected Alexander to take him on a ride in a canoe he'd recently purchased so he could take himself down the River Wey that ran along, and was accessed via, the rear gardens of his flat. It was another place of solitude, the need for which today he'd put to one side as he continued to reach out to my son and strengthen their friendship. Alexander's shoulder injury had healed, the ice hockey season was on its summer break and his exams were over: he couldn't have been keener.

'Are you sure it's big enough,' I'd asked doubtfully. 'I

know he's slender but he's six feet and still growing. Is there room for his legs? I don't imagine it takes too much for those things to topple over.'

They stood in front of me howling with laughter, sweetly disdainful of my efforts to explore the safety aspects of such an outing.

'Mum, don't be ridiculous, of course there's room,' Alexander had said, raising his eyes to the ceiling in exasperation. 'I'm almost sixteen. I can take care of myself, so stop worrying.'

John, much to Alexander's delight, added his own amusing observation. 'It's only the River Wey we're going on – not an Atlantic crossing.'

We all erupted in laughter.

Another two weeks passed, and another few days after returning from Ray, John was talking, unprompted again.

'What's strange is that the journey up of four hours feels so much longer. I play my music very loud and try to enjoy that – I even sing sometimes – but those three hundred miles seem like the whole six hundred. But when I'm driving back, I'm home before I realise I've set off. I don't play any music because I need to be alone with my thoughts, but it feels like I'm on autopilot and haven't driven at all. Very odd, and a complete blur.'

'I'm sure that's something to do with the distressed state you're in when you're returning home. Very distracted, I would think. Promise me you'll stop halfway and stay overnight somewhere if you're feeling tired.'

'I'll be okay. Don't worry.'

'I do worry. I don't want you falling asleep at the wheel exhausted with the emotion of it all.'

'You know what's really surprised me? I'm not a man who opens up easily and I'm in the company of a man I barely know, but after only three sessions I can sit in front of Ray and cry buckets, while he sits quietly opposite. In that room, with him, I can let it all go. I don't recognise myself sometimes.'

A pattern emerged; every two weeks he would return from his visit to Ray and disappear off the radar to be alone. His sessions, he said, engulfed him with renewed pain and were emotionally exhausting.

'I'm sorry I don't call straight after I get back, but the only thing I want to do is collapse in bed and sleep, and boy, the hours I sleep after seeing him. Anything between twelve and sixteen. Crazy stuff. My body feels so leaden I can hardly move. I don't think I've ever felt tiredness like it, or a sleep that's so heavy.

'I understand. I just want to know you're back safely, and the text you send is enough for that.'

'I need to be alone too. It's not about you. I just need to be in a space away from the world.'

I would watch him bounce back from his visits and naturally look for signs of change, not external ones but the small nuances that would suggest he was veering in a different direction.

But for the first few months at least, by the time he'd driven the return journey and hibernated for twenty-four hours, he was back to the John I knew, making a huge effort to face each day with a smile and to conceal whatever emotions he was experiencing.

It was reassuring to slowly watch him, with every passing visit, build a strong relationship with Ray, becoming further entrenched in the process and wholly committed to the long journey north.

'How are you finding the journey – are you okay doing it for a few more months?' I asked, after another two sessions had passed.

'It's crippling, and if it was every week I couldn't do it, but every two weeks I can just about manage. Your mum's right, though – I think he's worth it. I'm clearly not the expert in counselling, but whatever it is about him, I can walk into his room and can talk about every aspect of my life and feel comfortable doing it. For someone like me, that's quite something.'

I was conflicted. I wanted him to go to counselling and I wanted him to have this support, but I was now sharing him with a welcome, but invisible, visitor. I was not his only confidante any more, and the previous private intimacy of our lives together, and as lovers, felt intruded upon. I knew that although John had left the small room in the north, it had not left him. I suspected Ray had followed him down, and it was now the three of us, The Wise Man Of The North gathering greater importance with every visit, and with every compliment John vocalised on his return, his invisible image became insidiously larger in my overactive mind.

'He's one of those people that you probably wouldn't see in a crowded room,' John observed one day, 'because he's small physically, very understated and low key. But he's the sort who wouldn't have missed a trick with anyone else.'

'What, he'd be sitting in a corner somewhere?' I laughed.

'Yes, sitting very still and watching peacefully while none of us realised. I like that about him, and I genuinely look forward to seeing him. What's six hundred miles to sit with a man like Ray?'

I was becoming invisible myself, I thought wryly. The larger Ray became, the smaller I shrank. *You've only got yourself to blame*, I said to myself, *you pushed him up the M6.*

'Crikey, aren't you the sudden convert. A disciple in our midst! I knew you'd eventually see the light,' I joked.

'Steady, I wouldn't go that far. I'm just saying that Ray and I rub along very well, and your name for him – you know, The Wise Man Of The North thing – I've got to admit, he does come across a bit like that. One of these days I may be tempted to tell him the nickname you've given him.'

This small room in the north and the man who sat in it became a welcome and surprise sanctuary away from the world for John; this stranger who, within three sessions, John had become connected to and who elicited the most private and deeply felt feelings from him. His shattered life sat in pieces between them – pieces that Ray would help him to put back together.

The question was, while he did so, would the gentle waves of progress create cracks in my own foundations?

~

John's wasn't the only world shifting; mine was too. It was summer 2011 and time for another move. The town house with the balcony and river view was beautiful, but after two years I decided it was both too big and too expensive. We had thoroughly enjoyed living there but it was time for a different vista. I didn't feel compelled to buy another house, despite various people suggesting I should get myself back on the property ladder. I was thoroughly enjoying the feeling of freedom that this new style of living gave me. Just as importantly, if not more so, my son, now sixteen, was too. The world was our oyster … well, provided that oyster was within reach of his school.

As if by magic a top-floor flat in a two-storey building became free to rent in the same town. Within twenty-four hours of deciding it was time to move, I had viewed it with Alexander and agreed a one-year rental. It was modern, bright and open-plan, with another balcony, this time overlooking the River Thames. With a canoe club situated on the nearby banks and a busy bistro pub next door, it was another space in which to watch life go by while soaking up a river view and contemplating our own lives.

How incredibly fortunate we were to have stumbled on such a find; we were delighted. 'One of these days,' I said to Alexander, 'I quite fancy living on a boat. Maybe that could be our next step?'

'I'm not so sure about that one,' he answered dubiously.

Wherever we were going, the thrill of the impermanence of our situation remained. Here today, who knows where tomorrow. We were on another exciting adventure.

As I settled into our new home it occurred to me that the fluid and potentially changing circumstances that existed between me and John seemed to enhance our appreciation of each other's company rather than create an environment of unease. Perhaps, too, it was the novelty of our new relationship. We would regularly return to the local pub we had gone to the night before he had left for his travels, and enjoy romantic dinners out, walks in the Surrey countryside and the usual cinema and theatre forays. We also began to spread our wings in the company of my friends, and John spread his to join a golf club, where he began to build friendships of his own in the area.

Although we did not define our future, taking each day as it came, my probing nature threw up a subject that, as time progressed, I felt able to broach and which challenged the live-in-the-moment path we were on: could John ever contemplate having children again?

It was something I was keen to discuss honestly. It might not have been staring John in the face, but it certainly was me.

'Can I ask you something,' I said one afternoon, as we were curled up on the sofa reading the Sunday papers, my prying and serious tone immediately putting him on alert.

'That sounds ominous,' he jested.

'I know it's only been a year since you lost your boys, but do you think you'll ever want children again? I know another child could never replace Felix and Oscar, but I just wondered how you felt about the whole thing?'

He took a few minutes to answer downheartedly. 'I had

two gorgeous sons and being a dad was the best role in my life, one I miss every second of every day. But right now I don't see that happening.'

'I understand, but you loved being a dad so much it would seem very sad that you couldn't experience that in your life again.'

'Do you want more children?'

'I used to, when Alexander was much younger, but I didn't meet anyone I wanted to have a child with and now time's passed me by.'

'Is that why you're asking me, though?'

'No, not at all. If I'm honest, I think that in time you may come to a point when you *do* want another family. Who knows how you'll feel in a few years and, if we're still together, I'll be too old. I'm on the wrong side of forty already, and I don't know if I want another child at my age, even if it were possible.'

'I've had my time as a dad, Jill, so it's never going to be an issue. But if somewhere in the future I change my mind, which is highly unlikely, I wouldn't want them with anyone but you.'

'But if you ever did want more and I couldn't have them or didn't want them ... it's too important an issue. I just want you to know that I wouldn't stand in the way of you meeting someone younger who you could have that future with.'

'Don't say things like that. If it wasn't for you I wouldn't be with anyone right now, so I'm not about to go off in the hope of meeting someone younger. I'm not on the market for any such thing.'

'It's early days, John.'

'It's possible my view may change, but what won't change is that it could only ever be with you.'

Another session with Ray passed, and John emerged again. For the most part the detail of his sessions remained private. I didn't ask what they had spoken about and he didn't choose to disclose, and so when he did decide to share some aspects it was all the more surprising.

'Ray's asked me to write about my family,' he dropped into a conversation casually.

'Oh, right! Why's that?'

'Well, I've talked quite a bit with him about how distressing it is to me that I can't look back at all the memories of my family with any happiness, even now, over a year after they died. So he's given me some homework – I've got to write about them all separately, and when I next see him he wants me to read what I've written.'

'That's a big ask. Will you be able to do it?'

'I know, but yes, I'm going to give it a go. I'll try anything that he thinks may help. He's also suggested I go for long walks on my own.'

'I can understand why that might help.'

'I was telling him how I would walk for nine hours a day at Yosemite and what a powerful experience it had been – you know, being so close to nature and how it had suddenly made life seem worth living. He thinks I should try and do this regularly. That's why I went off all day walking on the one-year anniversary.'

He had disappeared some weeks earlier, on 30 June 2011, removing himself from everyone for twenty-four hours. He'd gone walking in local woods, completely alone with his family.

When he returned, he'd called me.

'They're disappearing, Jill. Their voices are slowly disappearing, along with how they smelt and how it was to cuddle them.'

I sat quietly listening, the thought of not being able to recall the smell and hugs of my own son illuminated in his pain.

'With every passing day it becomes harder to hold onto them. I don't want to lose the memories, but looking back to try and keep hold of them is such a painful space ...'

'You have the DVDs of them though, don't you, which you said you get huge comfort from watching?' I said, trying to sound positive.

'Yes, I have, but only two. They're mainly of Felix on a couple of his birthdays, two Christmas days with us all, Felix and Oscar in the back garden of our previous home and some of a holiday in Center Parcs. I can listen to their voices when I'm watching them, but outside of that it all just fades.'

'They're something to hold onto, though – at least you have them. You can see them playing and having fun, and Heather during her favourite time of the year.'

'It's the best I have, and seeing them alive and moving makes them very real and makes me feel as though it wasn't all a dream.'

Two inconspicuous, plastic, mid-blue DVD cases, but holding a beautifully framed small window through which he could replay snapshots of a previous life – a life that had taken on imaginary proportions. He could place his hand through this precious window and gently caress his family. But that caress came at a price: seeing them but not being seen, hearing them but not being heard, pain glistening on the glass as he looked through.

Closing my eyes, I dared to imagine, for the briefest of moments, walking in his shoes, into his darkness. I dared to imagine, for the briefest of moments, the cruel reality of two DVDs being the only window to my son; I dared to feel, for the briefest of moments, how he must feel, if it were even possible.

I could feel my anger rising.

If I were him, I'd be raging against the world.

If I were him, I'd find no comfort from old footage of my son, a son I couldn't smell any more, hug any more, touch any more … a son I could only see through a glistening prism of incalculable pain.

Who was I to suggest they were something to hold onto, however well-intentioned that suggestion may be? Who was I to suggest they had a value that would somehow appease his pain?

CHAPTER 24

He was packing his bags again, only this time I was packing mine with him. It was August 2011 and we were going for a one-week stay in a hotel on the edge of Lake Garda. It was six months after John's return from his travels and my son was away at a summer camp, so we had decided to seize the moment and escape together. Italy was our chosen destination, the country where we had shared our first kiss and, despite the fact that we were heading to a different location from that of our childhood skiing trip, it felt good to be returning together after all these years.

After a seamless breeze through the arrivals terminal, and after the requisite Italian stamp in our passports had been secured, we were driven by taxi to the hotel. It was a twenty-minute journey along high, winding, coastal roads and as we slowly descended, magnificent views of the lake below emerged through the open car windows. Before us lay a stunning and endless expanse of calm, sun-stroked water, glistening in the afternoon heat and surrounded by small hotels sitting closely side by side, their pastel paintwork, in soft pinks, blues and yellows, circling the lake like a vibrant rainbow and adding to the simple beauty of it all. Eventually we came to a standstill on a cobbled lake-edge path outside our hotel. A gentle bobbing sound from elegant boats with their tall masts, lined up along the water's edge, filtered into the car.

Moments later, and I was standing on yet another balcony looking out onto yet another waterside view. Balconies and water were becoming something of a theme in my life, but to suddenly find myself on a different one and in a different country was something of a welcome surprise. This was the smallest of all the balconies I'd had the good fortune to sit on but, boy, it had the biggest of waterside views. Lake Garda was literally a hop, skip and a jump away, a mere narrow, cobbled path lay below and between us; the water was tantalisingly close. As I looked in awe at the vision before me it was as though I was looking through a magnifying glass, and I felt myself and the balcony shrink to minute proportions, while the lake seemed to rise and move towards me, its vastness a giant, shimmering wall. Nature was yet again revealing its power and ability to seduce. I was mesmerised.

'Wow,' said John, squeezing my hand as he stood next to me. 'This is breathtaking.'

I turned towards him and beamed. 'Oh my goodness, how lucky are we to be here in such a beautiful, idyllic place. I feel quite overcome.'

He looked at me intently before kissing me softly on my lips. 'I love you, Jill – every sweet thing about you. We couldn't be in a more romantic place and it makes me want to tell you a thousand times that I do. You know I love you deeply, don't you?'

I smiled coquettishly. 'I love you too,' I said, squeezing his bottom playfully.

He laughed, pulling me through the large, open, ornate glass doors to the double bed only a metre or so away. It filled the small room and, lying on top of me as we fell onto its firm mattress, he stroked my hair tenderly.

'We're back, after over thirty years. We're back in the country where it all started and it all feels very special – just you and me and seven blissful, romantic days,' he said.

My emotions, however, had other ideas.

Three days later I sat sobbing uncontrollably on the closed toilet seat of our en-suite bathroom as a torrent of distress unleashed itself, raging unchecked through my body for a full twenty, soulful minutes.

Was it the comforting blanket of sun that had wrapped me up each day, quietly stroking my physical and emotional well-being?

Was it walking through a cocoon of gentleness: the hypnotic lake, the clear blue sky, John's loving embraces?

Was it the invisible and reassuringly protective arm of Ray telling me I could let go of the reins, that he now held them tightly. An unconscious act of transferral, perhaps?

Was it John's emerging emotional strength?

I didn't know – it had left me no time for thought. Whatever it was, the deeper recesses of my mind had awoken from their sleep and decided it was safe enough to rise up and demand a hearing.

Fourteen months of supporting and bearing close witness to the devastating consequences of John's loss had finally caught up with me, my emotions choosing this tranquil nirvana in which to burst the dam walls that had contained them, gushing forth and releasing the pressure of their previous confinement, in full, thunderous glory.

'What's wrong? Please tell me what's wrong?' he asked in desperation as he knelt on the floor in front of me, searching my tear-sodden face for some clue.

Struggling to breathe, I cleansed myself of it all as tears rolled down my cheeks, soaking my hands and dropping onto the bathroom floor. Choking and spluttering, Heather, Felix and Oscar finally broke free from my body as I crumbled in front of him and threw out rambling words that caught at the back of my throat.

'No more ... *enough* ...'

'No more what?'

'*Pain*. Absorbing ... your pain,' I sobbed.

'I don't understand,' he said in an increasingly worried tone.

'It's too much. Heather, Felix, Oscar ... how they died ... Lego coffins ... empty trampolines. Fourteen months ... absorbing all your pain ...'

'I'm sorry, I'm so sorry. I didn't realise—'

'I can't do this any more ... feel *buried*.'

'Jill, calm down, try to calm down. I'm listening,' he said, rubbing the side of my arm and anxiously pulling reams of toilet roll from the holder, scrunching it in a huge mound and placing it on my lap. 'Here. Here, have some tissues for your nose.'

'Are they out of the compartment? Are they in the compartment? Just *who* is out of the compartment? Constantly, constantly worrying if, if ... *you're* okay. Constantly worrying if I'm *saving* you or *supporting* you ... it's too, too much. Then Yosemite ... oh my goodness.'

I placed my hand to my mouth as my chest heaved with the recollection.

'Do you *know* how it made me feel? To think of you ... on that precipice ... *suicide*! I soaked *all* that up, like ... some huge porous sponge, and I'm *sat, sat* ...' I struggled to form this simple word, the one that singularly defined how I felt. The one I could have placed above my head on a placard while I sat silently below, the graceful curves of its letters beautifully depicting my drowning image.

'Sat, *saturated* ...' I finally spat out, 'just *saturated* with your grief.'

I could barely catch my breath, my mind exploding with the images that were rapidly descending, fighting for prominence: burnt houses, dalek coffins, mini towers of death, black holes, black hearts, silence, worry, silence, worry, his pain-ridden, disturbed face as grief strangled him, listening to his voice, again and again and again.

Listening to his tortured voice.

And now my own.

'Please. *Please* ... I need space. Just don't touch me,' I said, pushing his arm from me.

'Jill, I'm trying to comfort you. Please, come to the bed. I don't understand what's brought this on. We're in this beautiful place, having such a wonderful time.'

'It's not here. It's *inside* me. They're not my family, John, but I feel them … *all* the time … the tragedy of their lives … so, so *young*. I'm human, and every day I look at you and, and …'

'And what, Jill, and what?'

'I *see* them. I see them looking back, standing next to you, their lost lives just … etched in you, your face … leaking from your pores.'

He watched, wide-eyed, making no further attempt to intervene as I continued, my streaming nose now bringing a deeper, nasal tone to my words. I didn't care what I looked like, I didn't care what I sounded like.

'Every time I look at Alexander … I see them, John – the men your sons will never become. Every milestone he makes is one they won't. I *feel* that as you stand next to him … it *shrieks* back at me. How, *how* could it not? And then, oh boy … people asking if you have children, worrying about your reaction, their reaction … *everything*, just everything. *Anything* to do with fire – should I turn television over if … if fire comes on … like treading on eggshells. I'm *exhausted*. I'm so tired, so very tired of it all … I'm sorry, but I am. I'm *full* to the brim and I can't take any more. I just can't take *any more*.'

I was done. A metaphorical vomiting of my emotions straight into his stunned lap, leaving behind my fragile, drained form, immediately weakened from my purge.

I looked up slowly and held his gaze, his concerned blue-green eyes filled with tears at my graphic breakdown.

'Are you done?' he asked cautiously and so quietly I could barely hear him as tears began to roll down his cheeks.

I nodded.

He slowly leant in, wrapping his arms around me tightly and burying his face in my neck.

'I'm sorry, I really am,' he said, softly. 'I love you, Jill. I don't want to hurt you. I don't want to lose you.'

'I love you too,' I whispered in his ear, 'but—'

'I know, I know ... from now on things will change.'

As we lay spooning on the bed, his body protectively wrapped around me and facing the open balcony doors, an internal peace seemed to descend, bringing with it an exquisite sense of calm. As it rested on my weary form, I felt overcome with relief.

The ground beneath us had shifted again. Was it seismic fault lines I could see emerging, or mere tiny and inconsequential cracks that could be navigated without permanent damage?

I didn't know, and for once my mind was empty, resolutely refusing to open its door.

Breathing softly, I fell asleep to the sound of Italian voices from outside, floating through the balcony doors.

I woke the next morning as he emerged from the bathroom, his boundless energy catapulting us forward from the previous day's distress and filling the room.

'Come on, lazy bones, it's a gorgeous day and we've got lots to do. I fancy a boat ride to a different port. How about it?'

And so the rest of our week continued.

'Let's go on the cable car and have lunch at the top of the mountain.'

'Shall we go swimming in the lake and sunbathe?'

'I fancy going to that bar that's got a live jazz band on tonight, what about it?'

He was John at his best – wonderfully infectious, light-hearted and fun. I couldn't fail to be lifted from my earlier distress.

No talk of death, no talk of grief, no talk of Heather, Felix or Oscar. I didn't have the emotional strength to revisit my outburst, and crucially, without saying a word, he made it quite clear we weren't going to.

Food was our new emotional outlet: cold, sweet Knicker-bocker Glories eaten at a lakeside cafe, a favourite in the searing heat; authentic Italian pizzas and pastas at a variety of different restaurants in the evenings, all of which were buzzing with other tourists; sizzling steaks; early evening glasses of chilled white wine, enjoyed as the sun set and the world went by; sumptuous olives, oils and breads. And, best of all, a mouth-watering selection of cakes – which John convincingly sold as breakfast – enjoyed each morning with delicious fresh coffee as we sat in the early sun under the shade of a local cafe canopy.

And then our final night was upon us and the food of our final meal was before us. I looked down at my chosen risotto as it was placed by the waiter on the table in front of me. It was grey, distinctly unappealing and shared none of the obvious joys of my previous feasts. Slowly, I looked across at John's sumptuous bowl of cannelloni, lightly scattered with melting parmesan cheese, and our eyes met, my face unsuccessfully hiding my disappointment.

'Do you not fancy it?' he asked as he was about to take his first mouthful.

I grimaced silently, as I decided whether I would eat my own.

He put his cutlery, loaded with food, back down on his plate.

'Would you like mine instead?'

'I'd feel awful,' I answered unconvincingly.

'Really – I don't mind.'

I looked across at him and steadied my gaze. A moment's silence passed between us before I continued.

'Well, after the last few months it's the least you owe me, I suppose,' I said, winking affectionately as I lifted my plate of risotto and handed it to him.

He smiled a huge knowing smile and handed me his plate. 'Yes, it's the least I owe you – so enjoy.'

No talk of death, no talk of grief, no talk of Heather, Felix or Oscar.

Just one plain risotto conveying all that needed to be said.

We returned home. We were different. In my mind, I had cut John's ties to the life raft of Jill, symbolically setting him free. For all my relief, I had been shocked at the unexpected arrival and strength of my own feelings, but I had to listen to my own voice, to nurture the impact of providing prolonged support to John, and place a new, closer, protective boundary around myself, actively resisting my natural desire to enquire and probe and dig deeper while The Wise Man Of The North took full control.

It was a separation of sorts, essential for us both to clear the road ahead and have some chance of seeing clearly. I had broken free, and John, chastened by my outburst, began to actively steer a course to Ray in an effort to shield me.

I sat back and reflected. I was forty-six, and the therapist's chair was now worn from the seat of my own pain and confusion. But I had, during the last fourteen months, reached the end of my own road: the one marked 'saviour'.

CHAPTER 25

Celebrations filled our home with the sound of Alexander bursting through the front door and shrieking with joy that he'd passed all twelve of his GCSEs. His face beamed with his success and his vibrant energy filled the hall.

'Congratulations, you clever thing, I knew you could do it,' I shrieked back in excitement, opening my arms wide to embrace him.

'I couldn't have done it without you, Mum, all your huge support. I know I wasn't easy sometimes,' he said as he engulfed me, squeezing me tight.

My eyes welled up with his kind words and acknowledgement.

'What's wrong?' he asked as I pulled away and he saw my distress.

'I'm just completely overwhelmed with pride … you deserve them all. You worked so hard. They're happy tears,' I joked.

'You big softy,' he said, warmly.

'As for you not being easy sometimes … that's a bit of an understatement,' I laughed. 'Wow, twelve! How does that feel?'

'Awesome … and a massive relief.'

'You've just put a brilliant platform under your feet. Honestly, it's the best start you could have given yourself. We've got to go out and celebrate. Shall we see if John fancies going for a meal with us – your choice?'

'Sounds great. I can't wait to see his face when I tell him I got an A in Religious Education!' he said, mischievously.

As he reached his bedroom door he turned and, looking towards me with a big grin, added light-heartedly, 'While you're calling him, I'll just add up what you owe me.'

'Ah, you're calling in my debt already. You're going to clean me out, so dinner's definitely on you tonight!'

'I'm joking,' he said. 'I don't expect you to pay. I studied to pass them for myself, and for you.'

'No, that was the deal, so enjoy it when you get it.'

He came back to me, giving me another hug.

'I know I'm very lucky to have a mum like you.'

'I know you are,' I said, laughing.

As he walked away from me, my heart swelled as I looked on in admiration. He'd managed to do what I hadn't: to put the platform of exam success under his young feet, a strong platform to spring from, to open doors and to fill him with crucial confidence as he stepped out into the world. My boy had done himself proud. My boy had done me proud too.

I breathed in the heady scent of his success, the mist of my own regret still circling.

Meltdowns were clearly in season. A few weeks after our return and with one outburst already addressed, another voice decided the platform was free for a showdown and wanted to be heard, and boy, did it shout and scream. Only this time, it was John.

The gentle, kind man I knew was standing in my living room taking centre stage. Like a dormant volcano awakening from years of slumber, his red-hot lava gushed out, fury oozing from his every pore, his eyes, his nostrils and most of all his mouth, filling the room to explosive capacity as he paced unnervingly backwards and forwards. Who was this man in front of me? I didn't recognise him. I'd never heard him swear before.

'Fuck the world, fuck the fucking world,' he screamed, his every word filled to the brim with searing pain.

Thank goodness Alexander wasn't at home.

What had provoked the ferocious beast from within to finally emerge? It was a beast I had expected to meet many months ago as he grieved the loss of his family and spat back at the world, but it had lain in silent wait for its own moment.

He had invested some of the money he had received following his family's deaths in shares and had unwittingly become a victim of a substantial 'boiler room' fraud. Not only had he lost his family, he had now lost *their* money, money he'd received because of *their* deaths.

As he raged uncontrollably in front of me, the John I had always known disappeared and was replaced by an intruder baying for blood. If he could only get his hands on the individual who had dared to inflict an injustice too far and brought further misery to his door …

'The fucker, the absolute fucker. What sort of person does something like that? What sort of fucking individual thinks it's okay to steal such a large amount of money?' he screamed.

I didn't get a chance to answer, but regardless, I didn't have an answer that was going to help.

'What fucking justice is there? What sort of fucking mad world is this? God?' he shouted at me, eyes wild. 'You ask me if I believe in a god. What sort of god does stuff like this? What sort of god wipes out my whole family? What sort of *fucking* god has my wife and sons trapped in a house fire? What sort of god thinks it's okay to deal me another shit card? God? There's no such fucking person. I tell you, if I could get my hands on the fucker who's stolen my money I swear I'd *kill* him. I've never felt rage like it. If I had a gun, I'd be hunting him out, if it's the last thing I did on this earth.'

As I watched him unravel before me, I became increasingly frightened. He was spiralling rapidly downwards, vengeance leading the way. His face was red with the anger-fuelled force of blood being pumped vigorously around his body as he failed to find the release he wanted – the someone, the some-thing, the *anything* he could punch repeatedly to exact his revenge. His contempt and hatred of the world he found himself in hung menacingly in the air around him.

I stepped in front of him before he combusted.

'John – enough. *Enough*,' I said, raising my voice in the hope of being heard. 'Whatever's happened doesn't justify you making such threats. I'm not going to listen to you talk like this – you're frightening me. Do you understand – *you are frightening me.* Please, calm down.'

It was enough to bring him back from his seething trance and return his awareness to the room he was standing in.

'I'm sorry, I don't want to frighten you, but—' he said, his voice still raised and gladiatorial.

'No, there're no "buts". Stop talking like that – guns, hunting people down – are you mad? I understand why you feel so angry, but *please*, no more crazy gun talk. You're getting out of control. Take a breath, sit down for a minute, let's talk.'

'I can't sit down, I *cannot* sit still right now. I'm sorry if I frightened you.' His voice had calmed slightly, but as he continued to pace back and forth it was clear he was far from done. 'I have to go out for some fresh air. I can't stay in here.'

'I understand, but promise me you're not going to do something foolish?'

'I'll be okay. I just need to take myself off and deal with it alone. I know you're trying to help, but now is not the time.'

Seconds later he was gone, leaving an immediate and disquieting silence.

During the following days, utterly exhausted with the sheer force of his own anger, he fell crashing to the ground. This criminal act had become a catalyst for his buried fury, which, once unleashed, had become a tornado destroying everything in its wake, leaving disaster behind. He was flattened, broken into a million pieces and at risk of being pushed over the edge, into oblivion and beyond reach. I felt redundant and unable to offer wise words of reason that would help him make sense of what had happened. I was struggling to comprehend it myself, and I felt out of my depth. He needed hands beyond his own or mine to guide him. Ray stepped in.

Within weeks, John was departing again, only this time not to some sunny overseas clime surrounded by Western indulgences but on another long drive north, heading to a retreat run by Buddhist monks.

We had previously talked about the possible benefits of such a thing, or spending time alone in a secluded environment somewhere, but John had made no concrete plans. It was a sign of his emotional fragility that during his next session with Ray he had asked him if he knew of such a place and immediately booked a week at a retreat in the Lake District that Ray had recommended.

Set in the countryside and with beautiful circular views, it was a place that would bring him back in touch with nature and hopefully bring him back in touch with himself, just as Yosemite had done. Within this peaceful environment he could detach from the world and others, and lose himself in his surroundings without speaking a word to anyone throughout his stay if he chose.

'I'll call to let you know I've arrived, but then you'll probably not hear from me again until I leave.'

'That's good. I don't want to, unless you really feel the need to talk. The whole point of something like this is that you detach from the world.'

'I have Ray to call on too. He's been very supportive and it's reassuring he's close by if I need to call him, or go and talk with him while I'm there.'

I was hugely relieved that Ray would only be a short distance away from him and contactable. In keeping with my resolve to take a step back following our return from Lake Garda, I was circling John helpfully rather than jumping in with both feet. Ray's continued presence ensured I could stay in this new and healthier role.

Six hours later John called.

'I'm here,' he said, 'standing in the room I'll be sleeping in. Boy, it's basic – one single bed with a thin blanket, one bedside table, one sink, and the door has no lock. You'd be having kittens with such lax security,' he chided.

I laughed in acknowledgement.

'Basic is good. No distractions, then, and in keeping with that I'm going to go. I want to leave you to it and give you the space you need.'

I put the phone down and breathed a sigh of relief.

I was listening to his voice. He had called for the briefest few minutes after three days.

'I just wanted to say I love you, and although I miss you, it feels right to be here.'

'I love you too. How's it going?'

'Good. On the first day I walked the garden and woodland of the whole grounds, which run along the coastline, and on the last two days I've taken myself out to different spots and walked for about eight hours around each. So, alone with nature and my thoughts. The solitude is a relief. I've become a vegetarian who eats small portions because everything here is done in small measure. I've done guided meditation for the first time ever, which I found rather strange. The senior monk leading the group lost me when he started telling me to imagine a light coming out of the head of some mythical figure. But, hey, I had a go and I'm trying.'

'Are there many there?'

'A few in the meditation group, but other than that I've barely seen anyone. I can hear the monks chanting at certain times of the day, but outside of that it's beautifully quiet.'

'You're okay though?'

'Yeah, it's doing me good. I'm going to have another session with Ray tomorrow, and then the next day I've decided to go to Center Parcs, which is not far from here. I had many happy holidays there with Heather, Felix and Oscar and I want to spend some time retracing all the things we did together. I just feel the need to go back.'

'Well, take it easy. I'm going to go now. I'm here if you need anything.'

I cut the call short deliberately, determined to stop myself becoming immersed. This was his retreat, not mine.

I put the phone down and breathed a sigh of relief.

I waited with growing irritation outside a large, isolated, detached property for my errant son to emerge from a party with his friends where he was celebrating passing his GCSEs. It was one o'clock in the morning and he was now thirty minutes later than we'd agreed. The house, set back approximately five metres from its high perimeter hedging and with a wide gravel drive to the right-hand side, was positioned on an unmade road opposite a field. Lights adorned the front, illuminating the dark night, the lack of street lighting intensifying their brightness.

Parking spaces were in demand as other parents arrived, slowly driving down the narrow road, headlights shining as they tried to position their vehicles in spaces that didn't exist. Thank goodness I'd managed to secure one just outside.

Repeated calls to his mobile had, unsurprisingly, gone to answerphone.

As music boomed from the rear garden and the sound of high revelry spewed into the night air, I silently remonstrated with him, replaying our earlier conversation.

'*Twelve thirty*?' he'd stated incredulously, like I was some sort of jailer. 'That's *so early* ...' and had laughed as he added, 'Just because you go to bed at ten doesn't mean everyone else does.'

'Less of the cheek, and it's still a no. That's late enough.'

Realising I was not going to be moved he'd wrapped his arm around me, bringing out his best charm offensive as he'd attempted to coerce me gently into accepting his preferred timings.

'*Go on*, it's to celebrate my GCSEs. Can't we make it one o'clock? His parents are there.'

'Ah, sweet talk won't change my mind. Twelve thirty is late enough.'

He'd looked to the ceiling, exasperated.

And so the negotiations had continued, and he became increasingly frustrated at the boundaries I was imposing. Next on the agenda had been what alcohol he could take, as he assured me *everyone* else was taking *at least* a couple, and there would only be soft drinks at the house.

'Only two beers – are you *joking*? It's a party.'

'Three, and that's my final offer, take it or leave it. You're sixteen, not eighteen.'

As I'd moved onto the subject of drugs, I'd morphed into the most *absurd* mother. Didn't I *trust him* not to take that route?

Just checking.

As I'd moved onto the subject of girls, I'd morphed into the most *embarrassing* mother.

Just checking.

'It's so unfair,' he'd eventually said. 'Just because you're in the police, why should I suffer?'

I'd laughed at his favourite assertion. 'It's nothing to do with my job. It's called being a parent. One of these days you'll look back and thank me for it.'

And so it had been decided, or apparently unnecessarily imposed – twelve thirty, and the consumption of three beers only. Who was I kidding.

As I watched him suddenly emerge from the house at one thirty in the morning, attempting to focus on his surroundings, it was abundantly clear, as he stood still and gently swayed from side to side, that additional alcohol had been consumed. He slowly walked towards my car and I watched in resigned amusement as he tried to approach in a straight line to mask his inebriation. Moments later, the passenger door opened and he burst in, larger than life and smelling like a brewery.

'*Hello*, Mum,' he said affectionately, his pronunciation slow as he did his failed best to sound sober. 'I'm … going to go … in the back. So I can lie down,' he continued as he pushed the passenger seat forward and crawled onto the rear seat. His groaning immediately filled the small space as the motion of the car began to make him feel nauseated.

'Can you *not* go so fast over those speed humps,' he pleaded eventually. 'They're making me feel worse.'

I put my foot on the accelerator. That'll teach him, I mused, as I wistfully recalled that sweet six-year-old boy, poking his little finger into the new au pair's leg and telling her 'You've got *big* legs.' Boy, times had changed.

I was listening to his voice. Another three days had passed. He was talking about his visit to Center Parcs, his voice fragile.

'I walked for three hours through the grounds, revisiting the three different chalets we stayed in together, the swimming pool, the high wire that Felix had loved and the restaurant we used to eat at. We'd always sit at the same table and it was free, so I went and sat in the same chair and closed my eyes. For the first time since they died I took myself back to all those happy times. I could feel them all around me, like they were alive at the table – all their laughter and excitement at being on holiday, all their love, the boys chatting away as we planned our days. I was so lucky to have shared all that with them, and as painful as it was to go back, it was a relief to have found a space in which I could do that, to be able to surround myself with them and smile and feel close.'

'Thanks,' I said gently, 'for sharing such a beautiful and private moment. I'm quite overcome. What a special place that must have been.' I paused, wanting the significance of what he had just said to be silently acknowledged before continuing.

'I'm going to go and leave you with your thoughts and with your family. Take it easy.'

I cut the call short deliberately, determined to stop myself becoming immersed.

I put the phone down and breathed a sigh of relief.

His family, in the vast hole that was their absence, had proved to be his saviour, reconnecting him with what was to be truly valued, and facilitating his emergence, restored, from his dark space once more. He knew that the return of his stolen shares or revenge would not bring him happiness; more importantly, he realised that what had happened held no power to take from him the love he'd shared with his wife and sons.

Uncomplicated, was how he described his retreat – and surprisingly comforting. Set against a backdrop of post-autumnal, crisp, mainly sunny days, and with no expectation of conversation with others and no one to listen to, the solitude had been a relief. His anger, which had started to dissipate prior to his arrival, dissolved further amidst such a peaceful and calm environment.

I was listening to his voice. He was back and had called, and he was recounting the only conversation he'd had within the retreat.

'I was sitting eating alone and one of the monks came over and asked to sit with me. He said he was one of the senior ones there and asked me why I'd come. I told him about my family and how I was trying to find some meaning in life after my loss. He said he'd been on a twenty-year path seeking enlightenment and had yet to find it.'

'Right.'

'That brief exchange with him made me see that I'm just a novice. My hope of finding some wise answers right now or in the immediate future is unrealistic. I may never find them.' He paused momentarily before continuing in a considered and peaceful tone. 'I've got such a long way to go, Jill. The rest of my life probably.'

I put the phone down and breathed a sigh of relief.

CHAPTER 26

I sat on my balcony wrapped up from the cold autumn air and quietly reflected.

The John I knew had returned, leaving his vengeful one-man mission against the world, against the 'fucker' who'd fleeced him and against a God he didn't believe in, on the floor of the Buddhist retreat, on the floor of a Center Parcs restaurant, and under the very table he'd previously sat at with his wife and sons – a table at which, for the first time since they'd died, he'd been able to look back on happier times, to sit still, feel and embrace their sweet presence.

The Jill I knew had returned, leaving her saturated sponge on the floor of an Italian bathroom, on the floor of John's own life.

As I looked across at the river, the morning sun sending rays across the calm water, life felt good. We had emerged from our respective meltdowns together, stronger and with a deeper bond. The many long conversations we'd had surrounding his grief and his family, and that I had actively sought out, were placed gently to the side in a box marked 'Caution'. I couldn't grieve John's family any more, I couldn't grieve for John any more. He had to do this alone.

As I looked across at the river, the morning sun sending rays across the calm water, life felt good. The Wise Man Of The North had filled the many holes of grief left behind as I retreated and John moved firmly in Ray's direction, opening up a space in which we were slowly exploring the normality of life. It was a space in which the balance of conversation had started to move from multiple deaths, darkness and a million tears to the normal subjects of day-to-day life as John placed a protective boundary around me. Yes, we continued to talk about Heather, Felix and Oscar and how John was at any given time, but the intensity of the previous volume of these conversations had diminished. I breathed a sigh of relief.

As I looked across at the river, the morning sun sending rays across the calm water, life felt good. My old counsellor had referred to the way we interact with those close to us, and the way we receive from them in terms of *privileges* and *rights*. When we treat, inadvertently or otherwise, what is a *privilege* from any relationship or friendship as a *right*, we cross an unspoken boundary, we lose sight of the gifts offered and at once become a moral trespasser in someone else's land. I could see the box of gifts that John offered daily, marked 'Jill', slowly spreading its contents before me: kindness, he said, friendship, love and laughter to name a few. He would smile and wrap his arms around me, and whisper in my ear, 'I see you, Jill, I see all of you clearly.'

And if tomorrow he comes again, he will stand at my door, waiting for an invitation in.

∼

A month later, and we were strolling hand in hand along the River Thames in the cold winter air.

'Do you think you're ready to go back to work soon?' I asked.

'No, not yet. I need a bit more time to consider what I want to do. After a lifetime of cabinetmaking and shopfitting maybe it's time for a change. Something different. A project of some kind might be nice, though.'

'Project – what sort?'

'Buying a small property, possibly, and renovating it. That sort of thing. So I can keep myself busy and use the skills I have without facing a full-time work role.'

'That sounds exciting. I've always fancied doing something like that myself.'

He looked across at me seriously. 'We could always do it together – pool our resources and try and make a bit of money on something?'

'Blimey, where did that come from?' I laughed.

'I'm serious. Why not? We'll save the money on two separate rentals and can invest in a property we own.'

'Boy, we're moving fast. First, we're buying a property to renovate, then two steps later we're living together and not a sniff of sweet romance anywhere,' I ribbed.

He stopped, pulled me towards him and kissed me before we continued walking. 'I'm sorry. I didn't set off on this walk with any of this in mind. Our conversation has taken us here. But I wouldn't be suggesting it if I didn't love you,' he said.

'It sounds like a very exciting venture, but you're talking to a woman who hasn't lived with a man for fourteen years, so mentally that's quite a bridge to cross. But what's more important is Alexander. You have a lovely relationship with him, but I'm not sure how he'd feel about such a big change.'

'I understand, and don't want to tread on his toes, but if he's happy, I'm happy too. Come on – let's grab life right now and do something unexpected and fun.'

'On one condition.'

'What's that, then?'

'That we still walk together freely.'

'Ahh, you and this freedom stuff,' he said, playfully squeezing my arm.

'Buying bricks and mortar doesn't change my view on that – it's very important to me.'

'I know it is, but that's going to be difficult for me now.'

'Why? You understand what I'm saying, don't you?'

'Well, *sort of* … but remember the shopfront thing we talked about?'

'Yes, you're the master,' I laughed.

'I've let you into my shop now. I've locked the door and thrown away the key. So you're going to struggle if you want to leave.'

I stopped and looked at him. 'What a beautiful thing to say. That you feel like that.'

'I do. You're in here,' he said, as he patted his heart gently. I don't want to lose you. I don't need to be free from you. I love you dearly and I can't imagine not sharing life together.'

I kissed him briefly on the lips and smiled at him mischievously.

'Wow. I'm in the shop of John Bickley. Now that's quite some achievement! Are you sure there's enough room for one more?'

'I know – you're very lucky,' he joked. 'It's all that probing and digging you do. Look what you've done to me!'

'I'm really touched. What a special place to be.'

'Come on,' he said. 'Let's go for a coffee in that lovely cafe we like opposite Hampton Court. We're almost there. I'll treat you to a big piece of cake.'

'A piece of cake won't buy you my lifelong love, you know, but it'll buy it for today,' I teased.

'Cake, coffee, me … you know you'll never want to leave.'

Alexander quickly dispensed with any concerns I'd harboured about him protesting at such a move. This was not quite an abandonment of our cosy and secure life together, but more a complete embrace of John, a man whose company he loved. His overt pleasure was indicative of the warmth and affection he now felt for him.

'That's a brilliant idea,' he enthused.

'Well, I know, but it's a big change. We've lived alone for fourteen years in our little world and it would be different living with John.'

'Of course it'll be different, but I'm sure it'll be a lot of fun too. I think he's great and would love to live with him. Another man about the house would be pretty good, I think.'

After years of devotion I was being usurped.

'It might not all be a bed of roses, you know. He still has his bad days and probably always will, and that can be distressing to be around.'

'He's a great guy and he makes you really happy. You're like a pair of big kids when you're together. I've spoken about his sons with him and I'm cool with that. Anyway, you're the one who wants to live in the now, so let's do it.'

How old was he? Just sixteen. How he shone before me: mature, sensitive, full of his own fun and energy, and so decisive and clear about the path to be taken.

'He's rubber-stamped your arrival,' I joked later to John.

'Really? He's okay with me upsetting the status quo after all these years?'

'Oh, yes – he's clearly looking forward to some male company. I'm beginning to wonder if this is more an arrangement for the benefit of you two, rather than me and you,' I laughed.

'It's to the benefit of us all, Jill.'

The following day I watched the two of them walk towards one another in the living room of our flat, arms outstretched, and fall into the biggest bear hug. I could have cried at the joy between them.

'Alex, Alex,' John said, grinning widely as they eventually parted. 'Thanks for letting me join you and your mum. I know you're a close unit, so I feel really touched that you're happy to have me along.'

'No worries. I could do with another guy around here,' he said, gesturing towards me. 'You know, to help field my mum.

Did I tell you about her tracking me with postcodes whenever I leave here?' he laughed.

I could see how this was going to play out and smiled a huge smile.

Great highs are so often followed by great lows. I had just learnt that I had been unsuccessful in stage two of my Inspectors' promotion process, which had involved preparing a written submission covering six areas of policing, and evidencing previous work. It was useful, but didn't help my feelings at all to know that there were apparently hundreds of candidates for very few spaces and that I was not alone on the greasy pole of aspiration. It was simple – I was facing more of what I'd faced far too much of in my life: failure, rejection, more failure, more rejection. Adding further misery was that, unlike the regular stage one exam opportunities, this process was a random event based on supply and demand: no inspector vacancies, no process. I would now have to wait for some indeterminate amount of time to throw my hat in the ring once more. No wonder they gave you five years from passing 'stage one', not only to successfully get through 'stage two', but also to complete your first year in the rank.

I did some quick maths; it was one year since I'd banked my exam, which gave me three more years to successfully get through stage two, a process that might only be run once or twice in that time frame. The greasy pole of aspiration suddenly grew longer and greasier, testing my desire to cling on. I could hear Michelangelo's wise words, the ones that I'd been so keen to share with my son in the hope of inspiring him, and the words that I'd tried to live by myself:

The greater danger for most of us lies not in setting our aim too high and falling short, but in setting our aim too low, and achieving our mark.

Well, I'd aimed high and I'd fallen short, and right now, as I took another stinging slap in the face, it didn't feel so good. I wanted to inspire my son, not repeatedly show him how to be graceful in defeat. I wanted him to have a mum who aimed high and succeeded. For *once*, I wanted to aim high and succeed. I was so proud of *his* exam success and I'd wanted him to be equally proud of mine – even if it had taken me five decades to get there. But it wasn't to be.

As my hands slid slowly down the pole, I muttered under my breath, 'Bloody Michelangelo and his bloody wise words.'

A matter of months later, at the end of January 2012 and on the coldest of days, the three of us walked through the door of our new home, in our new town of Guildford and into a new period in our lives.

What had happened to my bid for freedom and becoming mortgage-free to consider an alternative way of life? It had been a move designed to cast off the societal burden of walking on a daily, unconscious treadmill in ultimate pursuit of a paid-off mortgage. Had I ditched my strongly held views and succumbed once more to the inevitable slavery of home ownership, waving my freedom goodbye as I signed on the dotted line? No, I had not. As much as I now owned a house, I was not owned by *it*. A subtle difference, but one which gave a whole new feel to the venture. We walked in through the door in the same manner that we had chosen to walk together – taking one day at a time. I'd also just had two and a half years of blissful balcony vistas in two very different homes. The nomad in me had been nourished and I was ready for pastures new.

As was to be expected, our new home brought a new energy with it, a breath of fresh air, and there was no better place to stand still and inhale it deeply than in our stunning back garden. Approximately thirty metres long by eleven metres wide, it was split into two grassy tiers, with a stone pathway running through the middle from the top to the bottom, where it tapered into a 'V'. Sitting majestically halfway down and to the left was a two-hundred-year-old apple tree. It was bare when we moved in, but as early summer arrived and its pink blossom emerged, it shimmered in its regal beauty and took centre stage, powerful in its stillness and bringing a tranquillity to the garden. Established and well-tended plants filled the upper borders which, as spring and summer dawned, revealed a rainbow of colour.

Surrounding it all, just beyond the perimeter fence, was an array of mature trees, host to a multitude of sweet-singing birds; as the sun rose each day and shone down onto this south-facing oasis of perfection, they filled the air with their morning song. This was the reason we fell in love with the house. To be able to walk out of our back door and immediately become touched by the close and hypnotic effect of nature was a gift. We felt very lucky.

Within a few months of moving in we had made the decision to add to our garden glory by building a summer house at the bottom that would make use of the 'V' section, and simultaneously create a living space that could be enjoyed by us all: a place where my son could relax with his friends, where John could play his music loudly, and somewhere for us all to party and enjoy a drink while socialising with family and friends. It would house a pool table, a bar and a music section for John's lifetime collection of CDs and records. John and his skills were to bring our vision to fruition, and perhaps this was where any individual want regarding its eventual use was inadvertently transcended by the positive experience that completing it ultimately proved to be.

As he built something from new with his own hands, something he had designed, the project delivered to John something far more profound. He says the summer house represents two structures: the first, its own physical one; and the second, far more powerful to him, an emotional one. It was the first time since he had returned from his travels that he had put his heart and soul into something that required a personal focus and physical investment and, when faced with buckling down to it, invest he did.

With dogged determination and exacting standards he threw himself wholeheartedly into every second it took to build. He was a man on a mission. All his blood, sweat and tears were sewn into the very fibre of the structure, finally becoming its beating heart in an embodiment of John, his grip on life and his future in it. Its finished beauty matches that of its surroundings and, as I watch him stand alone in the middle of his creation, it matches that of its maker.

It stands proud just behind the apple tree and, as the sun

bounces from its front floor-to-ceiling glass windows and doors, it is a constant reflection of hope.

As I lay under the warm quilt with my bedside lamp on, I heard the front door close, signalling his return from another long journey north. It was late and I was relieved he was safely home.

He slid into bed with none of his usual brooding darkness. This time he had returned more animated. He had been going to Ray for one year, and in recent months his mood on returning had slowly improved.

'Ray says that maybe I could drop to just one session a month.'

'How do you feel about that?'

'Well, if Ray thinks I'm good enough for that, then I'll be guided by him.'

'What else does the mighty Ray say?' I teased. 'I thought counselling was to supposed to have boundaries, but The Wise Man Of The North seems to have joined us in bed.'

He laughed. 'Ray says ...'

I smiled inwardly – I'd encouraged his presence in our home. He was a beast of my own making who would leave when he was ready and not before. Strangely, for a man I'd never met I'd grown rather fond of him.

CHAPTER 27

I was listening to his voice. He was travelling back from another session with Ray about two months later and, unusually, wanted to disclose what they had spoken about.

'I wanted to share this with you because it was something you suggested a long time ago.'

'Oh, what was that?'

'Remember when I was doing all the different activities: the bungee jumps, parachute jump, swimming with the sharks, all that stuff?'

'Yes, you madman.'

'You thought it was me testing my own mortality, which some of it was, I think. But there's another reason that came up today and it's about how guilty I felt, and still do, about not managing to get into the house on the night of the fire.'

'You can't punish yourself about that.'

'But I *was* doing, that's the point. It's guilt about not

coming home earlier and not being able to save them when I got home.'

We were on extremely delicate ground.

'Are you okay to talk about this when you're driving?'

'I'll stop if I start getting upset. It was just that it was a bit of a light-bulb moment for me, and because you'd questioned why I was doing all these things before, I wanted to talk to you about it. Do you mind?'

'No, of course not.'

'Ray suggested I may have been unconsciously setting myself challenges to overcome – you know, because I couldn't overcome the fire. So managing to complete them all was my way of trying to prove something to myself – to show I was courageous enough to face them all, however dangerous.'

'Do you think that's possible?'

'Yes, when I take myself back and think about how I was, I was most definitely pushing myself. I just didn't understand why.'

'Does it help you in any way?'

'It helps me understand, that's all. But the guilt I feel will never leave me – I couldn't protect them.'

I could hear his voice faltering and becoming weaker.

'This is such a sensitive subject. Come home and we can talk about it more when you're not driving.'

'Okay,' he answered as though in some other world, distant and no longer connected to us.

I thought I'd add one more thing in the hope he might digest some of it.

'You were a wonderful dad, John, and they all adored you. Try and focus on that right now.'

A couple of hours later and he walked through the door exhausted, taking himself straight to bed, a brooding and heavy look on his face. He'd emerge in his own time. I knew when to circle quietly.

Ray's continued support was proving invaluable as, despite John's fluctuating emotions, it was clear he was growing stronger.

This was evidenced a few months later when he climbed what almost two years earlier would have seemed an impossible wall. It was five months after we'd moved in, and the two young daughters of friends who had come to stay were running into the back garden and the summer sun. To what or whom were they running?

As I looked out from a rear room window onto the back garden, there stood John in the middle of a makeshift, but undoubtedly creative, campsite for two. Unbeknown to me, the previous evening he had promised them he would build them such a thing and, true to his word, there it sat. It was every child's dream: two separate covered sleeping areas side by side, containing sleeping bags, rolled out and ready to be used; a front deck complete with chairs to lounge in; and a superb sunbathing area situated at the side with mats to lie on. An Australian outback hat each, which they wore excitedly – one John had collected on his travels, and one a gift – completed the picture. This was a five-star camping site: a superior model.

How they revelled in the fun of it all, soaking up the enthusiasm, energy and joy of John. It was a wonderful scene of laughing, happy children who demanded his time and attention and on whom he showered it all. It will forever remain etched in my mind as a moment that defined just how John walks as a man. This was the second anniversary of his family's deaths, and the girls were aged ten and six – the exact ages of his sons when they'd died. Faced with creating an experience that was heartbreakingly reminiscent of precious times he had shared with his sons, and on such an upsetting day when inside he carried deep sadness and pain, he chose not to flee in the opposite direction. Instead, he stood fast and faced his nightmare head on, finding the strength to rise above his own internal distress, generously becoming absorbed in, and surrounded by, a mirror of what had been so cruelly taken from him.

Only two days earlier he had lain sobbing in my arms as the approaching anniversary grew closer. These two scenes were in stark contrast to each other, but they illuminated how far he had moved forward in his ability to confront his demons, and were indicative of his continued recovery and emotional strength.

Children were becoming a bit of a theme, and at forty-eight they weren't on my horizon any more. I had the large baby I wanted: he was a strapping six-foot-two eighteen-year-old, and from the moment he was born he'd been the brightest light in my life. I had known the subject of children might arise at some point between us, but until then it lurked in the deeper recesses of my mind in a box marked 'No'.

We had decided to take a holiday to Turkey with Alexander, staying in a hotel that sat on a cliff edge, with stunning, panoramic views of the Mediterranean Sea, a vista that was magnified by both the hotel's elevated position, and its proximity to the coastline. On an almost daily basis we relaxed in the open-air pool as a respite from the forty-degree heat, taking in the views of the endless blue sea and clear sky that surrounded us, moments when all seemed perfect in the world. Out of the blue one day, John made his announcement.

'I've been thinking about what we spoke about last year – you know, whether I'd like another child. It's over two years now since Felix and Oscar died and although I can never replace them, I'd love to feel the happiness that being a dad brings again.'

What an emotional milestone to have arrived at. I had never been quite sure if he would. His face beamed.

I glanced across at the pool bar where Alexander was sitting on a stool, larger than life, hairy-chested and broad-shouldered, short, dark, wet hair swept back, and drinking a cold beer as he eyed the array of young, bikini-clad girls around him. Baby, no; man, yes. He was a wonderful spirit, one that emptied my bank account with alarming ease, but nonetheless, a wonderful spirit. He had all my love, he filled my life, and gave me enough love to last a lifetime.

I rapidly processed the enormity of what John had just said.

'What a place to have reached. How does it feel?'

'Mixed. Painful, because it's moving on, and for a long

time I didn't want to. I didn't think I would ever feel able to contemplate fatherhood again. I suppose it's a positive thing too. What do you think?'

'I think it's filled with great sadness, but filled with tremendous hope too. I feel quite emotional.'

'You're supposed to be happy for me.'

'I am, I am – I'm just a little overcome. What a moment.'

'Anyway, you've mistaken what I was asking. I meant, what do you think about having another child – with me?'

My immediate inclination was to roll out my previous suggestion from a year ago – the possibility of a younger, fertile model, possessing eggs galore. And I wasn't joking either – this wasn't a joking matter. I'd always known that if he ever reached this point it would be a cruel twist of fate that he was with a partner whose age rendered this desire an impossibility.

'I feel a bit unprepared for such a big question, if I'm honest. I wasn't expecting it.'

I was floundering, struggling to provide an immediate response to a question that, from where I was sitting, didn't have a simple answer.

'Relax, there's no pressure,' he said, sensing my discomfort.

'I'm not sure if it would even be possible.'

'No, but you haven't reached the menopause yet, and you're in great shape.'

'But it'd be against the odds of nature, and I'm not really sure how I feel about having another baby. A few years ago, maybe, but now I'm heading to fifty … I feel awful talking like this after what you've just said.'

'I understand your feelings. But if it doesn't happen with you, it won't be happening.'

I was cornered and felt the weight of responsibility pressing heavily on my shoulders.

'I love you, John, but this is too important. I don't want to stand in the way of what could be a new family full of children for you. Life's too short – you know that. I said you were free, and this is exactly what I was talking about. You're young enough to go and meet a younger woman who you could have two or three children with.'

'I'm not interested in anyone else. I want to share life with you, be that with or without a child. If you don't want, or can't have, a child, it isn't going to affect what direction my life takes. Please understand that. If it happens I'll see it as a blessing, but if it doesn't then I'm cool with that, too.'

'But I'm not sure *I'm* comfortable with that.'

'Listen to me. I am *not*, repeat *not* interested in meeting any other woman just so I can have children. So stop telling me that's what I should do. Okay?'

'Okay. I just need some time to think about it.'

The issue had been well and truly aired. I couldn't see my view changing, but for now it seemed we were bigger than the issue itself. If it ever became bigger than us, then we would know we had reached a crossroad on our path.

John's ability to move forward in these ways, and in life generally, was without doubt assisted by the presence of Ray in his life. He had become a convert to the value of counselling, or specifically, the value of Ray, and the emotional riches he brought into his life with his wise guidance and still, powerful presence. To be able to sit in the company of a man who was not connected to his loss or life proved to be a great release. Ray created an environment of gentleness and safety in which John could unburden himself without risk of judgement or retribution, and which encouraged in him a growing openness and trust. He describes it as being 'at ease, with no pressure or scrutiny' and, in approaching it with an open mind and a receptive attitude, John found that the process elicited the most private of his thoughts, leaving no stone unturned. It was the most reparative of experiences.

Seventeen months after he had started his sessions, John returned once more from his long journey north. It was the last time he would make this journey.

He had arrived at Ray's door wanting a prescriptive and finite explanation. He had taken with him his many questions, his endless search to understand the randomness of life events and his quest to find a reason for life itself. Although counselling had not provided all the answers he'd been looking for, he had come to appreciate that perhaps there were none, and along the way Ray had helped him come to a place of acceptance about the loss of his family.

'How do you feel? Will you miss him?'

'I will, actually. I've grown very fond of him. To have had that space to retreat to, and to be able talk to him in a way was unable to talk to anyone else … it's truly been the best thing for me. Thanks so much for supporting me with it.'

'You've no need to thank me. You're the one who took yourself into that painful space with him.'

'But I wouldn't have done that without you pushing me in that direction.'

'Well, walking through his door was one thing. Sitting still in the room with him for almost a year and a half takes a lot of strength, and you managed to find it. I couldn't do that for you.'

He hugged me tight, whispering in my ear, 'I couldn't have got through it without you, though.'

'Do you mind me asking,' I said, pulling away, 'which bits of your time with Ray will you find the most helpful, do you think, in the future?'

'I suppose it would be to "sit" with my feelings rather than to fight them, and not to create expectations of myself that I may never be able to fulfil – you know, about looking back with happiness. Small things, but they have a big impact. Yes, I'll most definitely miss our chats. He's been an unexpected gift, has Ray.'

The Wise Man Of The North had left John's life, but he'd left mine, too.

I was going to miss him. He hadn't just been a gift to John.

CHAPTER 28

I sit and quietly watch him as he reads, sitting in the living room of our home. It is three years since his family died, and eighteen months since we bought our house together. We rose this morning and chose to walk together for another day.

He is my contradiction: filling me with both immense depths of sadness and immense depths of love.

He is my contradiction: bringing daily joy and hiding daily sorrow.

He is my contradiction: he brings tears, he brings a love I've never known.

He is my contradiction: my love for him will never be stronger than my love for his family, and my eternal desire that it is they who walk beside him, not me.

He is my contradiction: for our love to draw its breath, his family drew their last.

He is my contradiction.

He is undoubtedly a changed man; in facing the devastation of his loss he has emerged, in his own words, with his emotional 'shop door' open, far more receptive to, and affected and touched by, life's daily events. In his ensuing struggle for survival and to find a reason for living after the deaths of his family, he has had no choice but to dig deep and reach inside himself, and in doing so has found a complexity of emotion he did not previously know existed. He has been slowly resurrecting his life, placing its shattered pieces back together, pieces that will forever be etched with his pain and which no longer sit neatly together and at ease with the world. His wife and his sons are the fabric that joins them, the spirit within him, their very essence felt by him every moment of every day.

With Ray's guidance, he has managed to find a place from where he can look back and celebrate the twenty-three very happy years he shared with his wife, Heather. But has yet to reach this place with his sons, who remain a source of continuing distress to him. His Center Parcs experience was a rare moment of emotional freedom with them, and his memories of Felix and Oscar continue to be filled more with pain than with joy. He does not know that he will ever be able to embrace those precious moments with them and gain some comfort from the tremendous love, laughter and fun they all shared. For now, it is too big a mountain to climb, so he does not attempt to do so.

The overall value of his life has changed. A part of him has died; the light that shone with his family's presence has been extinguished and it will not glow again. That is not to devalue the richness of the relationships he has today – with his mum, his sister, myself and countless friends. He recognises that the sum of their individual parts continues to bring him happiness, but the totality of it all, the umbrella which sits over his life, has lost the lightness and freedom that walking through life untouched by tragedy and adversity can bring. It is to the richness of the individual relationships that he now turns his focus: these give his life a reason.

He credits his relationship with my son, Alexander, as giving him a 'sense of worth'. It is a relationship that he has invested in wholeheartedly, and an investment that is richly deserving of all the rewards it now brings into his life. My son has enormous respect and love for him, and gains simple joy in sharing John's time, and in seeking him out for advice and his opinion on all manner of things. They share a great camaraderie and humour, rubbing along together like two old friends who've known each other for years. They are at ease in one another's company and have an unspoken bond, and both have personalities that are sunny and laid back in nature.

His yardstick for what is important in life, how he views what is to be valued and what is unimportant, springs from the deathbeds of his family. Nothing, understandably, has the same importance any more. Nothing ever will.

I sit and quietly watch him as he reads, sitting in the living room of our home. It is three years since his family died, and eighteen months since we bought our house together. We rose this morning and chose to walk together for another day.

I am his contradiction: a figure of hope when all hope is lost.

I am his contradiction: a lush green field in a barren landscape.

I am his contradiction: offering a hand of friendship he would rather not be needing.

I am his contradiction: offering a hand of love as he holds tightly to the hand of another.

I am his contradiction: I am life, as he is cloaked in death.

I am his contradiction.

I am undoubtedly a changed woman; walking beside the ravages of multiple deaths has given me an uncomfortably close insight into John's life following his loss. I didn't know his wife or sons, but I feel them every day; their young, lost lives are like a mirror hanging on my wall. My desire to live in the moment is illuminated and crystallised in the shadow of their deaths.

John's yardstick in life is a daily aspiration to which some days I come momentarily close, but more often than not, lost in the minutiae of life, I fail to reach. I am human and, on occasions, that individual at the supermarket checkout just refuses to back up. I can only try harder. John generously tells me all things are relative, but he is a quiet and powerful presence by my side. Each day I watch his example and try to inch a little closer to it.

My own shift in life, that had started before John arrived, continues in harmonious tune with his own vision. One of these days I may well live on that boat and he may well be with me. One of these days we may well sell the house we bought and choose another venture; the idea of travelling the world without the burden of material possessions still beckons – just the open road and days full of possibilities. For now, my job and my love of and commitment to my son and his university education keep me anchored for a while longer.

It is without doubt that, in providing support to John, I took myself into complex waters. Were my actions entirely altruistic, or feeding my own unhealthy needs?

As I reflect on the last three years, for all my introspection I am aware of one simple fact: the lifeline I offered to John was unlike any I had offered to others before him. This one was different. Not because it was a convenient self-serving construction of mine in which my denial was firmly stuck in the sand with my head, but because as I reached out I knew exactly what I was doing, alive to what it was that I offered and, most importantly of all, I gave it freely. Like some sort of out-of-body experience, I watched myself standing before him as he took my hand.

This has not negated the need to check my own motivations, but by allowing myself to provide such support, with my own fear of repeating past mistakes ever present, I have emerged emotionally stronger.

I have given that which I wished to give while protecting and nurturing my own self.

I have given that which I wished to give, taking responsibility for myself only.

I have given that which I wished to give without attachment.

And in doing so I have set myself free.

Over time we have achieved a beautiful middle ground where our relationship can thrive. It was a balance that was needed and which, after Lake Garda and with Ray's support, we seem to have found. John's family sits between us. They represent a large part of his life, and will forever be part of him – a part of us. When I invited him into my life I invited them too, and their silent presence is humbling. I look at the few pictures of his sons that he can bear to have out – or not, when some days I note they have been returned to his drawer – and they smile back at me, sweet, happy and innocent, and at heartbreaking odds with the cruelty of their demise, their images a shattering reminder of life's vicious turns.

We continue to do what we have always done so well – talk about his family and his distress – when needed. He cannot hide; I sense him all the time, but the emotion of his loss has found a healthier space between us, perhaps because of the natural progression of time, but also as a result of John's own regained autonomy and determination not to rely on the previous level of support I gave him, to show me I'm not saving him. I watch as he saves himself daily. But he is honest, too, and says that in retrospect he was looking for someone to hold onto, someone detached and removed from his family, and my offer of support gave him that. He was unaware that I was feeding this need in him and accepts he was entirely selfish in the immediate aftermath of the tragedy, when he repeatedly brought his black life to my door. In return, he brought, and continues to bring, a multitude of gifts to not only my life, but also to my son's: the box marked 'John'. We regularly open and spread its contents before him: gentle, strong, relentlessly optimistic, loving and fun, to name a few. He keeps his own counsel and shields us. Perhaps he has moved too far in the other direction, at pains to show he didn't arrive just to take, unconsciously or not.

We continue to do what we have always done so well: talk about us and our continued wish to share life together. I tell him he is free, and he tells me he doesn't want to be and he doesn't need to be. He ribs me as he dismisses what he still affectionately refers to as 'this freedom malarkey'. He insists he has no desire to go in search of a different life, a different, younger woman who could bear him his much-desired child. I insist the door will always remain open should he change his mind.

'Why say that?' he admonishes tenderly. 'If I told you tomorrow I was leaving, you'd surely be upset. You don't want me to go.'

'Of course I would be upset. I love you and would miss you and all the riches you bring into my life, but I can't contain you. That's not love, is it?'

'I don't feel contained by you.'

'But that's my point.'

We continue to do what we have always done so well: laugh out loud at each other and at life, to be the big school kids that my son says we still are.

I love John's keep-it-simple approach to life, what he calls his 'empty mind'. It is at odds with mine, but all the more attractive for it. He tells me he wouldn't like to exist in my mind, constantly busy and turning over life. But without it, I doubt I could have provided him with the support that I have while simultaneously trying to understand the part I was playing in the script of John's life, and in the script of my own. The many long conversations I had with myself, the differing argumentative voices in my head shouting: *you're saving, you're supporting, you're saving, you're supporting*, have been placed in another box marked 'Peace'. I couldn't save John. He had to save himself. Only he could find his reason to live. Only he could choose to face another day.

For all my busy mind, I'm at peace with John. I'm at peace with myself.

To date, John and I have spent 2,737 days sharing life together.

The average lifespan for a female in the UK is approximately 31,930 days.

The average lifespan for a male in the UK is approximately 28,670 days.

Heather lived for 16,755 days.

Felix lived for 3,650 days.

Oscar lived for 2,195 days.

Days John will cherish for the rest of his life.

EPILOGUE

OCTOBER 2017

John: I knew you'd say yes.

Jill: You took long enough.

John: Where does that leave your 'being free to leave' position, then? I mean how can you say yes to marrying me but still talk of such a thing?

Jill: Because it's the premise of love. Marrying you doesn't change that. We're still free.

John: I love you and I don't want you to leave.

Jill: I love you too, and nor do I want you to leave, but—

John: Keep it simple, Jill, keep it simple.

Jill: Impossible.

John: You and your freedom malarkey.

Jill: You'll never change me.

John: I wouldn't want to.

KEEPING IN TOUCH

And the final words of our story come from my editor, Cally Worden, in emails she sent after she had first read my memoir:

On a genuine and very personal note – we moved into our new home here just under four months ago. We have a single smoke alarm downstairs that works, but is frankly inadequate for the size and layout of the property. There are two others (one upstairs, one down) that are linked and much better sited, but which were disabled for works that took place before we moved in. Re-enabling them has been on the to-do list for too long. Today (literally) I insisted my husband attend to this, and my family and I will sleep more soundly tonight as a result. Your story made that happen. Thank you xx

4th Nov 17

With regards to the house alarms, this is something we should have done ages ago but, like so many others, had neglected it ... always something else more pressing to do. But, as your story illustrates, this approach can have devastating consequences; reading it was the nudge we needed. I'm quite sure that once the book is published it will touch many others in the same way. Who knows how many lives will be saved as a result. The nature of prevention means you'll never know. But I'm certain others will act, as we have. In fact, my husband has this week gone to visit my mum and has strict instructions from me to ensure she, too, has a functioning alarm installed before he leaves. Two households within which Heather, Felix and Oscar have already made their presence felt, in the best possible way.

6th Nov 2017

These responses have been included as an illustration of one of the ways in which I hope our story will have a positive impact on the lives of those who read it.

The following email address is for readers who would like to share whether reading this memoir has resulted in their own installation of a smoke alarm or testing of a current one.

jillbarnesauthor@gmail.com

Visit www.cloakedinwrappedin.com for more information.

Jill Barnes was born in Manchester in 1965. Throughout her public-sector career she qualified as a psychiatric nurse and served in both the Royal Military and the Metropolitan Police. She retired from the latter as a Detective Sergeant in July 2016 after twenty-five years. Although born in the north, she has lived in the south for the past twenty-six years.

Printed in Great Britain
by Amazon

60880669R00241